Advance Praise for *After Evangelicalism*

"A first-person account of the rise and fall of evangelical Christianity, *After Evangelicalism* takes you on a poignant journey through history, theology, and politics that opens your eyes to just how far evangelicalism has strayed from the heart of what it means to be Christian. If your experience with evangelicalism has taken you through the mire of purity culture, white supremacy, patriarchy, LGBTQ exclusion or if it has just left you feeling disillusioned and exhausted, you can trust that Gushee uses these pages to set a foundation that will lead you out of this expired belief system and toward a refreshing and much more life-giving way of following Jesus."

—Amber Cantorna, national speaker, LGBTQ advocate, and author of *Unashamed* and *Refocusing My Family*

"As a self-identified 'evangelical' Christian who is not yet willing to abandon this religious identity, I cannot endorse the central premise of David Gushee's thoughtful new book. But I can fully endorse his diagnosis of the many problems facing American evangelicalism today. My fellow believers ignore this book at their peril."

—John Fea, Distinguished Professor of American History, Messiah College

"As progressive Christians exit evangelical churches and parachurch organizations in droves, many have felt rudderless, unsure of how to reconstruct their theological framework after saying goodbye to the worldview that has shaped them. *After Evangelicalism* is the compass they need, pointing the way toward a biblically rooted, pro-LGBTQIA, antiracist, justice-oriented, Christian humanism. If there is one book that ex-evangelicals need to read, it is this one."

—Chanequa Walker-Barnes, Associate Professor of Practical Theology, Mercer University, McAfee School of Theology

"Carefully researched, historically accurate, and convincingly reasoned, this is the road map for the soul to those of us who are now without a country."

—Gregory Thornbury, Vice President, New York Academy of Art

"*After Evangelicalism* is essential reading for those who have found white evangelicalism wanting. Drawing on his own spiritual journey, David Gushee provides an incisive critique of American evangelicalism. But this is not ultimately a work of deconstruction. Gushee offers a succinct yet deeply informed guide for post-evangelicals seeking to pursue Christ-honoring lives, and he does this with such eloquence that the book transcends its immediate purpose and speaks compellingly to all who are exploring how to be Christian in these times."

—Kristin Kobes Du Mez, Professor of History, Calvin University, and author of *Jesus and John Wayne*

"Since the evangelical revolution of the 1970s and 1980s, evangelicalism has given the impression that it is immune to the decline plaguing mainline Protestantism. That is, until now. As David Gushee's insightful analysis of the current post-evangelical moment suggests, US evangelicalism squandered its opportunity, and now people—especially young people—are leaving evangelical Christianity. As Gushee demonstrates, evangelicalism's wounds are mostly self-inflicted, originating in the move by straight white men to perpetuate structures that reinforce their power and dominance over the life of the church. Gushee is driven by a profound need to address the pastoral concerns of this growing post-evangelical movement and herein offers a combination manifesto, love letter, and game plan for fellow #exvangelicals. The rest of the church would do well to heed his words too. Gushee's spiritual inventory of this movement and his articulation of a post-evangelical theological framework serve as a road map for renewal for a fragmented and moribund first-world Christianity."

—Rubén Rosario Rodríguez, Professor of Theological Studies, Saint Louis University

"Thinking about Christianity after evangelicalism is neither trendy, alarmist, nor faithless, but rather it carves out a needed path forward for those millions of exvangelicals who have found the movement that birthed them to be irrelevant, traumatic, and even abhorrent and are seeking a place to land. Few have earned the right to speak to this topic with such prophetic clarity and practical insight, not to mention approachable writing style, as David Gushee."

—Peter Enns, author of *How the Bible Actually Works*

"If you're part of the growing number of post-evangelicals whose conscience resulted in living out your faith in exile, this is the book for you—especially if your spirit longs to move beyond the painful place we've come from and reengage your spiritual imagination to explore beyond the evangelical horizon."

—Benjamin L. Corey, author of *Unafraid: Moving beyond Fear-Based Faith*

"There is a growing number of people who identify as ex-Christians in the United States when in fact they are probably ex-evangelicals. It's not an overstatement to say that Christianity is better represented outside of that fairly recent, contextual, and reactionary movement. And for those who find themselves disillusioned with the evangelical brand of the Christian faith they once found meaningful, it may seem as though to leave evangelicalism is to throw away Christianity. In this book, Gushee gives a methodical account for why that is not the case. In *After Evangelicalism*, Gushee offers clear, comprehensive, theological content for Christians who follow after Jesus in a direction other than evangelicalism. And of the many books that David Gushee has written, this may be one of his most timely and most well-read books."

—Reggie L. Williams, Associate Professor of Christian Ethics, McCormick Theological Seminary

"Gushee's book provides an insightful analysis of the evangelical movement. *After Evangelicalism* is a helpful guide forward for those disillusioned with the church and looking to reconstruct their faith in Jesus."

—Sarah Bessey, author of *Miracles and Other Reasonable Things*

After Evangelicalism

After Evangelicalism

The Path to a New Christianity

David P. Gushee

First edition
Published by Westminster John Knox Press
Louisville, Kentucky

20 21 22 23 24 25 26 27 28 29—10 9 8 7 6 5 4 3 2 1

Book design by Sharon Adams
Cover design by Barbara LeVan Fisher, www.levanfisherdesign.com
Cover art © SilverCircle / Shutterstock.com
Interior art © Yuri Gayvoronskiy / Shutterstock.com

Library of Congress Cataloging-in-Publication Data

Names: Gushee, David P., 1962– author.
Title: After evangelicalism : the path to a new Christianity / David P. Gushee.
Description: First edition. | Louisville, Kentucky : WJK, Westminster John Knox Press, 2020. | Includes index. | Summary: "David Gushee offers a new way forward for disillusioned post-evangelicals by first analyzing what went wrong with U.S. white evangelicalism in areas such as evangelical identity, biblical interpretation, church life, sexuality, politics, and race. Gushee then proposes new ways of Christian believing, belonging, and behaving, helping post-evangelicals from where they are to a living relationship with Christ and an intellectually cogent and morally robust post-evangelical faith"—Provided by publisher.
Identifiers: LCCN 2020023998 (print) | LCCN 2020023999 (ebook) | ISBN 9780664266110 (paperback) | ISBN 9781646980048 (ebook)
Subjects: LCSH: Christianity—United States—21st century. | Christianity—Forecasting. | Evangelicalism—United States.
Classification: LCC BR526 .G865 2020 (print) | LCC BR526 (ebook) | DDC 277.308/3—dc23
LC record available at https://lccn.loc.gov/2020023998
LC ebook record available at https://lccn.loc.gov/2020023999

♾ The paper used in this publication meets the minimum requirements of the American National Standard for Information Sciences—Permanence of Paper for Printed Library Materials, ANSI Z39.48-1992.

For the post-evangelicals

Contents

Foreword

Brian D. McLaren

Years ago, an evangelical pastor told me of an exchange he had with a fellow pastor. They had attended the same evangelical seminary about a decade earlier. As he sat in his former classmate's office, he scanned his colleague's huge bookshelf filled with familiar evangelical titles by familiar evangelical authors. To his surprise, he noticed one my books, sticking out like a sore thumb.

He pulled it off the shelf and asked, "How did you like it?" "I didn't finish it," his friend replied. "Why not?" he asked. "I spent a lot of money and time on this library," his friend answered. "If that book is right, I would need to throw out half my library and start over again. That's not happening." That ended the conversation.

I kept thinking of that story as I read the book you're now holding. You might be one of those people who have invested a lot of money and time in evangelical Christianity. The thought of writing off that investment seems too high. Yet every day that passes, the cost of staying silent and therefore complicit rises too.

David Gushee has good news for you. Instead of writing off your whole evangelical investment as a total loss, you can shift your investment into a different kind of Christianity. He calls it *Christian humanism*, and if that term seems to entice you, let it. (And if it doesn't, let it anyway.)

I've had the honor of reading and endorsing several of David's books, so I've had a front-row seat in watching his transformation and migration. Step by step, he has made clear what he needed to leave, and in this book he makes it equally clear that instead of moving from one static location to another, he has moved from a static location to a dynamic peregrination, from a place to a path, from "Here I stand" to "Here is the path I am now following."

It's a good path, an honest and welcoming path; and by the time you finish chapter 9, there is a good chance you will feel drawn to join him on it.

Whatever else we might say about American evangelicalism, it's hard to deny that it has become uglier, more compromised, and less credible in recent decades, and especially since November of 2016. There is a certain point in the decomposition of a religious community at which its gatekeepers lose their authority. Like a bar of soap, it has been used up. They can scold, critique, and threaten even more loudly than before, but folks wonder, "And why should I care what *you* think anymore?"

I think we're at that point for growing numbers of evangelicals. If evangelical gatekeepers can swallow keeping children in cages, mocking the Sermon on the Mount, and following leaders in thrall to Trumpist bigotry, why would anyone respect their discernment, value their praise, or fear their critique?

For that reason (and many more), I think a lot of people are ready for this book; and if they start it, there's a high probability that they'll actually finish it, come what may. David writes so clearly and with such refreshing brevity that I feel confident in making that prediction.

After getting the lay of the land in the first few chapters, here are a few highlights you can expect:

In chapter 4, you will not be able to forget the "burning children test." Then, after David describes six strands of evangelical theology, you'll come to the dramatic watershed moment when he concludes, "*I need to state very clearly that I oppose every aspect of this version of evangelical Christianity.*"

In chapter 5, you'll find his exploration of "Jesus according to" highly compelling, not to mention comprehensive and insightful.

If you've been staying home most Sundays because church seems more and more like "a consumer culture" and an "outpost of a political party," you may discover in chapter 6 that your departure doesn't mean that you've actually rejected church, but rather that you've wisely turned away from "a negation of what Christ intended the church to be."

In chapter 7, what David means by Christian humanism will become starkly clear—in clear contrast to "inhumanity in the name of Christ," and you'll find his discussion about human sexuality to be refreshingly realistic and humane.

Then comes chapter 8, where David lays down this provocative gem: "There is no way that the Bible can be said to produce a single coherent political vision or ethic. It has proven to be usable for endless alternative politics: theocratic, royalist, authoritarian, fascist, ethno-nationalist, slavocratic, colonialist, Christian democrat, revolutionary, reformist, liberal, libertarian, socialist, communist, anarchist, quietist, millenarian, and even today's social-conservative white evangelical Republicanism."

I think that chapter 9 will be one of the most quoted chapters in David's body of work to date, outlining seven commitments for post-evangelical politics.

If a nonfiction book can be said to have a climax, you'll reach it in the final paragraphs where David offers a confession and apology that are sobering, pointed, and unforgettable . . . and, I hope, contagious.

For all these reasons and more, as much as I've loved all of David's books, this one strikes me as his magnum opus, the one most not-to-miss, the one that should not be put on your shelf until you have read through to the last page, come what may.

Thank God, David Gushee is right: there is indeed life after evangelicalism: life abundant, full, and free.

Acknowledgments

Every book is in some sense a communal process, and this one is no exception. I would like to express my deepest gratitude for the community that helped bring this book to life.

This begins with Mercer University, which granted me a desperately needed sabbatical leave, and whose students helped inspire and inform this book.

Isaac Sharp, my graduate assistant and protégé, commented on the first draft and contributed a massive amount of research.

Others who read part or all of the manuscript include Theron Clark-Stuart, Edwina Cowgill, Jeremy Hall, Alice Hunt, Kristin Kobes Du Mez, Noam Marans, Eric and Tessa McDonnell, Isaiah Ritzmann, Ron Sider, Steve Watson, Ken Wilson, and Reggie Williams.

My father, David Gushee, and mother-in-law, Lynnie Grant, read along as the book developed and contributed valuable suggestions.

My beloved wife, Jeanie, deeply committed to the pastoral purpose of this book, engaged every word of the manuscript carefully and more than once. I am so grateful.

I am very grateful to Isaiah Ritzmann, who contributed the insightful typology of post-evangelicals that I am including as an appendix.

As with every book, the responsibility for any omissions, errors, and misjudgments in the book falls fully on the author.

I would like to thank various audiences that have worked through this material with me prior to publication, including St. Luke's Episcopal Church (Atlanta), First Baptist Church (Williamsburg, Virginia), Word Made Fresh, Point Loma Nazarene University, Seeking the Kingdom class of First Baptist Church (Decatur, Georgia), Southwest region pastors of the Vineyard

Church, McCormick Theological Seminary, Dayspring Baptist Church, and Amherst College.

This is now the fourth book I have published with the estimable Westminster John Knox Press and its wonderful editor-in-chief, Robert Ratcliff. The support that WJK, Bob, and his team have offered to me during this set of book projects goes far above and beyond what I could have hoped or expected. My gratitude is very deep indeed.

Finally, I am grateful to everyone who has contacted me directly with questions emerging from evangelical and post-evangelical faith crises. Thank you for trusting me with your questions and your anguish. We are in this together. I hope that this book helps chart a path forward, for all of us.

Introduction

EVANGELICALISM'S CONSCIENTIOUS OBJECTORS

This is a book for people who used to be "evangelicals"[1] and are now post-evangelicals or ex-evangelicals or #exvangelicals or somewhere painfully in between.

I am one of them. One of you. In the United States alone, there are millions of us.

According to the Pew Research Center's landmark 2014 Religious Landscape Study, adults who had been raised evangelical but who had either switched to another religious tradition or no longer identified with any religious tradition comprised roughly 8 percent of the total US population. That's about 25 million people.[2]

White US evangelicalism, in particular, is in trouble. This comment is from Daniel Cox of Public Religion Research:

> Nearly one-third of white Americans raised in evangelical Christian households leave their childhood faith. . . . The rates of disaffiliation are even higher among young adults: 39 percent of those raised evangelical Christian no longer identify as such in adulthood. . . . As a result, the white evangelical Protestant population in the U.S. has fallen over the past decade, dropping from 23 percent in 2006 to 17 percent in 2016. But equally troubling for those concerned about the vitality of evangelical Christianity, white evangelical Protestants are aging. . . . The median age of white evangelical Protestants today is 55.[3]

Michael Gerson, a dissenting evangelical[4] who served as a speechwriter for President George W. Bush, also worries that evangelicals are in serious trouble as they hemorrhage their young people: "About 26 percent of Americans

65 and older identify as white evangelical Protestants. Among those ages 18 to 29, the figure is 8 percent. Why this demographic abyss does not cause greater panic—panic concerning the existence of evangelicalism as a major force in the United States—is a mystery and a scandal."[5]

Evangelicalism's recent declines take place against the broader backdrop of a declining Christianity in the United States. Various polls reveal that the number of people claiming Christian affiliation in this country has been dropping by just over 1 percent a year, and those claiming no affiliation are rising at almost the same rate—making it look like a direct swap of Christianity with disaffiliation.[6] It has also been clear for a while that millennials—those born between 1981 and 1996, now twenty-four to thirty-nine years old—are the least religiously affiliated group ever polled.[7] Early indications suggest that the generation rising after them—now called Generation Z, basically the college kids and younger seminarians that I teach—may be even less interested in religion.

For a long time, US evangelicals comforted themselves with belief in their immunity from the overall Christian decline. *We* were fine; *they* (those other, less faithful Christians) were in trouble, because of their liberal theology and lack of vitality. That was the story. But now, well, not so much. Evangelicals are experiencing the same downward trend.

People are leaving evangelical Christianity, young people most of all. That's a fact. Some are leaving their evangelical churches, families, and friends. Some are leaving evangelical theology. Some are leaving the evangelical subculture. And some are leaving God, Jesus, the Bible, the Holy Spirit, the whole thing, Christianity, all of it.

It must be acknowledged that every religious tradition produces dissidents and exiles. The faith with which one is raised does not always fit. And sometimes people leave their childhood faith as much as a declaration of independence from Mom and Dad as anything else.

Undoubtedly this helps to explain why evangelicalism is losing some of its young. But the evidence suggests that much more is going on. What we are seeing is not just rebellion against parents or normal ebb and flow. We are witnessing *conscientious objection*. Ex-evangelicals are leaving based on what they believe to be specific offenses against them personally, or against their family and friends, and specific experiences of trauma that have left lasting damage—like clergy sexual abuse, sexist exclusion and mistreatment, and every kind of indignity against gay, lesbian, and trans people. Some are leaving based on intellectual problems that they could not resolve within the evangelical tradition—like biblical inerrancy, evolution, and overall closed-mindedness. And some are leaving because they believe the ethical posture of evangelicalism—on sex, race, worldly politics—reeks with hypocrisy or is, in fact, unethical.[8]

This is a book about, and for, these people—evangelical exiles for reasons of conscience. I am not writing about, or for, mere religious preference-switchers. I am writing about evangelical exiles, trauma, and conscientious objection.

ARE/WERE YOU AN EVANGELICAL? TAKE OUR SIMPLE TEST AND FIND OUT!

Let's take a test to see if you qualify as an "American evangelical." Put a check in the box beside the item if you know what I am referring to in any of the following twenty-five references:

- ☐ "Lord, I Lift Your Name on High"
- ☐ John Piper
- ☐ Complementarianism
- ☐ 700 Club
- ☐ *The Message*
- ☐ Wheaton College
- ☐ Azusa Pacific
- ☐ Moody
- ☐ Veggie Tales
- ☐ Zondervan
- ☐ God didn't make Adam and Steve
- ☐ Christian Zionism
- ☐ Father, hold me
- ☐ Bob Jones
- ☐ Biblical inerrancy
- ☐ *I Kissed Dating Goodbye*
- ☐ John MacArthur
- ☐ Eugene Peterson
- ☐ Purity rings
- ☐ Reparative therapy
- ☐ Left Behind
- ☐ Hell houses
- ☐ Tim LaHaye
- ☐ Tony Evans
- ☐ The rapture

If you checked twenty or more boxes, you are, or were, an evangelical. Congratulations! Your prize is a boxed set of all the writings of John MacArthur!

Yes, if you checked most of those boxes, you know quite well the world we are leaving or have left. It wasn't all bad. But it is a world we cannot live in anymore.

But even those who know they must leave do not always know where they are going. Many individuals have made their decisions, of course. But overall, post-evangelicals do not know whether they are leaving church, or leaving evangelicalism, or leaving their denominations, or leaving faith, or leaving the Bible, or leaving Jesus, or just leaving. They do not know whether they are now to be mainline Protestant or Catholic or spiritual-but-not-religious or agnostic or just disillusioned.

This book is about where we might want to be going more than what we are leaving. And yet it is impossible to think deeply about where to go next if we don't think deeply about what went so wrong where we were. Throughout this book, we will need to do both.

MY JOURNEY OUT OF EVANGELICALISM

In my book *Still Christian: Following Jesus Out of American Evangelicalism* (published in September 2017), I told my personal faith story.[9] I hope you have read it or will read it soon! But here is a summary. I share it because it is always important to be honest about the experiences one brings into a book, especially one like this.

I was born into a Catholic family in northern Virginia and left the church at the age of thirteen despite the strenuous protest of my Irish Catholic mother. Three years later, I underwent a dramatic and most unlikely conversion to evangelical faith in a Southern Baptist congregation. I was all in from that point on, later attending Southern Baptist Theological Seminary and becoming an ordained Southern Baptist minister.

This means my first entry into an evangelical subculture was in the born-again Southern Baptist world of the late 1970s. I didn't know I had become an "evangelical." The term wasn't used at that time among Southern Baptists and had only just begun to catch on in national media.

The fact that I wasn't raised in an evangelical family, that I became a Southern Baptist, and that Southern Baptists really did not identify as "evangelicals" until they were led to do so by conservative Baptist leaders in the 1990s, makes my journey different from that of many other post-evangelicals. That I am old enough to have a history with evangelicals that goes back to the late 1970s gives me a somewhat longer historical frame than those who are younger. And finally, the fact that my evangelical experience was generally wholesome and untraumatic—until I took on controversial ethical issues as an adult—also shapes me and the approach I take here.

After seminary, at age twenty-five, I decided to attend the liberal Union Theological Seminary in New York, where I received doctoral training in Christian ethics and wrote a dissertation about Christians who rescued Jews during the Holocaust.[10] This dissertation became crucial in launching my career and forming my moral vision. I learned then to care deeply about the moral effects of Christian faith, for good or ill. I became certain that the goal is not just to make more Christians. The goal is to make better Christians.

During a pivotal two years of that six-year doctoral process, I worked on the staff of the estimable Ron Sider, who initiated me into the broader evangelical world of the early 1990s. His version of evangelicalism was derived from his Mennonite faith. It was hopeful (rather than pessimistic or angry), center-left politically (rather than right-wing), and oriented to peace and justice (rather than end times, abortion politics, or apologetics). Sider helped me figure out who I was going to be religiously.[11] It was under his influence that I embraced the evangelical label, both personally and professionally. His name will appear in this book several times. He is one of the best.

Gratefully accepting the only teaching job available to me upon graduation in 1993, I returned to Southern Baptist Seminary for a soul-testing three years. When I was hired there, it looked like Southern was going to become not just a Southern Baptist school but an explicitly center-right evangelical school. Part of the agenda of the new leaders at Southern was to bring Southern Baptists into the evangelical world, and to do that they were hiring self-identified evangelicals like what I had become. I hoped that my center-left evangelicalism would fit well enough and would allow me to find and hold a place there. But under then-youthful new president R. Albert Mohler Jr., the school lurched to the right and threw many of us off the bus. The pivotal issue at the time was women in pastoral ministry—which I was for, but Southern decided it was most definitely against.

As an imperfect but salary-paying escape hatch, in 1996 we moved to the Bible Belt town of Jackson, Tennessee, where I taught for eleven years at another Southern Baptist school, Union University. It was there that I became truly drenched in turn-of-the-millennium conservative evangelical culture—not just at Union University, but also in our Willow Creek–affiliated local Baptist congregation (which I helped pastor),[12] in the two very conservative Christian K–12 schools to which we sent our children, and in the evangelical establishment. By that, I mean the array of evangelical Christian colleges, seminaries, magazines, publishing houses, and other institutions that I began having opportunity to serve in my rising career and which will be an important part of the story told in this book. If you attended an obscure evangelical college somewhere in America, I probably lectured there between 1996 and 2007. If you don't remember it, you must have missed required chapel that day.

During the latter stages of this period, I became a visible activist on two causes that left Union University's 95 percent Republican constituency unhappy with me: climate change and post-9/11 US torture of prisoners in the "war on terror."[13] (I took the "liberal" position by being concerned about both and by calling evangelical Christians to resist Republican positions on both.) This was uncomfortable enough for all concerned that when a more politically diverse, moderate to liberal, post–Southern Baptist school, Mercer University, invited me to a distinguished university professor role in 2007, the answer was an obvious yes. Everyone breathed a sigh of relief.

Yet even here at Mercer, though our family moved out of the Southern Baptist and evangelical subculture in both church attendance and employment, I remained a self-identified progressive evangelical. I was still trying to call US evangelicals to essentially the same vision that Ron Sider had imprinted on me in the early 1990s, and I was still holding a national center-left evangelical audience that had been building for twenty years.

But then in 2014 I wrote *Changing Our Mind*, a book gently making a biblically based argument for full evangelical acceptance of LGBTQ people in church life on the same terms as straight people.[14] This work rocketed me—against my will—right out of the evangelical world that had nurtured me and that I had served for two decades. But this forced exit from the evangelical institutional world, the broken friendships, online attacks, and canceled speaking appearances, led to my entry into new communities of Christian exiles and dissidents. It also, quite gradually, opened my eyes to the deeper theological and ethical problems within evangelicalism that are the focus of this book.

I was "following Jesus out of American evangelicalism," as I said in the subtitle of that memoir. But the memoir was mainly about "out of American evangelicalism," not "following Jesus somewhere else." I had not developed my thinking about where to go next, and I was not sure I would write about it if I ever did. The wounds were still too fresh.

TODAY'S EXVANGELICALS AND THEIR PREDECESSORS

I might have left it there, but a remarkable experience at the American Academy of Religion meeting in November 2018 made that impossible.[15]

I was serving as president of this large global association of religion scholars, and my presidential address carried the announced title "In the Ruins of White Evangelicalism: Interpreting a Compromised Christian Tradition through the Witness of African-American Literature."[16] I will say more about that address later.

What struck me that memorable night in Denver was the rather substantial array of hungry young evangelicals and post-evangelicals who came to hear me. Gathering in the front rows of the lecture space, approaching me afterward, telling me their stories, these promising but troubled (ex-)evangelicals were all around me. They hailed from the best evangelical schools. They were pursuing or had finished doctoral programs in religion and theology. And, to a person, they knew that there was something deeply broken about white US evangelicalism. They were hoping for something from me, some guidance, analysis, or hope. This became apparent in numerous conversations that night and in the days that followed, in person and online.

That is how the seeds of this book were planted. Since then, I have looked around a bit more and seen the signs of distress everywhere. One might even call it a movement.

Depending on how far one wants to zoom out, one can see a US evangelical dissident and exile population, and people trying to chart paths forward into something like post-evangelicalism, extending back quite a while. In this book we will meet evangelical dissenters and exiles—based on politics, race, sex, gender, doctrine, and more—going back many decades.

More recently, the emerging church movement that began in the early 2000s, centered around figures like Tony Jones, Doug Pagitt, Ray Anderson, and Brian McLaren, now looks like an early expression of post-evangelicalism.[17] Authors like these, as well as those who have followed, like Rob Bell, Nadia Bolz-Weber, David Dark, Jennifer Crumpton, Deborah Jian Lee, Peter Rollins, and the late Rachel Held Evans, all seem to belong in a post-evangelical space.[18]

I meet scholars of religion everywhere who came through evangelicalism and left it behind. Visit a religion department almost anywhere in the United States and you will meet some post-evangelicals. Their existence offers happy evidence of evangelicalism's vitality but sad evidence of the difficulty many of evangelicalism's most thoughtful young people find in remaining within their tradition.

Throughout this book, we will keep in mind the complex relationship of evangelicals of color in the United States (and abroad) to white US evangelicalism, which holds most of the power within the evangelical world. While, based on a theological definition, many millions of non-US evangelicals, as well as African American, Latino/a, and Asian American Christians, would count as evangelicals, the power structure and cultural ethos of evangelicalism has been very much US-white-dominated since the birth of the modern evangelical movement in the 1940s. A less polite way to say it is that many evangelicals of color find white evangelicalism hopelessly American and hopelessly racist (see chap. 9).

Relatedly, the very visible, very conservative, very moralistic politics of white evangelicals has both attracted nonwhite evangelicals and repulsed their own dissidents. In other words, moralistic, politicized conservative evangelicalism continually creates and then sheds dissidents. This has been going on for a while. But it certainly seems that the dissident population is growing from all racial and ethnic groups within evangelicalism. The all-powerful, mostly male, white, and American evangelical power structure is being challenged as never before.

Recent dissenting or post-evangelical events such as the Evolving Faith and Liberating Evangelicalism conferences are emerging exactly at this sore point.[19] Meanwhile, black and Latino/a liberation and womanist theology teems with people raised as evangelicals and now definitely post-evangelical, in large part due to white evangelical racism but sometimes also due to black and Latino/a evangelical sexism and rejection of LGBTQ people.[20] We will engage a number of these voices in this book, for they have much to offer all post-evangelicals.

While this book will mainly concern US evangelicalism and its exiles, at least a brief further word about global evangelicalism seems appropriate. My lectures have taken me to Great Britain, Canada, much of Europe, South Africa, Australia, and New Zealand, with a dip into Latin America. I have learned much on these travels.

My impression is that Australia is the nation whose dynamics in relation to evangelicalism—in terms of both religious life and worldly politics—most resemble those of the United States. In both countries, the LGBTQ issue has been both a political issue and a religious one. The press for gay marriage, for example, has led to stark challenges to the evangelical establishment in Australia, which in turn clamps down hard on dissent, which in turn produces exiles, which in turn leads to reconsideration of evangelicalism. Keith Mascord, whom I met in Sydney, has written two books documenting this exact journey.[21] One difference in the Australian context is that the evangelical power structure in Australia is dominated by official Anglicanism, and the issues are uniquely connected to the politics of global Anglicanism.

Overall, no issue is more certain to produce evangelical exiles than resistance to LGBTQ inclusion, and the dynamics are similar in much of the world. My experience is that eastern European and global south evangelicals are more closed to any reconsideration of that issue than are those in other contexts I have visited, with Africa the least friendly context. Indeed, while my *Changing Our Mind* book is currently being translated into Swahili, the identity of the translators is being closely held for their protection. That translation project is being undertaken to ameliorate the great suffering of LGBTQ people in Africa, whose life-threatening situation is partly caused by fundamentalist and evangelical Christian zealotry.

Most everywhere, I see a recurring pattern. When LGBTQ evangelicals, their families, and allies start pressing for dignity and even full inclusion, they begin their arguments from within an evangelical theological framework. Eventually they tend to discover that evangelical ways of reading Scripture and, more broadly, of observing reality and discerning truth, may themselves be the problem. This then tends to move some from a dissenting posture within evangelicalism to self-exile from evangelicalism.

Before the LGBTQ inclusion fight created such heartburn, a similar story played out in relation to full equality, dignity, and service for women. Among evangelicalism's exiles from the 1980s and 1990s (and on till today) have been many, many women. Evangelical women often have been blocked from pastoral service, and in some traditions have been consigned rather roughly to existential spiritual inferiority. This is a global pattern, and global evangelicalism has thus produced a boatload of female exiles, who are now providing leadership in the post-evangelical space; that is, if they have not felt the need to leave the Christian world altogether.

One more foray well beyond the bounds of evangelicalism may be helpful. In conversations with friends who occupy leadership roles in the Jewish community in the United States, I have learned that some similar patterns have become visible there. At least part of the Orthodox Jewish community relates to Jewish faith and tradition in an analogous manner to how many evangelicals relate to Christian faith and tradition. It is interesting, then, to discover a dissenting and post-Orthodox Jewish trend, also especially among the young. The issues tend to be similar: the role of women, LGBTQ inclusion, and politics. For both Jews and evangelicals, how one relates to the policies of the State of Israel is another point of anguish and division.

Do you notice a pattern beginning to develop here? To the extent that US and global evangelicalism (and beyond?!) have been dominated by straight white men, and to the extent that these leaders have interpreted Scripture and tradition in a way that reinforces their power, they have produced exiles from the margins of their community—those who are not white, not male, and not straight. Today, it seems to me, these exiles are being joined by more and more straight white male exvangelicals, sometimes in solidarity with those already pushed out, and sometimes for their own reasons.

In the United States, the precise post-evangelical moment we find ourselves in seems to have begun in 2016—that fateful year—mainly under the #exvangelical label. Blake Chastain created the hashtag and now runs a podcast under that name. Spoken-word artist Emily Joy was involved in starting the #ChurchToo movement to address sexual abuse in evangelical churches. Religion scholars Bradley Onishi and Chrissy Stroop are ex-evangelicals who are writing about the growing movement.[22] At the most recent American Academy of Religion meeting, post-evangelicalism received its own session for the first time. Something is in the air right now—that's for sure.

I feel a profound sense of responsibility to help this surging population of evangelical exiles chart a way forward, if I can offer something that might be of value. I first felt called to be a Christian pastor when I was seventeen years old. Throughout my career I have been responding to a pastoral call. "Feed my sheep," Jesus said (John 21:17), and that is what I have tried to do. This book is an expression of that calling. *I feel called to help shepherd the lost sheep of post-evangelicalism, especially the most recent exiles*—so many of them heartbroken, angry, and alienated from their churches, their families, and their God. This book is for them.

OUTLINE OF THE BOOK: AUTHORITY, THEOLOGY, ETHICS

That's enough background. Now here's a snapshot of where the book will go. The book consists of three sections, each three chapters long. The sections are called "Authorities: Listening and Learning," "Theology: Believing and Belonging," and "Ethics: Being and Behaving." I am making proposals for post-evangelicals in all three arenas.

Part 1: Authorities. How do we learn God's way forward for us? To whom, to what authorities, do we listen? In this section we will consider the history of evangelicalism, the nature and role of Scripture, and the value of other resources and ways of discerning God's will.

Part 2: Theology. What shall we believe and do about God, Jesus, and church? These chapters take a close look at the major narrative threads of the Old and New Testaments and the God we meet there. The church chapter offers some theology and practical discussion of churchgoing options for post-evangelicals.

Part 3: Ethics. What should our character and behavior look like in the arenas of sex, politics, and race, three of the most important ethical concerns driving people out of evangelicalism today?

Those who are at all familiar with my books will see that I am plowing considerable new ground here—only the ethics section reflects much earlier work on my part. I am excited about that. I have learned a great deal in the process, which is one of the main reasons to write a book. Each chapter reflects engagement with a specific, separate scholarly literature—stacks and stacks of books that you will mainly meet in the footnotes. Feel free to engage this material as much as suits you.

As a Christian ethicist by training, I hasten to add that I do not claim special expertise in evangelical historiography, biblical hermeneutics, or theological method. (Fancy words, huh?!) I have done the best that I can outside my specialty, within the limits of my competence. I hope that others will build on what I have attempted to do here.

FINDING OUR WAY OUT OF THE MAZE

A friend of mine proposed an image to describe what he sees going on right now: Young evangelicals began life on a path that their parents and pastors said would take them all the way through the journey, with Jesus and Truth intact.

Maybe about the time they entered college, they found themselves in a maze of questions and problems. I picture one of those massive garden mazes like the one at Hampton Court in England, in which the hedges are so tall that you cannot come close to seeing over them. You just try to make your way through this massive maze and eventually come out on the other side. It is surprisingly difficult.

As adults, my wife and I tried the Hampton Court maze. We really had trouble finding our way. I remember feeling just the beginnings of genuine panic when every path we took within the maze led to a dead end. I began to fear that we would never get out, that in the end we would die in the garden maze of Hampton Court, our flesh to be eaten by proper British vultures.

OK, that's a bit over the top. But it was a relief to get out, I can tell you that.

I meet people all the time who can't find their way out of the evangelical maze. They got stuck in the northwest corner over biblical inerrancy, or in the northeast part over male dominance, or in the southern region over sexual purity. They can't get out, can't go back to where they came from, and can't move ahead.

The goal of this book, then, is to offer clues for getting out of some of the most difficult spots in the evangelical maze, in order to come out on the other side—not just alive and intact, but still interested in a relationship with Jesus. It is a tall order, because among the worst failures of evangelicalism has been the damage done to people's opinions about Jesus himself. Evangelical leaders wanted to be understood as speaking for Jesus, and unfortunately, many have accepted that claim and therefore rejected both them and their Jesus.

Jesus himself needs to be re-presented and reconsidered, and I will do that here. A term I will offer to describe the vision of Jesus I am embracing is *Christian humanism*. It is a new term for me to use in my work, though not a new term in Christian history. It basically means orienting our lives by a version of Christian faith that is compassionately realistic about the human condition, reflects the best of human knowledge, and enables all kinds of human beings to truly flourish. It's humane and for human well-being. I have come to believe that something that might be called Christian humanism offers a good way forward for post-evangelicals. I am confident it reflects Jesus' own way of treating people.

Many readers will have encountered the word "humanism" only in negative connotations, as a way of claiming that only humans matter and that God does not. But I will draw on older, more inclusive uses of the word that celebrate human life and the best human values as gifts from God.

Whether that concept works for you or not, whatever path you pick for getting out of the maze, I invite you to come along with me on a journey into a future that is post-evangelical but still centered on following Jesus, hopeful of making Christians into better human beings, and committed to making the world a better place.

PART I

Authorities: Listening and Learning

1

Evangelicalism

Cutting Loose from an Invented Community

Ah, evangelicalism. We can't move on without a serious look back. We can't think clearly about where to go next without thinking deeply about where we have been—and who we have been. At least I can't. And so, once more, we plunge into the effort to understand evangelicalism. It is no small task.

For twenty-five years I described myself as a centrist or progressive evangelical ethicist. In several previous books I offered my own brief take on evangelicals and evangelicalism,[1] always dissenting from conservative evangelicalism but until 2017 happily claiming the evangelical label on its progressive side. Now that I have left, I offer a final interpretation, at greater length and depth. Perhaps it will be helpful to other post-evangelicals. I hope so.

My core claim is that the modern American evangelicalism that so many of us are now abandoning was a brilliant social construction, an invented religious *identity*, that over decades yielded something like an actual religious *community*.

This is a provocative claim, because most observers have been treating this the other way around all along, as though an evangelical community existed, and the definition of its identity was the needed project.

My claim is indeed just the opposite.

The modern evangelical *identity* was invented through a historical retrieval and rebranding move undertaken by an ambitious group of reformers within the US Protestant fundamentalist community of the 1940s.

The modern evangelical *community* was the eventual product of their entrepreneurial efforts, with an assist over several decades from journalists, historians, pollsters, marketers, consumers, congregations, denominations, parachurch organizations, and regular Christians that all intersubjectively decided to accept the existence of evangelicalism or to identify as evangelical.[2]

The fallout of the invention of modern American evangelicalism has been profound. As a critic I know that by now I mainly notice what has gone wrong, which will be detailed painstakingly in this book. But it would be unfair not to acknowledge at the outset much that has also been good. This includes considerable Christian evangelism, personal discipleship and spiritual growth, church building, education and research, child care and family counseling, relief and development, public policy advocacy, and cultural production including books, music, and art. And the very achievement of modern evangelicalism—the creation of a religious identity that came to dominate the perceived landscape of not just American Christianity but also much of world Christianity—is truly staggering.

EARLIER EVANGELICALS

The *term* "evangelical" was by no means created out of whole cloth in 1942 when the National Association of Evangelicals was created, which is the beginning point of the main story that I want to tell.

Usage of the word "evangelical" does have a long, traceable history.[3] It once had distinguished Protestants from Catholics in Europe, Puritans and Methodists from Anglicans in England, and revivalists and Pietists from nominal, rationalist, and formalist Protestants everywhere.[4] Numerous specific groups of considerably different character called themselves, or were labeled, evangelical (an adjective), or sometimes evangelicals (a noun).

Despite these usages, I side with the scholarly skeptics on the question of whether there really was anything that could fairly be described as "evangelicalism," or an "evangelical community" before the term was retrieved and reinvented by the "new evangelicals" in the 1940s. Certainly there were groups that described themselves, among other ways, as being evangelical, or having an evangelical character, and in turn they have often been described by historians as evangelical, or as evangelicals, or as part of an evangelical "movement" or evangelical "coalition." But I think what happened in the second half of the twentieth century in America was the purposeful creation of a new religious identity and community, which was gradually embraced by all kinds of people, including academics, missionaries, pastors, media, pollsters, and regular believers.[5] Complexities about these historical and definitional matters abound, and I send you to the sources listed in this endnote for more.[6]

THE NEW EVANGELICALS

The Greek etymological origin of the term "evangelical" offers a clue to why the reformist fundamentalists of the 1940s turned to it for self-definition. Derived from the New Testament term *evangelion*, meaning "gospel" or "good news," evangelical is (or has been, or once was) an appealingly laudatory self-description. To be evangelical was (is) to be a gospel Christian, a good news Christian, a New Testament Christian—basically, one of the good, true, authentic Christians. It has almost always been deployed as a contrast term against other versions of Christianity—Catholic, Anglican, scholastic, liberal—viewed as less than ideal.

With polite skepticism, mainline scholar Gary Dorrien argues: "There is an element of presumption in the attempt by any group to claim the term [evangelical] exclusively for itself"[7]—and, I would say, any attempt to contrast *our group* as gospel Christians over against *those lesser Christians*. This has not prevented its use for precisely that purpose, historically and today.

There were certainly appealing qualities to many of the Christian groups that had been identified as evangelical in the past. Especially because the groups claimed as evangelicals were so very diverse, one could reach back into history for any number of examples matching one's preference in launching a new movement. If what was wanted was doctrinal rigor, belief in a completely error-free Bible, warmhearted evangelistic fervor, sacrificial missionary service, personal moral commitment, social-justice reformism (or quiescent social conservatism, take your pick), one could find it.

Both the etymological and the historical appeal of the term help explain why the terms "neo-evangelical" and "evangelical"[8] were deployed by that small but talented and determined group of Protestant fundamentalists in the early 1940s to advance what amounted to, in that moment, a new religious identity, and in the end yielded something like a new religious community. These men (and they were almost exclusively male) had profound ambitions for rescuing Christian witness in a world, and a church, in crisis. The world in which they emerged was torn by catastrophic global warfare and genocide. The onlooking churches had been divided and weakened for decades and had been powerless to prevent a second world war just two decades after the first. These leaders wanted to contribute to renewing American, Western, and human civilization. They went back into history for the best examples they could find.

These leaders who eventually called themselves evangelicals—including Carl F. H. Henry, J. Elwin Wright, Harold John Ockenga, E. J. Carnell, Charles Fuller, and eventually Billy Graham—distinguished themselves as gospel/evangelical Christians from three other types of Christians, some of whose versions of Christianity were believed to be so deficient as not to qualify as Christian at all.

They self-defined as faithful evangelical Christians by contrast with what they viewed as the terrible errors of *Roman Catholicism*. Evangelical anti-Catholicism once ran very deep, and sometimes still does.

They self-defined as faithful evangelical Christians by contrast with the *mainline (and/or) liberal Protestants* who then dominated the Protestant and much of the American scene.

And they self-defined as faithful evangelical Christians by contrast with the militant *Protestant fundamentalist movement*.

Let's go a bit deeper on the two main Protestant groups from which they were trying to distinguish themselves.

Mainline (sometimes also called ecumenical) Protestants then and now are generally understood to be those Protestants found in denominations that are a part of the National Council of Churches (NCC) and the global ecumenical movement as expressed in the World Council of Churches. In the United States, the membership of the NCC has grown to include the United Methodist Church, the United Church of Christ, the American Baptist Churches, the Brethren in Christ, the Episcopal Church, the Presbyterian Church (U.S.A.), the Evangelical Lutheran Church in America, the Reformed Church in America, the Friends (Quaker) churches, most historically black Protestant denominations like the African Methodist Episcopal (AME) churches, most Eastern Orthodox communions, as well as immigrant church groups from Korea, Syria, Poland, Moravia, Hungary, Egypt, and Armenia.[9]

Some of these churches are among the oldest in the United States. Each has its own complicated institutional history, usually involving multiple splits and mergers. Representative congregations are found all over the United States. The beliefs of members and clergy could, and can, vary dramatically. Today, they represent around 14 percent of the American population, down from 24 percent just twenty years ago.[10]

At the time of the engineered birth of modern evangelicalism, these denominations, their seminaries, their top theologians, and the National Council of Churches itself were perceived by fundamentalists to be both ascendant in US religion and culture and dangerously compromised by liberalism.

Mainline Christianity was viewed as liberal *methodologically*, having adopted biblical criticism and modern evolutionary science and now testing biblical claims according to these sciences, rather than the other way around. It was viewed as liberal *theologically*, having abandoned in some cases core beliefs like the virgin birth and the bodily resurrection of Jesus in its effort to modernize and rationalize Christianity. And it was viewed as liberal *politically* and *ethically*, having embraced reformist politics of a Progressive movement, social gospel, and later New Deal type. This latter worry signaled a grave misunderstanding of the main thrust of biblical teachings about economic and political life, which survives to this day in much of US evangelicalism.[11]

But fundamentalist concerns over mainline theological method, and its doctrinal results, were not ungrounded. While my own current theological thinking will be unpacked later in this book, here I will say that taking modern biblical studies and science seriously, as mainline Protestants did, did not have to result in the abandonment of belief in the inspiration and truthfulness of the Bible, the veracity of miracles, the virgin birth, Jesus' resurrection, or the reality of the Holy Spirit. But it often did. The fundamentalists were worried that the liberals were modernizing Christianity to death. Though mainline Protestant theologians varied considerably in their approaches, the broad fundamentalist concern about the direction of liberal theology was not unreasonable.

So much for the liberals. What about the other side, the fundamentalism that the new evangelicals were also concerned about?

Conservative Protestant Christianity, of course, has its own long history, and in America you never had to go far to find some expression of it. Zeroing in on the late nineteenth century, it is fair to say that the US religious coalition that became fundamentalism began as a motley array of movements emphasizing, among other things, global evangelism and revival, personal holiness (and eventually, for some, the "Pentecostal" experience of outpourings of the Holy Spirit), dispensational premillennialism, and a resolute defense of biblical inerrancy.[12] It included Calvinists and Arminians, Wesleyans and Baptists, Congregationalists and Pentecostals, and many others. Whatever their differences, these groups noted with growing concern the rise of Darwinism, biblical criticism, and theological liberalism in the seminaries and churches, and threats to shared Protestant values in the public arena and public education. (Of course, some historians group all of these together simply as "evangelicals" or, at least, as conservative evangelicals.)

After World War I, "fundamentalist" became the primary self-designation of a militant cohort of these traditionalist Protestants who were ready to do battle with the liberals both in church and in culture. *Defending the fundamentals* became the battle flag they carried into combat in the 1920s as vitriolic internecine conflicts about the direction of American Protestantism tore apart many denominations, churches, and schools.[13] Fundamentalists also contested the teaching of evolution in the public schools, a fight that attracted global attention in the 1925 Scopes Monkey Trial. By this point fundamentalism had become defined by its fighting spirit, intellectual defensiveness, and opposition to modern ideas.

After many defeats both in these Protestant denominational battles and in the broader culture, fundamentalism had to regroup. Historian Joel Carpenter has described what happened next in rich detail.[14] Having lost control of mainline denominations and their agencies, fundamentalists created, or expanded, a substantial religious subculture, including Bible institutes, conferences, magazines, radio programs, seminaries, books, Sunday school literature, mission agencies, and more. Many fundamentalists withdrew from mainline Protestant institutions that they believed did not represent their core convictions, but others remained connected as a dissenting minority holding more conservative beliefs.

The new evangelicals came to believe that the overall spirit of fundamentalism had become counterproductive, too militant, separatist, and hunkered down. They wanted to distinguish themselves from that spirit and present a new face to the world.

But this was not a symmetrical third-way move, splitting the difference between liberalism and fundamentalism. The new evangelicals didn't come from nowhere—they were intrafundamentalist reformers, aiming for a better brand, spirit, and strategy to defeat Protestant liberalism, recover true orthodoxy, and take leadership of American Christianity for evangelistic and missionary purposes.[15] As George Marsden, one of the leading historians of evangelicalism, has written, they "were not breaking away entirely from original fundamentalism since original fundamentalism included the very orthodoxy they were attempting to recover."[16]

Though eventually fundamentalists and the new evangelicals from whom they emerged split along many lines, Jon Stone is right in claiming that "the evangelicals were not altogether able to escape the fundamentalist orbit."[17] Historian Donald Dayton suggests that this was especially because core neo-evangelical leaders remained predominantly influenced by the fundamentalist neo-Calvinist theology of late-nineteenth- and early-twentieth-century figures like B. B. Warfield, Charles Hodge, and their ilk, long after they made their mid-twentieth-century break into evangelical identity. In other words, they called themselves evangelicals, but they thought like fundamentalists, never developing a different theology.[18] The most skeptical interpretation is that the new evangelicalism was simply strategic rebranding, a "change in strategy rather than a change in substance."[19]

The reformist fundamentalist effort to rebrand as evangelical and to build a grand evangelical coalition, or even an evangelical community, succeeded far beyond what they could have imagined. The retrieved term "evangelical" graduated to become a real contemporary religious identity and then a community that people eventually came to talk, write, poll, and politick about as if it has always been a real thing in the United States and the world.

One of the most profound ironies facing post-evangelicals is coming to terms with the invented nature of the religious identity (and purported heritage) that so many of us had embraced, as well as the relatively short history of the religious community that the neo-evangelicals created and we came to join. Perhaps better understanding the origins of modern evangelicalism will make leaving it behind a little bit easier.

AMERICAN EVANGELICALISM ON THE MARCH

The rebranding and aspirational creation of American evangelicalism has now had seventy-five years to work itself out.

At one level, the social construction of modern US evangelicalism was fabulously successful. A term used for a reform movement and religious rebranding within the fundamentalist orbit became the term of choice for millions of flesh-and-blood Christians to describe their core religious self-identity. As D. G. Hart has written: "Almost by sheer tenacity neo-evangelicals had created a new religious identity, and evangelical was its designation."[20] This kind of thing does not happen every day. Joel Carpenter sums it up: "That they . . . convinced many that there was such a thing as evangelicalism [was a] major [feat] of religious imagination and statesmanship."[21]

Not only did they convince many that there was such a thing as evangelicalism, they attracted many to want to join up. People who once described themselves as Lutherans or Pentecostals or Baptists or Calvinists or born-again gradually also, or instead, claimed an identity as "evangelical." Congregations, colleges, seminaries, parachurch organizations, and even denominations did the same. Sometimes they changed their mission statements and their names. Other times they changed their faith statements and creeds. What emerged was a new religious identity that gradually gave birth to what amounted to a vast religious community of sorts.

It must be emphasized that numerous religious traditions, denominations, and organizations that *predated* the efforts of the "new evangelicals" of 1942 gradually chose to join the increasingly robust evangelical coalition-cum-community, in ways both formal and informal. Denominations joined the National Association of Evangelicals. Pastors read *Christianity Today*. Seminarians attended Fuller Seminary. Colleges joined what became the Council for Christian Colleges and Universities. Everyday Christians read Francis Schaeffer and Carl Henry. Scholars produced faith statements intended to offer a shared evangelical theology.[22] Authority figures of all types attempted to conform their institutions to the norms of evangelicalism as now defined.

This evangelicalism-building process involved the partial or total submerging of older sectarian distinctions under the new umbrella of evangelicalism. In the end, scores of religious subcultures of wildly divergent character joined to create one vast new evangelical culture, with its own (marketable, consumable) version of everything—books, music, theology, conferences, study centers, you name it.[23]

Sociologist Christian Smith described the success of the project this way:

> What the evangelical movement *did* accomplish was to open up a "space" between fundamentalism and liberalism in the field of religious collective identity; give that space a name; articulate and promote a resonant vision . . . that players in the religious field came to associate with that name and identity-space; and invite a variety of religious players to move into that space. . . . These evangelical activists created a distinct, publicly recognizable collective identity.[24]

Lots of prior subcultures did survive. You could be a Holiness Christian in Kentucky and an evangelical, a tongues-speaking Virginia Pentecostal and an evangelical, a California Vineyard Church believer and an evangelical, a Grand Rapids Dutch Reformed and an evangelical, a Pennsylvania Mennonite and an evangelical, a Chicago Evangelical Covenanter and an evangelical, a Florida Baptist and an evangelical. Every evangelical's experience of the evangelical culture was and is mediated through their particular denominational or church subculture—that is, if they continue to remain engaged in their specific tradition while also becoming a part of evangelicalism writ large.

But from a certain perspective, a perspective from below, as it were, it is not cynical to suggest that evangelicalism eventually became a *conquering power* within the US and eventually global religious landscape, grabbing territory and gobbling up older identities wherever it did not face significant resistance. The new evangelicals initially wanted a big-tent coalition. But sometimes they operated as if they were building an empire.

Donald Dayton rightly suggested that this hegemonic postwar evangelicalism had some profoundly damaging effects. A specialist in nineteenth-century Wesleyan-Holiness and politically progressive evangelicalism, Dayton lamented the way the new evangelicalism obscured (purposely, in his view) not just the significance but the quite distinctive qualities of some of the traditions that predated it, including especially the progressive and egalitarian traditions in which Dayton was particularly interested.[25]

Dayton also believed that the post-1942 new evangelicalism essentially infected (my word, not his) these older traditions with its unhelpful core of fundamentalism. For example, traditions that had never used the language of inerrancy to describe the Bible now felt the need to write one of fundamentalism's core tenets into their faith statements. Traditions that had long-standing commitments to gender and economic egalitarianism and social-justice activism were now compromised by the sexist, hierarchical, and conservative religiopolitics of the regnant new evangelicalism.[26]

The striking irony here is that where smaller, previously distinctive religious communities embraced the new evangelical movement, perhaps to become a part of a religious group with a reach much longer than anything they had ever experienced, many ended up losing their distinctive identities in the process. One might say they gained the world and lost their souls.

In 1991, Dayton suggested that the term "evangelicalism" had outlived its usefulness as a theological or analytical category.[27] Dayton's critique came from the left. D. G. Hart's critique of evangelicalism came from the right, from the tiny denomination called Orthodox Presbyterianism (OPC), but it was remarkably similar. For Hart, evangelicalism had little coherence as a religious identity, was "a parasite on historic religious communions," and could even be described in the language of injustice. "It is curious that the evangelical movement in the United States is so oppressive that it can claim even those who do not want to belong to it."[28]

These two very different thinkers had united around a common conclusion: evangelicalism was both incoherent and oppressive. The category (and identity, and "community") should be deconstructed entirely and purposefully abandoned.

Listening to this history, perhaps we can learn that one aspect of a way forward for post-evangelicals is to renew earlier traditions and distinctives, throwing off the hegemony of establishment evangelicalism in the process. Let Wesleyans be Wesleyans, Anabaptists be Anabaptists, Brethren be Brethren, Calvinists be Calvinists, charismatics be charismatics—and so on. These traditions, especially the minority traditions, appear to have been healthier on their own than within the evangelical coalition. Their theologies, approaches to church life, and ethics were more coherent, added a spicy diversity to American Christianity, and enriched the life of their adherents and Christianity as a whole. Evangelicalism has weakened these traditions through its energetic, homogenizing, and politicized coalition-building efforts.

AN UNWIELDY EVANGELICALISM DEFAULTS TO CONSERVATIVE POLITICS

As the years passed and evangelicalism coalesced as a recognized religious community, it seemed to become more difficult to define its center and boundaries. It was much easier to know who was a Catholic, Orthodox, Baptist, Methodist, or Lutheran Christian than it was to know who was an evangelical. Every effort to define evangelicals failed to convince somebody else who was doing their own defining.[29]

Constant power struggles erupted over who counted as a real evangelical, who should make evangelical doctrinal decisions, and what boundary lines they were drawing. Judgments by "important" voices within the evangelical world that an individual or group had drifted into heresy gained the power to ruin people's careers. Perceived doctrinal slippage within the big evangelical tent played a key role in the high evangelical anxiety about definitions. But there had never been a shared evangelical creed or confession, and therefore never much clarity about who counted as an evangelical.[30] Historian Molly Worthen correctly suggests that at the heart of evangelicalism lies a "crisis of authority," which has constantly manifested itself.[31]

Then, oddly enough, American politics intervened and, in a sense, solved the evangelical identity problem—at grievous cost.

The emergence of a highly visible partisan evangelicalism in the 1970s, with the birth of what was originally called the New Christian Right, turned the focus of many evangelicals, and the understanding of US evangelicals from outside the community, away from evangelism and theology toward politics. I will treat this matter at length in chapter 8. Here it is enough to say that white evangelicals gradually became identified as, and with, socially conservative Republicans—and eventually with any old kind of Republican, in a process that can be described as *identity fusion* between "white evangelical" and "Republican." This move may have provided a welcome shared identity and purpose for most white US evangelicals, but it shattered the earlier big-tent coalition, at least insofar as it had included many nonwhite and politically progressive evangelicals. It also deeply compromised the religious identity and mission of evangelical Christianity. Incidentally, it has also erased any meaningful distinction between evangelicalism and fundamentalism; at least on the political front, that distinction has collapsed.[32]

The partisan politicizing of the evangelical label in this way did not cohere with the original plan of evangelical strategists in the 1940s. They wanted to move fundamentalists out of their bunkers and into "biblical," effective, social-ethical-political engagement. Their agenda was generally conservative but not partisan. It was a different era in any case. There were liberal Republicans and conservative Democrats then. America had not sundered into totalistic left-right tribalism.

Still, the signs were there. The political statements and involvements of postwar American evangelical leaders were consistently politically conservative from the beginning, as had been earlier fundamentalism when it attempted to engage the politics of its time, and this pattern carried forward right through the 1960s.[33] And when, after that, American politics turned sharply binary—left-right, blue-red, Democratic-Republican—white evangelicals were easily persuaded to turn right. They had been there all along. Long before the Moral Majority existed, authoritative white evangelical leaders were already anticommunist, nationalist, antiliberal, antifeminist, antigay, anti–civil rights movement, Eisenhower/Goldwater/Nixon Republicans.[34]

In the election of 2016, evangelical politics took a disastrous turn in its overwhelming support for Donald Trump—including 81 percent of the voters who identified as evangelical, with considerable cover from highly visible "evangelical leaders" like Franklin Graham, Paula White, and Jerry Falwell Jr. This Trumpist turn became a bridge too far for many who had hung in there as evangelicals previously, especially for the young.[35] Seventy-five percent support for the evangelical president George W. Bush was one thing. Eighty-one percent support for Donald Trump was something else.

With Trumpism, American evangelical politics reached its nadir.[36]

A RETROSPECTIVE ON MODERN AMERICAN EVANGELICALISM

In a brilliant recent dissertation on evangelicalism, one of my graduate students, Isaac B. Sharp, looks closely at the course of the modern US evangelicalism that I am describing.[37] However invented it may have been in the beginning, says Sharp, evangelicalism did come to exist as a real thing in the world, just as its World War II–era founders had hoped.

But the new evangelicalism "faced a profound identity crisis from the outset."[38] This contributed to another critically important development—an informal, ever-shifting cast of power players constituting a kind of self-appointed evangelical council of bishops continually set itself the task of policing evangelical boundaries.

Evangelical identity, which was initially defined quite generically in order to build a broad coalition, gradually narrowed as internal challenges were continually met by exclusion of dissenters: African Americans and other nonwhite evangelicals when they challenged white evangelicalism's racism, feminists, non-Calvinists (Methodists, Arminians, Anabaptists, etc.), political liberals, followers of Karl Barth and neoorthodoxy, LGBT people and their allies, and others. These "other evangelicals," says Sharp, were marginalized, were excluded, or chose to leave as they kept losing power struggles within evangelicalism. The pattern is clear: *dissent, lose, and leave* (or be forced out). Evangelicalism has been shedding disillusioned exes for a long time, as

David Hempton showed a decade ago.[39] That tendency has only accelerated in recent years.

Sharp's thesis is that "over the course of the 20th century, mainstream evangelicalism [became] increasingly homogeneous along ideological, social-cultural, theological, political and racial lines" due to the outcomes of these conflicts. Evangelicalism's original breadth gradually narrowed.

Sharp shows that every effort to develop a truly postfundamentalist evangelical theology, and social ethic, has failed—and that the sources of its failure go well beyond theology alone. Gary Dorrien had warned already in 1998 that "if evangelicalism is to become something more than fundamentalism with good manners . . . it must become clearly distinguished from fundamentalism in its approach to core theological issues."[40] Profiling a host of thoughtful evangelical theologians at that time, Dorrien was hopeful that this could happen. But twenty years later it is clear that evangelicalism has failed to meet his challenge. The wreckage left by those who tried and failed to reform evangelicalism is visible everywhere.

Muslim scholar Ibn 'Arabi (1165–1240) wrote, "Every branch reverts to its root."[41] It is possible to look at today's American evangelicalism as reverting to its root, its founding Protestant fundamentalism—or as never really having left, despite its public claims and self-understanding.

And it hasn't reverted just to its founding theological fundamentalism. It has also reverted to its founding cultural fundamentalism, rooted in its founding social location and politics. American fundamentalism in the 1940s was dominated by socially conservative, antiliberal, antimodern, deeply nationalist, patriarchal, middle-class, straight white men. Their assumptions always colored their theology and do today. As Jacob Cook argues, these men didn't see the significance of their social location. They attributed everything to their (right) theology and their adversaries' (wrong) theology.[42] We see with somewhat more critical eyes today. Any post-evangelical American Christianity of any significance will have to grapple with social location, with race, sex, gender, and class.

It may be that former GOP vice presidential candidate Sarah Palin was right about something. She liked to say that you can put lipstick on a pig, but it's still a pig. Maybe evangelicalism—at its core, at its immovable power center—never was more than fundamentalism with lipstick on.

All of this, ultimately, helps explain why I believe now that we must leave evangelicalism behind. I first encountered a loving, devout, evangelistic, unpolitical, Southern Baptist version of evangelicalism. I didn't even know it was called evangelicalism, and it didn't matter. I became a believer and disciple of Jesus there. About a decade later, as a doctoral student, I again encountered evangelicalism, now in the loving, devout, egalitarian, feminist, pacifist, social-justice–oriented progressive version of Ron Sider and friends. It was, again, deeply appealing.

But now, twenty-five years later, both these versions of evangelicalism have been marginalized, if not pushed out entirely. Isaac Sharp aptly describes what remains: "Evangelical identity [became] closely associated with its most fundamentalist and conservative, Reformed and Republican, straight, white, and male leaders."[43] There is nothing in this for me, or for millions of others. We must leave.

But this means that I and other post-evangelicals have some work to do. We need to develop, or discover, a version of Christian faith and ethics that finally leaves all vestiges of this subculture behind—without leaving Jesus behind.

BEYOND DISILLUSIONMENT TO A NEW PATH

The sense that card-carrying American evangelicalism now requires acquiescence to attitudes and practices that *fundamentally* (aha!) negate core teachings of Jesus is fueling today's massive external criticism, internal dissent, and youthful exodus from evangelicalism.

This disillusionment is especially a challenge for the young and those without theological education. This is because—as I often tell my ministerial students—for most people the only version of Christianity that they know about is the one we are giving them. If that one available version of the faith, *the version that we offer them*, is corrupted, then our people may naturally conclude that they had better flee before church itself damages their one and only soul.

I see the fallout every semester among my undergraduate students at Mercer University, where serious religious commitment has moved from common to exceptional within the span of my twelve years at the university. (I do not believe it is all my fault, as some claim.) Some of these students are making their own exodus from a fundamentalist or evangelical upbringing. Others have gained their allergy by watching the news or their friends. I encounter such young people all over the country.

No Christian pastor can rest easy with people walking away from the faith—the gospel, the good news, that we promise at our ordination to advance. This is especially true when what is driving people away is not Jesus, but a particularly damaged version of Christianity that has prevailed over Jesus' own teaching and way.

Rather than simply lamenting our losses and critiquing evangelicalism, it seems important to try to articulate a more faithful version of faith. This is the post-evangelical task. It is where we will go from here.

TAKEAWAYS

- Modern American evangelicalism circa 1942 was an invented religious *identity*, retrieved from the past, that over decades yielded something like an actual religious *community*.
- "Evangelical" sometimes has been a congratulatory self-description, often used to contrast *our group* as gospel Christians over against *less faithful Christians*.
- The new evangelicals were in fact fundamentalists, many of a doctrinaire Calvinist/inerrantist type traceable to Old School Presbyterian theology. They were aiming to reform fundamentalism from within.
- The evangelicalism-building process involved submerging older sectarian distinctions. One aspect of a way forward for post-evangelicals is to revive earlier, healthier, pre-"evangelicalism" traditions and distinctions.
- Since the 1970s, white evangelicals have gradually become, and become identified with, socially conservative Republicans. Indeed, they have gradually become identified with any Republican, including Donald Trump.
- Contemporary American evangelicalism appears to have reverted to its founding theological fundamentalism, and its founding social location and reactionary politics, despite many dissenters.
- The sense that card-carrying American evangelicalism now requires acquiescence to attitudes and practices that negate core teachings of Jesus is fueling today's massive exodus.

2

Scripture

From Inerrancy to the Church's Book

Some of evangelicalism's most important problems relate to the Bible, and many people have left evangelical Christianity or even lost their faith entirely over Bible-related issues. As someone whose mornings begin with reading the Bible, whose writings are rooted in the Bible, and who preaches and teaches in a basically expository fashion from the Bible every weekend, this is not an assertion I am happy making. But I believe it to be accurate. This chapter will attempt to diagnose what has gone wrong in the relationship between evangelicals and the Bible, and offer a post-evangelical path forward that retains Scripture as sacred while making a variety of substantial changes to reading and learning from the Bible.

I want to make clear from the beginning that I am not joining that great cloud of skeptics who laugh off the Bible as some ancient book of mumbo jumbo. Nor am I joining that group, also sizable, who demote the Bible to occasional ceremonial use.

That is not my world, and that is not what I am going to recommend.

Still, I am going to argue that evangelicals inherited from fundamentalism profound problems in their understanding of the Bible, and these need to be identified and resolved in a healthy move forward toward a post-evangelical future. I join many other current post-evangelicals in making this move—scholars like Peter Enns and Christian Smith, pastors like Brian McLaren, Rob Bell, Emily Swan, and Ken Wilson, and popular authors like the late Rachel Held Evans.[1] Their work, along with that of both Jewish and Christian biblical scholars and theologians to be cited below, will inform our conversation here. This is the first of several chapters in which issues of biblical interpretation will be heavily engaged.

EVANGELICAL BIBLICISM

Let's start by thinking about the average highly devout, nonscholarly evangelical believer. In thinking of this believer, I want to paint a portrait of what we might call garden-variety evangelical biblicism. My thumbnail definition of biblicism is a stance in which the Bible is understood as the definitive, if not the only, source of authoritative guidance for life, sometimes tipping over into near idolatry of the Bible. Ex-evangelical sociologist Christian Smith has not yet been topped in his more formal definition of biblicism:

> By "biblicism" I mean a theory about the Bible that emphasizes together its exclusive authority, infallibility, perspicuity, self-sufficiency, internal consistency, self-evident meaning, and universal applicability.[2]

OK, this sounds pretty technical. There are millions of regular evangelicals who may not know what all those words mean—but they are biblicists nonetheless. They love the Bible; read it daily; memorize it deeply; and attempt to live by its teachings.

There are strengths to this way of life. Many of us have seen these strengths at work in real people's lives. "Biblical" people are often very well-grounded. They have clarity about what they believe and why they believe it. They have a sense of purpose in life. They sustain churches through their faithful commitment. Even those of us who have moved into a post-evangelical space can acknowledge these regularly visible strengths of the faith tradition we have left behind.

So, then, what's the problem? One way to say it is that despite its profound meaning and historic role, the Bible cannot bear the weight that evangelicals expect it to bear. I will name six core problems and then propose what I suggest is a post-evangelical way forward.

INERRANCY AND INFALLIBILITY

Many evangelicals have been taught to embrace a theory about the nature of the Bible called *inerrancy*. Inerrancy can be defined in various ways, but the simplest is that the Bible is *without error in anything that it states*. Infallibility is a term sometimes used interchangeably with inerrancy, sometimes treated as a logical consequence of inerrancy, and sometimes functioning as a slightly softened version of inerrancy. This last approach is how I want to use it, to describe the belief that the Bible is without error or fault (only) on theological, moral, and spiritual matters (sometimes defined as *theological inerrancy*).[3]

On this definition, inerrancy is the hard-line position, while infallibility is a modest amendment to make some allowance for concerns about, for example, ancient cosmology versus modern science. In the fierce definitional battles of the last fifty years within evangelicalism, no position to the "left" of infallibility has ever survived as a broadly accepted evangelical option.[4]

Some version of inerrancy often serves as the explicit or implicit foundation for the evangelical belief in the utter authority, trustworthiness, and reliability of Scripture. In a world filled with bad ideas and crazy theories, it is believed, the Bible alone is without error, entirely trustworthy, and absolutely true.

The most difficult problem for a theology of biblical inerrancy (or infallibility, but we will focus on inerrancy) is resolving the respective divine and human roles in the writing of the Bible. Belief in biblical inerrancy depends on something like the idea that the Holy Spirit took such entire control of biblical writers that everything they said was a flawless expression of God's Word. Even though the so-called dictation theory of inspiration was largely abandoned as too mechanistic, the alternative view, often called verbal plenary inspiration, still faces the same problem. It makes of the Bible a divine-human miracle not that different from the incarnation of Christ, to which it is in fact often compared.[5]

It is not easy to believe that any book written by humans could bear the weight of such claims. And when you dig into the Bible, you find much that is abundantly human, and indeed deeply problematic.

C. S. Lewis, long a popular thinker among evangelicals, once wrote:

> The human qualities of the [Bible's] raw materials show through. Naivety, error, contradiction, even (as in the cursing Psalms) wickedness are not removed. . . . We might have expected, we may think we should have preferred, an unrefracted light giving us ultimate truth in systematic form . . . [but] we cannot, for the life of us, see that [God] has after all done it.[6]

Lewis is saying that God has not "after all done it." The Bible was quite manifestly written (and *edited*—can editors also be inerrant?) by a diverse cast of *human beings*, reporting aspects of their experiences of encounter with God and what they believed God told them or gave them to say to others.[7] As Rob Bell says: "The Bible did not drop out of the sky; it was written by people."[8] Any book written by people is a human product. Any human product is subject to human limits and various kinds of error.

Theories of inerrancy are defensive products. They give off the scent of fear. Peter Enns puts it this way: "This view of the Bible does not come from the Bible but from an anxiety over protecting the Bible."[9]

It is natural to wonder whether the church has always embraced such a brittle posture.

The answer is no. Despite very high claims about the inspired nature of the Bible through most of church history, the concept of inerrancy is not part of the church's most ancient tradition.[10] Some scholars date it to anti-Catholic polemics during the post-Reformation period.[11] Others say that it took hold as a response to the first rise of modern historical-critical treatment of the Bible.[12] Others simply trace it to the fundamentalist/Reformed Princeton theology of Charles Hodge and B. B. Warfield, which came forward into evangelicalism.[13]

Whether as a response to the conflict with Catholics over where authority truly lies in church life, or in reaction to the challenging findings of modern biblical studies, or as a tool to define evangelical boundaries and win denominational battles, inerrancy has proved useful. The problem is that it tends to dissolve on contact with what is in the Bible itself, thus propelling many devout young believers into unnecessary crises of faith.

The Bible does not make comprehensive claims about itself like infallibility or inerrancy. That's partly because the anthology of texts that became the Bible offers very few examples of self-reflection on what it means to be part of sacred Scripture. Writings became Scripture in the canonization process of Israel and the church, which occurred long after the texts were originally written (and long, long after most were originally *spoken and passed down orally*, well before they were written).[14]

That's why there are so few biblical verses to cite that might yield an overall doctrine of biblical inspiration. One possible exception is this widely cited text from 2 Timothy:

> All scripture [is] inspired by God [and is] useful for teaching, for reproof, for correction, and for training in righteousness, so that everyone who belongs to God may be proficient, equipped for every good work. (2 Tim. 3:16–17; cf. 2 Pet. 1:21)

I have added the brackets because the two uses of the verb "is" are not in the Greek. A note in the NRSV gives the following as a possible reading: "Every scripture inspired by God is also useful for teaching . . ." This alternate reading suggests that one way to think about biblical inspiration might be that *some scriptural texts consistently demonstrate that they are inspired by God because they prove so useful in Christian experience for drawing people to Jesus and his way.* Other texts, it is quietly understood, do not demonstrate that effect and are not asked to bear that weight. This has sometimes been described as a theory of limited inspiration. If one needs an inspiration theory, it makes the most sense to me.[15] There is consistent evidence over two millennia that a limited but still large number of biblical texts prove deeply useful for what 2 Timothy calls “training in righteousness.”

I suggest that this approach more accurately reflects most of our real experiences with the Bible. The Sermon on the Mount is more useful than Paul’s regular defenses of his ministry, the psalms are more instructive than the lists of kings, and exhortations to love are more edifying than exhortations to kill. Another way to say it is that we all have a working “canon within the canon.” Few of us like to acknowledge it, but it is a fact.

The good news is that the canon within the canon can be so vast. You can build a life on it. Of course, you need to know where to look to find the criterion for creating that canon within the canon. I believe Jesus himself settled that matter when he offered the Great Commandment as the heart of the Law: love God with everything, and love your neighbor as yourself (Matt. 22:36–40).

Even if we take the NRSV majority reading and the Christian tradition that reflects it, the most that this one verse in 2 Timothy says about Scripture is that it is inspired by God and useful for Christian instruction. It doesn’t say Scripture is infallible or inerrant.

Inerrancy is an extrapolation of a miraculous understanding of the divine inspiration of the Bible. But it creates constant problems for those who attempt to make what we find in the Bible fit with their absolutist theory. All it takes is one counterexample—trivial ones such as conflicting dates, more serious conflicts such as the different accounts of the resurrection, or profound theological issues such as the challenge by the book of Job to the theology of the book of Proverbs.[16]

Watch what happens when conflicts are discovered—either (a) stretchy, highly creative ways of interpreting texts are invented to avoid any perceived problem or conflict, or (b) scholars and pastors quietly soften the interpretation of inerrancy to account for the real problems involved, or (c) the whole house of cards falls, the Bible loses all credibility, and people walk away from Christianity, because it hinged far too much on a rigid theory of inspiration.

Christian Smith put it this way: “In order for evangelical biblicism to *appear* to work . . . those who believe in it have to engage in various forms of textual selectivity, denial, and contortion—which actually end up violating biblicist intentions. Most of these are practiced covertly.”[17] But when these moves are discovered, the consequences can be devastating. John Goldingay talks about the slippery slope that leads from legitimate doubts about inerrancy to uncertainty with and abandonment of the rest of Christian belief and life.[18]

That experience can look like an awful faith crisis, as in the late Rachel Held Evans’s poignant words about her journey:

> With each question, the voice of God grew quieter and the voice of others grew louder. These were dangerous questions . . . forbidden questions, especially for a girl. They told her to fight against her doubts, but her sword grew heavy. They told her to stand strong in her faith, but her legs grew weak. Words that once teemed with life nettled her mind, and stories that once captured her imagination triggered her doubts and darkest fears. . . . There was no map for a world suddenly rearranged.[19]

These gymnastics, and these miseries, are not necessary. There is a better way.

COMPOSITION, CONTEXTUALITY, AND DIVERSITY

As a collection of texts written long ago, the Bible cannot be read apart from understanding the composition and editing processes behind its multiple texts, the vastly divergent contexts of its writing and editing, and the great and irreducible diversity of its content.

The Bible is a collection of texts, not one text, written over fifteen hundred years, in three languages, and from very different political and cultural contexts. As Brian McLaren and others have pointed out, the Bible is better viewed as a library of books than a single book.[20] Finding coherence and consistency in this vast and diverse collection of texts is not easy. Indeed, in some areas, finding coherence is impossible. The reality very often looks more like sharply diverging perspectives. This could be troubling, if our theology requires that the Bible speak with one voice. But what if that's the wrong expectation? To the contrary, the Bible is an extraordinarily diverse collection of texts by any measure—genre, context of composition, authorship, and purpose.

The Bible has historically been ordered according to sections (Law, Writings, Prophets, Gospels, Epistles, etc.), but the sections are uneven in terms of their purported commonality. Meanwhile each book of the Bible is so clearly its own work of art that each has its own scholars who specialize in studying it. Even the best efforts of these scholars leave plenty of room for educated guesses about the most basic matters of context and composition.

Interpreters struggle to make sense of the very ancient languages the Bible was written in (Hebrew, Aramaic, Greek), the many mysteries and question marks related to authorship, and the multilayered, sometimes multicentury editing process that is apparent in a close reading of most biblical books. This is not even to speak of the problems in the transmission of hand-copied written texts tracing back several thousand years. This accounts for the strained effort to restrict inerrancy claims to the "original autographs"—which no one has seen for millennia—and obscures both the writing and the editing processes clearly at play in biblical texts.

It is also a fact that every act of translation is already debatable, because languages reflect worlds of thought that differ dramatically across cultures. Don't miss the stark reality that the evangelical versus mainline versus fundamentalist division is even reflected in preferred Bible translations. Which version of the Bible shall we trust as offering the infallible English translation?

Even a freshman biblical studies course poses serious threats to the "God said it, I believe it, that settles it" understanding of the Bible—as many post-evangelicals can attest. It would be far better to find other ways to treat the Bible as sacred.

THE INEVITABILITY OF INTERPRETATION

All texts are products of authors, who wrote specific documents that must be interpreted by readers. As with any text, the Bible cannot interpret itself. The long history of Christianity clearly reveals what Christian Smith calls "pervasive interpretive pluralism,"[21] the constant and irreducible differences in how people interpret the Bible. This seriously undercuts biblical inerrancy.

This suggests another grave problem with declaring the Bible inerrant. Such a move tends to obscure the role of the interpreter in a fog of exalted dogma around the Bible itself. Biblical scholar Dale Martin puts the point quite trenchantly:

> The people who talk most about the Bible "speaking" are often those most guilty of ignoring or masking their own agency in biblical interpretation. . . . We cannot allow the . . . masking of human interpretive practices that are the actual agents that produce those "meanings" of the Bible so many people point to in their attempts to oppress other people.[22]

Whatever claims we make about the Bible's truthfulness, in the end we must face the fact that the Bible is being interpreted by Joe Pastor or Josie Sunday School Teacher, deploying whatever (usually very limited) interpretive skills they might have developed along the way, and exercising profound communal power as they do so.

The populist nature of American evangelicalism—which is an unusually democratic faith tradition—combined with the influence of low-church traditions like the Baptists and so many baptistic nondenominational church start-ups means that millions of evangelicals are set loose on the Bible believing that they need no help to interpret it. Of course, most people find the Bible at least somewhat confusing, so they do need help. That is where preachers, Sunday school teachers, and celebrity authors and pastors come in. The problem there, though, is that many of the most popular leaders that evangelicals turn to are . . . let's say, fairly limited in their skills. Joel Osteen. Kenneth Copeland. Paula White. I mean, really.

There is also the problem that the "plain commonsense," straightforward, populist reading of the Bible has often proved disastrous.[23] This was a huge issue in the pre–Civil War context when the Bible was used to defend slavery. Taken at its face value, the Bible does not condemn slavery. When abolitionists argued that the deeper message of the Bible was clearly against slavery—as Mark Noll points out—they were viewed as suspiciously unfaithful to the Bible.[24]

By contradicting the *plain teaching* of the Bible, many abolitionists were viewed as challenging biblical authority. The argument that "won" for many prewar Americans was the one that seemed most democratically and straightforwardly easy to understand and defend: God is OK with slavery because the Bible never condemns it and indeed actively teaches it (see chap. 9 for more).

Interpreters read through their own lenses, which consist of social location, level and type of education, sources consulted, Bible translations, religious (sub)traditions, and a thousand other factors. *Nowhere is the role of power-in-community more obvious than on this issue of interpretation.*[25] Whatever this or that evangelical understands God's Inerrant Word to mean has probably come to them through the authoritative interpretations of their most significant pastors, teachers, authors, musicians, bloggers, podcasters, Veggie Tales episode, or youth group moms and dads.

Meanwhile, as noted earlier, evangelical Christianity as a whole has been shaped by its collective social location, power, and self-interest—quite notable in relation to race, gender, sexuality, political loyalty, and nationality. But all of this is obscured when the Guy at the Front waves his Bible around, claiming to announce the simple, unadulterated Word of God. No. What he is offering is *his interpretation* of God's Word. What he does not offer (often because he does not realize it) is that he inherited this interpretation from some pastor or teacher himself. Nor does he admit that the interpretation will likely bolster his own power in the church and community.

A healthy post-evangelical approach to the Bible will heighten realism about the fact that the Bible is always an interpreted text, and that we flawed, limited, self-interested people are the interpreters. It will demythologize claims to authoritative truthfulness on the part of all interpreters, including those who claim the greatest authority in any given context. It will emphasize a communal process of interpreting Scripture, which occurs in an ongoing conversation between individual Christians, clergy, scholars, and the historic church, with the help of God's Spirit. Which leads to the next point . . .

THE CHURCH'S BOOK

The Bible was developed first by the Jewish people and its leaders and then expanded and reshaped by the Christian church and its leaders. For Christians, as the church's book the Bible cannot be fully understood apart from the church's history and tradition, including the forming of the canon, transmission and translation of texts, and scriptural interpretation, all in the context of the real power dynamics of Christian communities. Accepting that the Bible is the church's book does not have to diminish its sacredness, because the Bible is sacred to the church. But it does offer greater realism about where the Bible came from and what it is. It also helps the Bible remain sacred for us even when it is viewed as irrelevant (or worse) in secularized cultures.[26]

Perhaps the following almost-never-cited lines from 2 Timothy, just before the passage I quoted earlier, help us understand what we should take the sacredness of Scripture to mean:

> But as for you, continue in what you have learned and firmly believed, knowing from whom you learned it, and how from childhood you have known the sacred writings that are able to instruct you for salvation through faith in Christ Jesus. (2 Tim. 3:14–15)

Writing, according to most scholars, late in the New Testament period, the author offers a glimpse of the meaning and context of sacred Scripture that feels very much like what later developed in Catholic (rather than Protestant) tradition. The "sacred writings" (probably the Septuagint translation of the Hebrew Bible)[27] were passed on to Timothy from trusted elders, beginning in childhood. The texts were treated by these trusted elders as sacred.

In other words, *certain texts were treated as sacred and thus became Scripture for a family and community of people, because they were believed to bear witness to Jesus and to help people find salvation through him.*[28] Apart from the attestation of actual believers, the Bible would just be an ancient book. But because of the church's witness to the Bible's significance, it becomes plausible to treat these texts as "Scripture."[29] That is how texts became scripture, and how they remain Scripture. As Robert Jenson puts it, "It is only because the church maintains the collection of these documents, with the texts they presented, as the book she needs, that we are concerned for their interpretation" today.[30]

Even if the faith community decides to call certain texts inerrant, it is still the faith community that makes this declaration. The Bible is the church's book. The church believes the texts it calls Scripture to be sacred; to be, somehow uniquely, a bearer of the word of God, when read in contact with the Spirit of God. But this is still the church's decision. Speaking as a Jew about the Hebrew Bible, Marc Zvi Brettler makes the same point: "The Bible is the collection of ancient literature that my community has sanctified."[31]

I am suggesting that post-evangelicals do not need to abandon the Bible or a concept of sacred Scripture. But I am also suggesting that hints offered in 2 Timothy, as well as what we know of the canonization process, give us another way to hold the Bible as sacred—a way that does not require a brittle dogma of inerrancy. This way is to recognize that the Bible is and always has been the church's book. Ever since the canonization decisions were made by the church, the Bible has, with the help of the Holy Spirit, been continually forming the church that itself canonized these texts. It is a loop between church, Spirit, and Bible, and it is enough.

THE HEBREW BIBLE—AND THE JEWISH PEOPLE'S WAY OF READING IT

Three-fourths of the Christian Bible is what Christians have historically called the Old Testament, scholars usually call the Hebrew Bible, and Jews mainly call Tanakh (from the first letters of Torah [Law/Teaching], Nevi'im [Prophets], and Kethuvim [Writings]) or just "the Bible."[32] From there, the complexities only deepen. I want to camp out here for a moment and talk about some of those complexities, which are almost never mentioned in evangelicalism—and about how much post-evangelicals could learn if we listened to our Jewish sisters and brothers.

Judaism and Christianity are two of humanity's handful of major living world religions. Christianity emerged out of the ancient or "biblical" stage of Judaism. It began as a Jewish movement centered around belief in the Jew Jesus. This movement believed the crucified and risen Jesus to be the Messiah sent by God, and it believed the church to be the new Israel.

Both Jesus and the church were therefore viewed by Christians as the true fulfillment of God's relationship with the Jewish people—notwithstanding majority Jewish disagreement with such beliefs. The Jesus movement began as a Jewish movement in Palestine, became a Jewish and Gentile movement in the diaspora,[33] and finally became a largely Gentile movement with considerable anti-Jewishness embedded in its teachings.

Because of its origins, the church decided (not without fierce argument at times) to retain Jewish sacred writings as the first part of the Christian canon, calling this collection the Old Testament and interpreting it through their experience with Jesus, later reflected in the New Testament.

Use of the terms "Old" and "New" was not value neutral or merely chronological. Just look at the Letter to the Hebrews for a systematic Old Covenant–New Covenant paradigm (Heb. 7–8). That move left its unfortunate mark on Christianity as a whole. Jaroslav Pelikan put it this way: "The contrast between 'the old' and 'the new' unavoidably carr[ied] with it connotations such as 'the superseded' or at least 'the updated.'"[34]

Judaism is a living tradition. It did not wither and die in the moments after the birth of Christianity. What the early church did was something like digging up and replanting a rose bush out of someone else's garden without their permission. The church claimed for itself a version of the Jewish canon as it was developing at the time of Christianity's birth and inserted this literature into the Christian Bible as our part 1. It was a fateful decision.

Later Jewish sacred writings developed ways of reading the Hebrew Bible that would have been hugely helpful if the church had been paying attention. The primary example is the Talmud, which itself became authoritative, and yet Christians generally have no contact with it whatsoever.[35] Put simply, the Talmud contains discussions and debates among rabbinic authorities about how to interpret Hebrew Bible texts. The Talmud is a sacred book that enshrines argument and question into religious tradition itself. The way that the highest respect is offered to Scripture is by debating it and its interpreters.

But the concept of dialogue goes even further. Writing of Jewish theologians Martin Buber and Franz Rosenzweig, Paul Mendes-Flohr says: "Their overarching premise was that the Hebrew Scripture is at root a record of the dialogue between God and Israel."[36] Not a dictation. A dialogue. The Bible records the dialogue between God and God's people. It also records the dialogues among God's people.

Certainly, this is not the way that all Jews understand the Bible. Jews have their inerrantists and dictationists as well. But my understanding is that this has been something of a minor strand among even traditional Jews while it has been the dominant approach among evangelicals.

It would have been so nice if evangelicals could have known of the Jewish traditions of dialogue, debate, argument, questioning. Instead we got inerrancy. Inerrancy made it wrong to question the literal face-value reading of any biblical text—ranging from the Sodom and Gomorrah story to Joshua's holy war texts.

This created a lose-lose problem for us when we read such texts. Either we experienced what we feared was illicit moral resistance to morally troubling texts, and finally found we needed to leave the Bible (and faith) behind, or, we felt we needed to *discount our own moral resistance to scripturally recounted acts like divinely ordained genocide*, and so damaged our moral sensibility. We abdicated our moral responsibility to read texts in ways that bless rather than harm human beings.

Reinterpreting sacred texts in the name of fidelity to God and kindness to neighbor is precisely what the Talmud does, and many Jewish scholars do, to this day. If we had paid attention, we could have avoided the problem caused by our theological rigidity about how to read Scripture. And we might have avoided other harms that we did in the name of the inerrant Word.

Holocaust survivor, memoirist, and theologian Elie Wiesel described his approach to Scripture this way:

> If even the most authoritative teaching, the most sacred text, leads to dehumanization, to humiliation, to harm, then we must reject it. The Bible itself shows us how to do this. . . . [The rabbis] worked to align the text with their moral understanding. And in doing so, they gave us permission—no, an obligation, to do the same. . . . Our role in reading sacred scripture is to ask two questions: "What does the text say?" and "Who may be harmed by this text?"[37]

Christians took terrorizing texts and attempted to read them as if they were not. We did this even though much of Jewish tradition did not read its own texts that way. If we had instead privileged Jewish readings of Jewish texts—if we had even listened to them—we might have avoided a multitude of disasters.

EPISTEMOLOGY: THERE ARE MANY OTHER WAYS OF KNOWING

The Bible cannot be the primary source of knowledge and criterion of truth in all areas of importance. The evidence is clear that the Bible constantly reveals its inadequacy to bear this weight.

Stepping back for a broader look, here we are dealing with the issue of epistemology, or how human beings know things that we know, how we discern reality, how we distinguish truth from error.

There is a universe of things to know and understand and a variety of ways to pursue knowledge and understanding. There was a time—in the premodern world—when entire cultures accepted that the Bible (and the church) held the keys to all knowledge: about the universe, the earth, the animals, human nature, human history, theology, morality, and everything else. That time has passed, but most evangelicals have remained stuck there.

I will argue in the next chapter that post-evangelicals need to do some fresh thinking about other ways of knowing—indeed, other ways of hearing God address us. These include tradition, science, reason, experience, intuition, community, and relationships. The power of a narrow evangelical biblicism must be broken, but you can't replace something with nothing. We need to open ourselves to other ways of discerning truth.

ANOTHER WAY: CHURCH, LECTIONARY, AND LITURGY

I attend Catholic Mass most weeks. I want to conclude this chapter by talking about how Catholic liturgy treats Scripture and the constructive lessons to be learned from this. Much of what I say will also apply to other liturgical traditions.

In Catholic liturgy on Sundays, four Scripture passages are presented. (Actually, Mass is celebrated daily, so the schedule of readings is also daily.) The four readings are an Old Testament text, a psalm (usually sung), a non-Gospel New Testament reading, and a Gospel reading. The four texts are established by the lectionary, which for Catholics is set by the Catholic Church but largely overlaps with the same lectionary readings offered by the ecumenical Protestant churches.[38]

The lectionary itself signals the respect of the church for the Bible. But it also reflects the church's authority to develop a schedule and arrangement of texts. Even in the entire three-year lectionary cycle, *the Bible is being curated by the church*. Some principle of priority and significance is operating, and a vast array of texts are never read. Taking the Sunday and weekday lectionaries together, one analysis finds that 13.5 percent of the vast Old Testament is read (excluding the psalms), 55 percent of the non-Gospel New Testament, and 90 percent of the Gospels.[39]

Embodied gestures of respect are part of the reading of Scripture. Readers approach from the congregation, bow at the altar, read reverently, and conclude by saying, "The Word of the Lord," to which the people respond, "Thanks be to God."

The Gospel reading is the climax of the liturgy of the Word. More elaborate gestures signal the heightened significance of Jesus and his stories and sayings. All rise. A preparatory song is sung. The Bible is lifted above the celebrant's head and then brought down, sometimes to be kissed. An embodied gesture by all participants communicates their prayer that the Word would be in their minds, on their lips, and in their hearts.

The homilist then offers a reflection on one or more of the texts. Homilies are usually far shorter than evangelical sermons and do not attempt comprehensiveness or rhetorical cleverness. The Catholic Church wants to signal more attention to the text and less to the preacher.

Other biblical texts of special significance are woven into the rest of the liturgy. When one experiences this on a weekly basis, one senses the wisdom of the church in selecting the handful of biblical texts that will be embedded into worship. These texts make the cut because of their extraordinarily inspiring quality. These include the Lord's Prayer, as well as an abundance of statements in the eucharistic liturgy.

It seems ironic to acknowledge that a Catholic Mass almost certainly contains more Scripture than the average evangelical service. Scripture is quietly but profoundly treated as a trustworthy vehicle for encountering the word of God, surrounded with embodied gestures of reverence and receptivity.

The Catholic Church does not feel the need to pump up its language about the Bible. In a Catholic Mass, the Bible feels like what it is, the much-beloved sacred Scripture chosen, transmitted, and honored by the church. The church wants to immerse its people in as much Scripture as possible, but it subtly curates the people's exposure to the canon. Those many Scriptures that are recognized as most edifying are presented to the people, and *by* the people, day by day.

This lectionary-based, worship-centered approach is at least one way that the Bible can remain sacred for post-evangelicals. Without the weight of all knowledge placed on it; without need for unsustainable claims such as inerrancy; with a discipline provided by church tradition; with an implicit willingness to acknowledge gradations in the edifying power of different Scriptures; with Jesus always central; with a readiness to hear God's word in the mix of texts that are presented when the people gather.

That's a long way from throwing the Bible out with the bathwater, which is the sad choice many post-evangelicals have felt the need to make in light of the reign of terror and error that they have experienced at the hands of people claiming to be offering God's Holy Word.

Instead, post-evangelicals can continue to believe that God wants to speak to people in various and sundry ways. One of these ways is through Scripture. It is right to approach Scripture, in community, with receptive hearts and open minds listening for God's word. It is also right to remember that there is a substantial gap between what the God of the universe wants to show us and what human beings see. As Paul said, "We see through a glass, darkly" (1 Cor. 13:12 KJV). If we remember that, we might be able to avoid turning our fallible interpretations into infallible declarations of God's truth. And yet we will continue to seek God's truth, in the Bible and beyond.

TAKEAWAYS

- Despite its profound meaning, the Bible cannot quite bear the weight evangelicals expect it to bear.
- Inerrantist claims go beyond the Bible's own claims for itself and often create unnecessary faith crises for believers.
- Some scriptural texts consistently demonstrate that they are inspired by God because they prove so useful for teaching.
- A healthy post-evangelical approach to the Bible will heighten realism about the fact that the Bible is always an interpreted text, and that we flawed, limited people are the interpreters.
- The Bible is the church's book, and in a complex and morally ambiguous way, a borrowing of the Jewish people's ancient book.
- Instead of ignoring Jewish interpretation of their own Bible, we should pay attention to the Jewish tradition of dialogue with the text and each other.
- Use of the lectionary and rituals around Scripture demonstrate that the texts are curated by the church and received with openness for forming and governing Christian life, with the aid of the Holy Spirit.
- Post-evangelicals can set aside inerrancy without abandoning Scripture.

3

Resources

Hearing God's Voice beyond Scripture

BEYOND *SOLA SCRIPTURA*

Post-evangelicals are no longer able to accept exaggerated claims about the inerrancy and all-sufficiency of the Bible. If we hang in there with Christianity, we will need a new approach to listening for God's voice and discerning God's will.

It may be, though, that we don't have to start from scratch. There are plenty of resources available to aid our discernment. None of them, individually or together, can offer ironclad certainty that we are thinking (or living!) rightly. None of them, individually or together, can offer the authoritative doctrinal pronouncements that many of us heard (or offered!) within evangelicalism. They are resources for our best and most conscientious discernment, with the help of God's Spirit and Christ's example. In a postmodern, post-evangelical context, that is the best that we can do.

There is much packed into that last paragraph. I am saying that Christians have many resources for listening to God's voice and discerning God's will. But given human limits—even as humans with Jesus in front of us, the Bible open before us, and the Spirit within us—I am rejecting any inerrant path to infallible doctrine. I am emphasizing an open-ended and open-minded discernment process, individually and in Christian community, drawing on the best resources we can muster. I am noting the central role of conscience, that fallible but still essential moral rudder that God has given each human being. And, while specific confessional traditions do have agreed doctrinal statements and official structures of doctrinal authority, I am not proposing that post-evangelicals as a whole should adopt one of these confessional traditions.

And so, we continue.

Critical distance enables us to see that there has always been a gap between what evangelicals say about the Bible and what they do. I am not talking about the garden-variety moral hypocrisy common to all humans. I am talking about how evangelicals learn things.

The Bible is so often claimed as evangelicals' sole source of knowledge about God, but it does not appear to work quite this way in real life. Those who go to church the most and study the Bible the most know (even if they won't admit it) that the Bible contains substantial material that is barely understood, internally contradictory, morally problematic, and far removed from the concerns of life today.

These realities may not change official evangelical claims to *sola scriptura* (only Scripture is authoritative) or inerrancy, but they are reflected in the *functional role of certain other authorities* in evangelical life.

Evangelical Christians, just like other Christians, depend upon official and unofficial leaders who interpret the demands of the Bible and who create accepted patterns of reading and interpretation. Evangelicalism certainly does have its own clergy, its unofficial bishops, cardinals, and contenders for Evangelical Pope. Though their role is obscured by their lack of official status, and though they can never finally resolve the constant crisis of authority in evangelicalism, they do wield considerable power.

The actual daily life of believers also requires considerable access to other sources of knowledge. Christians who want to function in the real world do go out and study and learn from modern knowledge, while also making use of their own human capacities.

All of this is veiled from evangelical eyes by the fact that when they gather together, it is almost always the Bible that evangelicals study, the Bible that they elevate as holy, the Bible that is claimed as the source of ultimate knowledge. Evangelicalism has made it an article of faith to believe that the Bible can do more than it does. Meanwhile, back in the real world, anyone who has been to very many evangelical "Bible studies" can attest that what happens in those meetings is often more about the sharing of people's socially located biases, ideologies, and politics than close exegetical study of Scripture.

Where do we go from here? Into skepticism, atheism, or spiritual-but-not-religious? Into just making it up as we go along, or rejecting any concept like "authorities" for religious knowledge?

I take it as a given that because of the gap between an infinite God and finite people, and because human beings are both willfully sinful and unconsciously misdirected, there is no perfect or risk-free method when humans listen for God's voice. There is no foolproof formula, no guaranteed result, no absolutely sure foundation for knowledge. Dale Martin is right about the dangers whenever anybody promises "more security than is actually possible in interpretation . . . [through] appeal to a particular 'method.'"[1]

I believe that given human finitude and the way sinfulness distorts our cognitive processes, *the best approach is the most comprehensive*. We need to cast our nets as broadly as possible for truth, for direction, and for wisdom. We need to go for both-and syntheses, not either-or binaries. Heaven knows we need all the help we can get. The approach I will propose seeks all the available help, all of it critically engaged—with the ultimate goal being to gain the direction that we need to best love God and love neighbor, as Jesus taught (Matt. 22:36–40).

This chapter will offer reflections on three types of resources for Christian thinking and living: those *internal to the church*, those *wired into human nature*, and those *external in human intellectual life*. We will also see that this vision can connect to broader paradigms for how Christians should orient ourselves to the world in which we live, one of which is called Christian humanism.

INTERNAL ECCLESIAL RESOURCES: TRADITION, CHURCHES, AND THEIR LEADERS

I want to make two kinds of claims when it comes to the role of Christian tradition and other internal Christian sources.

My *factual claim* is that in almost every Christian setting, the interpretation of the Bible is mediated to believers through some version of Christian tradition, which itself is mediated and interpreted by recognized religious authorities, usually pastors or teachers. I will call Christian tradition, the various churches, and their spiritual and intellectual leadership our *internal ecclesial resources*.

My *normative claim*, or proposal, begins with this idea: post-evangelical Christians should allow *explicit engagement* with these internal conversation partners to inform our reading of the Bible and our efforts to follow Jesus faithfully, rather than pretending that tradition and church leadership are not mediating biblical interpretation. We need to "own" the role of tradition and leaders in our religious life.

Evangelical Christian biblicism has obscured the role of tradition and church leaders in shaping what we think we know. Evangelicals tend to leap back and forth between biblical texts and contemporary interpretation, with what James McClendon (nonpejoratively) called a "this is that" or "then is now" mind-set.[2] The apostle Paul addresses a comment to Corinth about marriage, we read it in our Bible over coffee one morning, and we leap over two thousand years to act as if Paul is addressing us exactly as he was addressing his original readers.

Sometimes reading the Bible does feel like that, and those leaps across the chasms of time are not dangerous. But actual Christians live in historical realms, not mythic ones. Part of this history is that we read biblical texts mainly as we have been taught to read them. We may think it's a direct line from Paul to us. It's not. We need to work hard to overcome our naiveté about the voices shaping, and sometimes misshaping, our reading of the Bible.

That's my first proposal. Here's my next one: post-evangelicals can and should join those evangelicals who have made a turn toward retrieving ancient Christian Tradition. But we must do so without falling into the errors so often visible in that retrieval process.

By capital-T Tradition here I am referring to the authoritative postbiblical creeds, conciliar texts, confessions, declarations, essays, treatises, and sermons that survive from the first seven centuries or so of the church's history. Let's call this the ancient Christian Tradition. This ancient Tradition is a shared legacy of early Christianity. It is the taproot of all specific Christian traditions that came forward into our world, including Eastern Orthodoxy and Roman Catholicism—as well as various forms of Protestantism insofar as they remain in living contact with that taproot. It is therefore appropriate to speak about a shared ancient Christian Tradition and specific traditions flowing out of it. Evangelical Protestants have often expressed little interest in either.

I should hasten to add that the distinction between Scripture and Tradition is itself debatable, and the debate is illuminating. Texts produced by early church leaders that the church decided should make it into the canon became Scripture; some texts produced by other early church leaders around the same time were not selected by the church for the canon. So, for example, 2 Peter is in the canon, and the *Didache* is not—yet which text is more inspired, or at least inspiring, is certainly arguable.[3] I believe that Dale Martin is correct in declaring that the New Testament is the first layer of Christian Tradition, rather than entirely distinguishable from it. Martin's overall approach to tradition closely tracks with my own:

> Tradition is the flow, the changing current, we, as Christians, *live in*. It cannot be separated from scripture because scripture is the early Christian tradition (or at least a few strands of it that survive in texts). And we never interpret scripture except from within tradition. Tradition is simply the church in its memory and presence.[4]

The recent turn to Tradition has reflected the welcome recognition that evangelicals would benefit from studying church history, historical theology, and major theologians far more than has been typical. Given the idiosyncratic and frankly absurd biblical interpretations that sometimes emerge in evangelical Christianity, this turn to Tradition is a welcome corrective. As evangelical historian D. H. Williams has argued, "As Protestantism confronts the post-denominational and . . . post-Christian world of the twenty-first century, it is vital that its future identity not be constructed apart from the fullness of its historical foundations."[5]

The historical turn in evangelicalism has gone further than mere resourcing, however. Theologian Robert Webber's *Ancient-Future Faith* project aimed to resolve the various problems created for Protestant Christianity by modernity (including various unhelpful conservative Protestant reactions) by retrieving as far as possible the ecclesiology, worship, spirituality, and mission of the ancient church.[6] Thomas Oden's retrieval of orthodoxy (sometimes called paleo-orthodoxy) had a more pugnacious edge, emerging from the mainline side of Protestantism and especially oriented to defeating prevailing theological liberalism, away from which Oden had famously converted.[7] Both projects were Protestant, though one was (post-)evangelical and the other was postliberal. Both have left their traces. An enduring Protestant engagement with the wellsprings of ancient, premodern Christian Tradition continues today both in scholarship and in some church contexts. This is a welcome development in many ways.

Still, in the ancient-church-retrieval project one catches a whiff of the romantic, an apparent yearning for the aura of sacred antiquity not that different from the feeling one gets in an old French cathedral. Those wandering an old cathedral, or digging in ancient textual sources, must be wary of imposing their own assumptions and needs onto what they think they are discovering. In much of today's turn to premodern orthodoxy, one spots the definite hope that these ancient sources can be played as the trump cards to resolve challenges facing a theologically and ethically divided postmodern church. These sources must be considered, but I do not believe they should have, or do have, that kind of adjudicatory power.

Not that the effort hasn't been made. An appeal to the ancient Tradition to guard evangelical boundaries and set definitions certainly has been a feature of recent decades. Conservative evangelical leaders find it helpful to cite "what the church has always and everywhere believed" in their battles against dissenters. It is indeed powerful ammunition when one can cite not *sola scriptura*, but Scripture and Tradition, to support one's positions. I often found myself on the receiving end of such arguments after publishing my 2014 call for full LGBTQ inclusion in the churches.[8]

The turn back to Tradition often seems to be a way of resisting the turn to the margins demanded by liberation theologians and other voices focusing on current oppression, especially oppression by the church. Instead of attending seriously to these contemporary claims, neo-traditionalism retreats more deeply into the past.[9]

Whatever value a turn to Tradition has offered on the liberal Protestant side, on the evangelical side it has reinforced white (straight, male, US) evangelicalism in its tendency to ignore scholars of color, liberation theologies, and anyone other than either modern evangelicals or the ancient church fathers. (Post-evangelicals whose reading was constrained by these boundaries will have a lot of catching up to do, by the way.)

After my bracing doctoral experience at the liberal/radical Union Seminary in New York in the late 1980s, my first discovery of Thomas Oden's paleo-orthodoxy was appealing. I felt the need for clearer doctrinal authority and deeper theology. I recoiled at content-free preaching in some liberal churches, and when I reentered the evangelical world I shuddered at the sentimental cotton candy so often offered. Oden (and Webber) charted a way forward, by going backward.

But once I had experienced paleo-orthodoxy used against me as a sword, I was less enamored. It seemed to me that a new (old) kind of infallibilism was cutting off needed debate and harming real people. The *return* to the sources was preventing a *turn* to the suffering human being. And the church's early Tradition simply lacked the purity claimed for it. It too was flawed. The most obvious example was its theological anti-Judaism. Those supposedly pristine early church fathers frequently radiated contempt for rabbinic Judaism and the Jewish people. The documentary evidence is beyond question, and these early church writings had disastrous results in encouraging the development of Christian hatred of Jews. Once one has taken that evidence seriously, it is impossible to romanticize this first layer of Christian Tradition.[10]

When you read in paleo-orthodoxy long enough, it becomes clear that often what scholars find in the Tradition is confirmation of theological commitments they have already made. But these commitments are obscured by the supposed methodology of simple historical retrieval. Meanwhile, Spirit-led, communally mediated, and theologically informed discernment of the Tradition itself is made more difficult by romanticizing it. Augustine's denigration of women is no less objectionable than John MacArthur's, no matter how venerable Augustine's writings might be.

So: paleo-orthodoxy is not what I am proposing for post-evangelicals. But I am still calling for a *historical turn*. I counsel post-evangelicals to become more serious about Christian Tradition and traditions—not to bow before tradition, or to dismiss it with a sneer, but to understand its shaping role in creating Christianity as we know it.

Deepening our sensitivity to the historical nature of Christian tradition and the mediating role of Christian leaders can help us think much more clearly about our realities and responsibilities today. We can situate ourselves within the flow of Christian history, better understand where our particular version of Christianity fits within the broader tradition, and think seriously about what the responsible transmission of Christian faith to the next generation ought to look like.

Instead of running from our responsibilities both to the past and to the future, we can own up to these responsibilities. If we break with majority Tradition, we will fully understand the gravity of doing so and give good reasons for it. If we affirm majority Tradition, the same applies. We can pay due homage to the Tradition of Christianity. But we will not ask it to absolve us of the necessity to think for ourselves and to take responsibility for what we decide.

LIVED HUMAN CAPACITIES: REASON, EXPERIENCE, INTUITION, RELATIONSHIPS, AND COMMUNITY

Fundamentalist and evangelical biblicism taught believers to overplay the Bible and underplay extrabiblical ways of learning and knowing. The Bible was treated as trustworthy in a way that other human products were not, because it was not viewed as a human product. Human reason was generally treated as untrustworthy, human experience as irrelevant, human intuitive capacity as damaged, and human relationships and communities as extraneous. This was a grave mistake. The church was overly optimistic about Scripture and overly pessimistic about human intellectual capacities. (And, to top it all off, we can now see that the church was naive in believing that what happens when people study the Bible is simply objective exegesis of the Bible, unaffected by human reason, experience, intuition, relationships, and social location in particular communities.)

If these human capacities, with all their limits, are always at play, we might as well own that and think about them systematically. So let's do that.

Human beings have been given *profound rational capacities* by God, if only we will develop them. We have the means to study, reflect, and reason our way to truth, or truths, however partial and provisional any human discovery of truth might be. Human reason is, or can be, a profound source of knowledge. We each have a responsibility to develop our intellectual capacity to the best of our ability. After all, Jesus did say, "You shall love the Lord your God . . . with all your mind" (Matt. 22:37), and Paul talked about the "renewing of your minds" (Rom. 12:2). A substantial strand of the New Testament features an emphasis on damaged and renewed, broken and healed human rationality.

Human reason is never infallible, though, including the reason of Christians. The church was not wrong in claiming that human reason's functioning is deeply tainted by sin—like everything else about us. That fallibility is visible every time we watch ourselves or someone else rationalize wrongdoing. Recent research by scholars such as Jonathan Haidt reminds us of the extraordinary complexity of human mental functioning, including the way emotions so often drive our reasoning processes. The irrationality of group behavior, such as in mass politics, gives plenty of evidence here.[11]

But still, I accept the Catholic view that human rationality remains at least potentially good, even if damaged by sin and potentially gravely misdirected.[12] Any human being's exercise of reason reflects their entire embodied selfhood, the state of their character, loyalties, relationships, and learning.[13] Wouldn't it be nice if post-evangelicals decided to devote at least some of our worship and study time to developing healthy and mature expressions of human rational capacity, rather than just one more Bible study?

Reason is *always touched by human culture and social location*. It is historical and contextual like every other human thing. But the evidence (however uncomfortable for pious ears) is that, sometimes, human reason offers not just solid insights but better access to truth than ancient biblical texts.

For example, it is our stubborn rational capacity that makes us notice logical contradictions. If God is love, love never harms a neighbor (Rom. 13:10), and the Bible depicts God ordering the slaying of all inhabitants of entire cities, as in the early chapters of Joshua, one of these things is not like the other. They can't all be true. But evangelicals are taught to pretend that there is no contradiction, because the Bible must not be questioned. It would be better simply to say that the contradiction is real and that committing genocide in God's name is never God's will. But this would require us to trust a source within us rather than accepting this part of the Bible.

Human rationality drives our powerful desire to come to a clear and accurate understanding of reality and to behave in accordance with what we discover. Grasping reality matters deeply to human functioning, even to human sanity. When what we are offered in the Bible or what is reinforced by Tradition seems to contradict what we observe to be real, evangelicals have often been taught to submit to Scripture and Tradition and ignore the facts in front of us. But this kind of religiosity not only takes us into intellectual dead ends, it can also hurt people—as when our texts seem to require us to put a grossly negative moral construction on the fact of nonheterosexual sexuality.

Human rationality has never completed its work. It will be developing as long as humans do. As individuals, cultures, and humanity, we are always learning. Civilization at any given moment reflects all that humans have learned so far, for good and ill. Stasis never arrives—humans are always seeking new knowledge.

This is one of the most remarkable and productive features of human reason. But a certain kind of religious textualism and traditionalism fosters a perennial drive to look backward for the truest and most important knowledge, rather than forward for the development of new knowledge. Certainly, there is much truth to be found in Scripture and Tradition, and religious life finds anchor there. But it is difficult to look backward and forward at the same time. The neck gets tired. Post-evangelicals, I hope, will learn to look around and look ahead quite a bit more.

Human rational capacity includes *the ability to learn things through experience.*[14] Sometimes these are contrived experiences, such as scientific experiments and computer simulations. But I am mainly speaking here about the experiences that come to us in everyday life, including family experiences, generational experiences, national experiences, travel and cross-cultural experiences, and experiences of extremity, trauma, and suffering.

Through experience, children learn language, warriors learn about war, spouses learn about marriage (and sometimes, about divorce), artists learn about the creative process, travelers learn from cross-cultural encounters, entrepreneurs learn from starting businesses, and athletes learn from performing under extreme pressure.

Some things that can be learned through experience cannot be learned any other way. Athletes offer one of the best examples of the indispensable role of experience. Throwing a curveball, serving a tennis ball, and shooting free throws are among those things that simply cannot be learned from a book. One can read and master all the rules of a game, even becoming the foremost authority on strategies and tactics, and not be able to play it with any kind of prowess, because only experience teaches one how to play the game. All apprenticeship programs are based on this discovery, that the best learning comes through doing.

Experience turns out to be one of the most reliable ways humans come to know things. Even though the lessons one draws from life experience are fallible like any other human endeavor, experience is a crucial teacher. Certainly, anyone attempting to understand an issue, to speak or teach or write about it, simply must seek the insights that can be offered by those who have the most direct experience.

But evangelicals elevated Scripture and downplayed experience. This often has proved disastrous in relation to real people's lives. I think of pastors sending battered spouses back into abusive marriages because they listened to what they thought they heard Scripture saying rather than listening to the terrorized voices of the abused. And pastors telling abused children to subject themselves to their parents rather than listening to the children's experiences of mistreatment and abuse. And pastors who once told slaves to submit to their masters. And, yes, biblical scholars and pastors and parents and teachers and friends and everyone telling LGBTQ Christian teenagers to disregard their experience of their own sexuality, personhood, and suffering.

Human beings also learn things through *intuition*, flashes of insight in the blink of an eye that lead to breakthroughs.[15] Intuitive learning is very hard to quantify but is an important part of most human lives. It is another way of knowing. Such intuition is not confined to what happens when we open the Bible, though that can happen, of course. But intuition may at times challenge the Bible.

All branches of historic Christianity have minority traditions that have emphasized the ineffable and intuitive dimension of Christian spiritual experience. Some specific traditions—such as the Quakers, the Pietists, and the charismatics/Pentecostals—feature very strong emphasis on the Holy Spirit. The Quaker tradition essentially teaches that the Bible was written to help believers interpret the movement of the Spirit, not the other way around, which is one reason why Quaker worship services feature spiritual listening more than preaching. Pietists of all types emphasize the centrality of the Holy Spirit for Jesus himself, for Christian discipleship, discernment, and community.

This is as good a place as any to mention that charismatic/Pentecostal Christianity is the fastest-growing religion in the world, and for good reasons.[16] Human life is broken and needs the healing power of God. Human beings are more than reasoners; we are souls, and we need God's Spirit. Pentecostalism occupies the odd position of being seen as both part of evangelicalism but in some ways also a very serious challenge to it. I have had just enough breakthrough experiences of God's Spirit in my own life to take the Spirit with utmost seriousness. I encourage the challenge that all Spirit-oriented forms of Christianity bring to doctrinaire text-and-tradition evangelicals—even while seeing the dangers and follies in Pentecostalism as everywhere else.

I think of how my community of Baptists privileges intuition and listens for God's Spirit. Not long ago I participated in an ordination council for a ministerial candidate. In our tradition of local church autonomy, the decision to ordain is left to the local congregation. The congregation in turn establishes its own criteria for ordination. In every ordination process I have been a part of, a candidate does not get into the ordination council without the congregation's positive intuitive read of their spirit, gifts, character, and readiness. Doctrinal questions are offered at the ordination council, but this follows a more intuitive assessment. This assessment is mysteriously communal. We do it together. Is it infallible? Absolutely not. But it is indispensable.

This of course reminds us that people are *embedded in communities and cultures*. We are born into or choose to join these cherished (or oppressive) contexts for living our lives, and no one easily breaks free of them. We learn from our communities, cultures, and traditions, the languages they teach us to speak, the way they teach us to read and describe reality. This means that no one approaches Scripture as an unmediated individual reader. We are enculturated and traditioned members of communities, and we read how they taught us to read—until we possibly get to a place where we learn to read in a different way.

Indeed, our communal experiences deeply shape every aspect of how and what we know. If this is so, any effort of Christians to discern truth should include all participants naming and examining the communities that shaped them. It should also include the commitment, in any major decision-making or discernment process, to bring a group together who come from a diverse range of communal backgrounds—that includes the voices brought together to form a syllabus in any academic course.

Human beings, finally, learn through *interpersonal relationships*. There is no "me" apart from "you," no "I" apart from "Thou," as Martin Buber so memorably explained.[17] Some of the most profoundly important things we learn in life are learned in the most intimate of our relationships. But evangelical biblicism is not able to account for that, either overriding the significance of relationships or pretending that they do not affect interpretation of the Bible.

In sum: Evangelical biblicism teaches people to downgrade or even dismiss the significance of what human beings can (and really must) learn from our own God-given capacities. Instead, evangelical biblicism claims to ask a very ancient collection of texts to provide knowledge that these texts cannot really provide—or cannot alone provide—and then claims to offer the single truthful account of what these sacred texts mean. The exclusive franchise apparently granted to Scripture (even if supplemented by Tradition) blocks off critical insights that can be gained through other resources, including ourselves and our own minds and hearts.

Seminary-trained people may recognize that so far in this chapter I have been reflecting on what has for a long time been called the Wesleyan quadrilateral—Scripture, tradition, reason, and experience.[18] But I have added explicit attention to the role of church leaders, intuition, community, and relationships. And now we add another set of resources available to post-evangelical Christianity.

EXTERNAL INTELLECTUAL RESOURCES: THE ARTS AND SCIENCES

Many evangelicals have been sent off to college or seminary with a warning along the lines of "don't let them ruin you up there." That is telling, isn't it? Distrust of higher education has been an enduring feature of fundamentalism and evangelicalism. This distrust has led some to steer away from any kind of higher education. It has led others to support Christian colleges and universities but only insofar as those schools constrain the academic disciplines taught there under the authority of a "Christian worldview." In general, evangelical fear of liberal learning has contributed to what Mark Noll properly described as "the scandal of the evangelical mind"—which is, in Noll's immortal phrase, "that there is not much of an evangelical mind."[19]

For those who avoid college because someone might get ruined, I have mainly pity for the young people affected. The same is true for those who will only send (or go) to Bible colleges with their Bible credits and little else, as if all one needs to learn for adult life is further details about biblical genealogies.

The more interesting question is the evangelical Christian college. I have written extensively elsewhere about the Christian college project, and I certainly do not dismiss a context in which I spent much of my career.[20] In this discussion, I am indebted to recent work by Harold Heie, a stalwart of evangelical higher education and an honest man.[21]

At their best, evangelical Christian colleges provide an environment in which Christian faith and values are treated with respect, numerous cocurricular opportunities exist to grow in Christian maturity, and the curriculum effectively engages the world's knowledge—governed by a broad Christian framework, but still permitting scholarship and teaching to proceed with an open mind.

At their worst, however, evangelical Christian colleges tumble forward into Christian triumphalism or backward into fundamentalist rigidity, offer juvenile or cloistered cocurricular activities, and constrain scholarship and teaching so much that faculty academic freedom is strictly limited and the curriculum barely engages current academic disciplines. Christian colleges are also proving susceptible to the confusion of white evangelical political proclivities with Christian orthodoxy.[22] Heie's overall conclusion, though very carefully written, is devastating: "My perception that the ideal for a discernment process . . . is difficult to attain at an orthodox institution further reinforces the conclusion I have reached (after serving my entire career at orthodox institutions) that the 'conversation toward Truth' ideal that I embrace for Christian higher education has greater potential for realization [elsewhere]."[23] Heie is basically saying that the kinds of schools he served his entire career have not proved hospitable for the kind of higher education that he most values. Ouch.

That's because administrators are trying so hard to protect the tender faith of their young charges. But it's not working: "Research shows that students at CCCU [evangelical] schools are more likely to face a religious crisis than their secular counterparts."[24] Based on her analysis of more than fourteen thousand responses to the College Student Beliefs and Values Survey, Jennifer Carter, an assistant professor of leadership at the evangelical Southeastern University, found "unique patterns of religious struggle" among students at evangelical colleges, which reflected her experience as a student at Valley Forge Christian College. As reported by *Christianity Today*, Carter found:

> At most institutions, rates of religious struggle decrease between the first and third year of college. Freshman [*sic*] have a lot of questions. Juniors feel more settled in their beliefs.
>
> But for students at schools affiliated with the Council for Christian Colleges and Universities (CCCU), it's the other way around. They tend to feel secure in their faith at the start of college but three years later, they're in crisis. . . .
>
> "I was raised in a Christian family, went to a Christian college, and had a lot of questions—and felt a lot of guilt and shame about that," [Carter] said. "I thought when I left college I'd have this really solidified faith, and I left with questions and doubt. I didn't know that was really normal."[25]

I call post-evangelicals, while in school or far beyond those years, to embrace an expansive and fearless engagement with the humanities, social sciences, and natural sciences, all of which offer meaningful ways of learning, knowing, and flourishing in the real world. Let us read world literature; engage global art, sport, and music; explore philosophy and world religions; take on modern languages; study anthropology, sociology, political science, and psychology; plumb national and world history; and learn from biology, chemistry, physics, math, and their subdisciplines and offshoots. Evangelical college guru Arthur Holmes was famous for saying, "All truth is God's truth."[26] It would be good if post-evangelicals made progress in addressing the world that way.

A FURTHER WORD ABOUT SCIENCE, WITH AN EXCURSION INTO CLIMATE CHANGE

Post-evangelicals are sometimes "post-" because of the subpar treatment of science that they endured in a mediocre Christian school somewhere. This has had disastrous effects on the retention of Christians as believers. Feeling as though they have to make a choice between the Bible and credible modern science, they have chosen science.[27]

It is true that science has seemed like a nemesis to traditionalist Christianity since about 1500. It was science that first began to break the church's (and the Bible's) monopoly on knowledge. Early scientists discovered better ways of understanding facts about the universe than what could be gleaned from the Bible. Scientific breakthroughs over the centuries continually challenged how the church read the Bible—and were regularly understood as challenging Christian faith itself. The church's sometimes violent efforts to force modern scientists to abandon their quests and renounce their discoveries failed, and deeply discredited the church.[28]

Science gradually solidified its place as a formidable body of practices and methods for discerning reality within its range of expertise. (The effort of some scientists to make authoritative declarations about areas outside their expertise, including the validity of believing in God, is sometimes called *scientism*. That is overreaching, and it is not the same as science.) The scientific method could not claim infallibility, but that was part of its genius and part of what set it apart so laudably from Christian infallibilist claims.

Science involves a commitment to constant research, data sharing, peer review, error correction, public hypothesis testing and revision, and the ever-present possibility of new discovery. Science's open-ended, exploratory way of learning is very different from backward-looking biblicism or Tradition, and the conflict has been obvious from the very beginning of modern science. To many of us, it looks as though science has mainly won that argument, though not even science itself can be taken uncritically. It has its own history of errors.

The problem of global environmental challenges, including climate change, comes to mind as I think about the intersection of faith and science. American fundamentalists and evangelicals have lagged behind most others in taking these challenges seriously.

Conservative Christians have been a retrograde force on the environment for various reasons. They have believed evangelism and personal morality mattered more. They have feared that environmentalism was a Trojan horse for pantheism or nature worship. They have sometimes held to an archaic human-dominion-over-the-earth theology. They have believed Jesus was coming back soon so the fate of the earth was irrelevant. Their theological drama was a drama of personal salvation and could not broaden to include the cosmos. Some have believed that God has promised not to allow catastrophic harm to come to the earth, because God is in control and will end history only at the divinely orchestrated apocalypse. And when environmental concern became more strongly identified with Democrats and political liberals than conservatives and Republicans, that sealed the deal.[29]

Today climate change has come to dominate the environmental agenda. It is essential for more Christians to engage the scientific conversation seriously. That includes the overall theory behind the worry about climate change—that the human release of massive amounts of greenhouse gases is projected to heat the earth's atmosphere to a dangerous point for human well-being and even survival. This theory and its critics both need attention, as does everything else related to climate change, including models of what the effects of various levels of temperature rise likely will be, the state of the actual temperature evidence so far, claims about the already visible effects of climate change, and the main proposals for how to slow the release of greenhouse gases, adapt to the climate's current and future changes, and deal with the economic consequences of dramatic changes in energy use.

Most people get their understanding of climate change from news stories. News stories are very brief summaries of someone else's summary. A news story may report on a press conference in which a few scientists offer top-line claims from an executive summary of a report, which may include projections of what might happen rather than facts about what has happened. Few people bother to go to the full executive summary at its source to read it for themselves. Fewer still will read the complete report. Almost nobody will dig into the footnotes. And that is not even to mention accessing alternative accounts of the evidence or alternative models.

We can hardly expect every Christian to do this kind of digging. But we do need some Christians who have the capacity to do so. On climate change, informed conclusions about all kinds of specifics may vary once that digging is done. But that would be informed engagement.

My own current provisional judgment is that climate disruption in many parts of the world certainly appears to be not just happening but accelerating; that it is causing considerable damage to people, ecologies, and communities; and that a significant body of climate scientists are convinced that the theoretical model is bearing out, while a minority of serious scientists dissent.[30]

But I also observe that the specter of relatively imminent, irreversible, civilization-destroying climate change catastrophe has now been accepted as a fact in large parts of global culture, rather than as a deeply alarming potential outcome of projected human choices in the next several decades. This is contributing to despair, and to an apocalyptic turn in theology, ethics, culture, and politics.[31] I think that this despair and this apocalyptic turn may in fact be morally disempowering, just as (from the very opposite direction) evangelical climate-change denial is also morally disempowering. We—all of us—need reasons to act in responsibility, not await the apocalypse in passivity.

I may revise these judgments next week, because they are based on my limited, amateur engagement with the science, which is always evolving. Still, what I am offering is a long, long way from just saying that God is in control, God promised not to send another flood, Jesus is coming back soon, and climate change is a liberal hoax. That's just bad theology and ideology foreclosing serious engagement with the complex evidence. Post-evangelicals will have to do better than this.

TOWARD CHRISTIAN HUMANISM VIA ERASMUS

The world is complex, and it faces staggering problems. It needs Christians who are up to the task of making a constructive contribution, intellectually ready for the challenges that all humanity faces, deeply motivated to love God and neighbor with all our minds.

The transition to post-evangelicalism offers many of us exiles a golden opportunity to rethink our epistemology—how we know what we think we know, to whom we talk when we are seeking truth, how we listen for God's voice. I am arguing that we abandon fundamentalist/evangelical dogmatism and biblicism, replacing it with a humble, expansive, open posture to the quest for knowledge. Scientist Charles Pasternak says that *quest* is the essence of humanity.[32] Christians need to be *part of that human quest*, not hunkered down in fearful, backward-looking defensiveness.

I am attracted to the Renaissance term *Christian humanism* to describe the spirit I hope will be embraced by post-evangelicals. I want to suggest that we seek a spirit that is *Christian*, centered in Jesus and anchored appropriately in our theological sources, and *humanist*, in seven senses:

- Rooted in a sense of common humanity and a quest for human unity;
- Hopeful about the moral potential of human persons while realistic about human sinfulness;
- Respectful toward and engaged with the common human intellectual enterprise of the past and today;
- Resolute in recognizing and respecting human free will, freedom of conscience, and the proper independence of the human mind;
- Concerned with the holistic well-being of all humans in this world, and not just their souls in the next;
- Committed to seeking common ground and peaceful solutions to human problems;
- Understanding Christianity to be *for humans* (and the creation),[33] not mainly about protecting Christian doctrinal purity, ideology, or the church's self-interest.

For this paradigm I am indebted to Desiderius Erasmus (1466–1536), the founder of Renaissance Christian humanism. A giant of learning, pioneer of modern critical thinking, and model of a European-cosmopolitan vision, Erasmus combined a Jesus-centered Christian piety with rich classical learning and a humane and pacific spirit. Still one of Europe's most celebrated figures, Erasmus was a both-and rather than an either-or thinker. When the Reformation came, and the new Protestants battled to the death with Catholic traditionalists, Erasmus earnestly sought a path forward where the streets would not run with blood. His was the road not taken. Just compare the seven-point list above with what happened during the wars of religion after the Reformation. Erasmus and his vision lost; and yet his example lingers on.[34]

Evangelical Christianity has far more often exhibited the combative spirit of Martin Luther rather than the pacific spirit of Erasmus, narrow biblicism over expansive Christian humanism. Stefan Zweig summarized their difference: “For Luther the religious was the thing of greatest importance on earth; for Erasmus it was the human.”[35] But Erasmus’s humanism was not disconnected from his love of Jesus; it was an expression of it. The whole history of the West might have been different if Erasmus had prevailed. The crisis of evangelicalism in our time provides an opportunity for a do-over in the spirit of Erasmus.

TAKEAWAYS

- There is no perfect or risk-free method when humans listen for God’s voice. Given human finitude, the best approach is the most comprehensive.
- Post-evangelicals need to name the role of tradition and leaders in our religious life and come to understand this role more fully.
- The turn to early church tradition has value but risks substituting one kind of infallibilism for another.
- Human reason, experience, intuitive capacity, communities, and relationships are valuable sources and contexts for theological and moral discernment.
- Post-evangelicals should embrace an expansive and fearless engagement with the arts and sciences, all of which offer meaningful ways of learning, knowing, and flourishing in the real world.
- We should abandon fundamentalist/evangelical dogmatism, replacing it with Christian humanism in the spirit of Erasmus.

PART II

Theology: Believing and Belonging

4

God

In Dialogue with the Story of Israel

This chapter begins the second of three parts in this book, involving my attempt to offer elements of a post-evangelical theology.

Cut loose from the constraints of fundamentalist/evangelical orthodoxies, what account of God, Jesus, and the church might be open to post-evangelicals? That is the question that motivates this chapter and the two that follow.

Post-evangelicals have many options for how to move forward theologically. I will offer my path, reflecting the mix of theological influences that have shaped my service as a Christian ethicist—someone for whom theology proper is a minor rather than major emphasis. Let's call what I am doing in the next several chapters something like constructive theology rather than anything like systematic theology. It will be clear how little modern fundamentalist or conservative evangelical Protestant theology appeals to me in terms of charting a path forward. And yet, several of my significant theological influences do intersect with evangelicalism at points.

SIX KEY STRANDS OF THEOLOGY

My higher education occurred in the 1980s and early 1990s. Upon reflection, six strands of theology (with related ethics) have predominated, mainly dating to those days.

1. *Kingdom of God theology.* Main idea: Jesus came preaching the kingdom of God, which meant God's reclaiming and transformation of this world in line with the promises and demands of the prophets. Glen Stassen and I eventually developed this concept for our textbook *Kingdom Ethics.*[1] It was based most explicitly on Stassen's findings in biblical studies. In terms of the development

of theology, probably the primary source for the recovery of Jesus' kingdom message was critical biblical studies, which then affected nineteenth-century Protestant theology, including . . .

2. *Social gospel theology*. Main idea: The gospel should be understood as thoroughly social rather than individual, which affects every aspect of doctrine and mission. The theology and social ethic we developed in *Kingdom Ethics* bears a close resemblance to the late-nineteenth- and early-twentieth-century social gospel theology, most famously articulated by Baptist historian and theologian Walter Rauschenbusch.[2] Though Stassen and I did not derive our kingdom-of-God vision from the social gospelers or Rauschenbusch, we came to very similar conclusions.[3] It should be noted that social gospel theology emerged from late-nineteenth-century Protestantism, and many social gospelers could be fairly described as evangelical Christians. But their this-worldly, social-change–oriented theology, and their socially progressive politics/ethics, were explicitly rejected by the other party within a splitting Protestantism.

3. *Holocaust theology*. Main idea: The Nazi genocide against the Jewish people (1939–1945) must be central in any further theology and ethics.[4] Those who made the greatest impact on me in this arena include Jewish writers Elie Wiesel and Irving Greenberg, and Christians Franklin Littell[5] and Dietrich Bonhoeffer. Writing during the Nazi regime with growing knowledge of its atrocities, Bonhoeffer is probably the most important Christian theologian in my life.[6] His was not Holocaust theology, but I place it in the same frame. Meanwhile, any theology deeply affected by the Shoah[7] is eventually going to make its way back into the ongoing Jewish-Christian dialogue, which affects my theology.[8]

4. *Liberation theologies*. Main idea: God stands with the oppressed of the earth and acts alongside them as liberating deliverer, and religious ethics must join in this liberative project. Emerging since the 1960s from the world's oppressed, liberation theology has become a major force in theology and ethics. Partly because I have spent my life mostly in the American South, I have been most affected by black theology and womanist theology. Major voices influencing me include Martin Luther King Jr., James Cone, and Howard Thurman,[9] and womanist thinkers like Katie Cannon, Emilie Townes, and Stacey Floyd-Thomas, whose vision is related but distinct.[10] Liberation theologies have been met with a cold shoulder by most white evangelical authorities.

5. *Catholic social teaching tradition*. Main idea: The church should engage politics, economics, and culture with a constructive social ethic advancing human dignity and social justice. Modern Catholic social teaching began with the launch of the papal encyclical *Rerum Novarum* in 1893 and extends to this day.[11] I also have long been attracted to the "consistent ethic of life"

articulated by Cardinal Joseph Bernardin and John Paul II.[12] Evangelicals largely dismissed Catholic theology and ethics until the culture wars erupted, at which time conservative Catholic sexual and life ethics became very interesting to them, and some partnerships began to be formed.

6. *Progressive evangelical social ethics*. Main idea: Close study of Scripture shows that God calls Christians to a social-justice–oriented ethical engagement in the world. The origins of this tradition (in recent white evangelicalism) centered around three primary figures whose work began in the 1970s: Mennonite historian Ron Sider, Baptist sociologist Tony Campolo, and social-justice activist Jim Wallis.[13] As already noted, this strand emerged from traditions—like the Anabaptist and Wesleyan—that predated the birth of modern evangelicalism.

Together, these rich theological and ethical influences have helped to produce what I am calling here, for the first time, my *Christian humanist* vision—which I named in the last chapter and which I will continue to unpack in what follows.

This book provides opportunity for me to consider why so little of conservative evangelical thinking has made it into my theology. The answer is instructive, I think.

In retrospect, it seems that my conversion into Southern Baptist life in the late 1970s brought me primarily into contact with a pietist tradition mixed with pop theology, rather than into any engagement with serious evangelical theology. Being "born again" meant having a personal relationship with Jesus and walking with him daily through Bible study and prayer. We focused on personal holiness, evangelism, church life, and world missions.

Dispensational theology also made inroads on that church. Hal Lindsey, that charlatan, was making millions selling his *Late Great Planet Earth* franchise, which included terrifying books and movies.[14] Church folk gave me that book and had me watch his movie and sing those wretched songs about the rapture. Lindsey, like his dispensationalist predecessors, cherry-picked Bible verses, read them against the background of the day's news, and generated pessimistic and politically laden scenarios of the imminent and inevitable end of the world, cutting the nerve of any progressive social-moral effort in the process.

Six years later, at the Southern Baptist Theological Seminary of the mid-1980s, I was not taught evangelical theology. I was primarily drawn into the orbit of Glen Stassen's Baptist progressivism in ethics and exposed to various options in mainline theology. Then I went off to Union Seminary, learned some liberation theology, and made the deep dive into the Holocaust.

It was not until my return to Southern Seminary as a professor in 1993 that I unhappily engaged the newly normative evangelical theology there. Under

Al Mohler's presidency, still ongoing as of this writing, this became a starchy scholastic neo-Calvinism, including the demand for an affirmation of biblical inerrancy and an all-male pastorate. Being politically conservative was also most helpful, especially for an ethicist.

In the succeeding twenty-five years, I have witnessed various protest and reform efforts in relation to this dominant version of evangelicalism. Isaac Sharp has done the best job at naming them all.[15] Recall that they include pre-1930s "evangelical liberalism," Barthianism, black evangelicalism, evangelical feminism, Wesleyan-Arminian-Holiness evangelicalism, contemporary progressive social justice evangelicalism, and lately, LGBTQ-affirming evangelicalism.

Gary Dorrien, writing in 1998 and thoroughly familiar with the main strand of US evangelicalism, which he called fundamentalist evangelicalism, expressed the hope that Wesleyan, Arminian, progressive, and other then-emerging theological challenges to dominant evangelicalism could be accepted as legitimate alternatives.[16]

Writing twenty years later, his student (and mine) Isaac Sharp, surveying these and other dissenters, has shown that this did not occur. Reformed, inerrantist, anti-Barthian, anti-Wesleyan, anti–social gospel (and usually anti–social justice), deeply and obliviously white, antifeminist, politically conservative, and anti-LGBTQ inclusion—that is the contemporary American evangelicalism that has won.

I need to state very clearly that I oppose every aspect of this version of evangelical Christianity.

Looking back, I pay homage to several generations of evangelical dissenters and reformers. Some of them kept the evangelical label; others had it stripped from them or abandoned it. Among those not mentioned so far, they include John Alexander, Greg Boyd, Stanley Grenz (gone far too soon), Nancy Hardesty, Paul Jewett, Roger Olson, Tom Oord, William Pannell, Clark Pinnock, Virginia Ramey Mollenkott, and Tom Skinner.[17] If I were to add the names of dissenting pastors, the list would quadruple in size.

The theological forays that follow will primarily reflect the impact of the six major strands that shaped my theology in its formative years. But the dissenting evangelicals, some of whom were affected by some of the same influences, have also left their mark.

BURNING CHILDREN IS WHERE I BEGIN

If you ask me what I most urgently believe about God, my story really begins in ninth grade, before my conversion. That was when the gifted young teacher of my freshman history class at Oakton High School hit us with a gruesome Holocaust documentary.

Night and Fog (1955) consisted most memorably of grainy footage of dead bodies.[18] I remember black-and-white images and French and bulldozers and corpses and the irreversible moral shock of a certain innocent ninth-grade boy. Since then I have seen many horrifying Holocaust documentaries, but this first one left a traumatic mark.

I felt compelled to return to the Holocaust at each stage of my education: a Judaism class in college, a paper on the problem of evil in seminary, a comprehensive exam on Holocaust theology at the doctoral level, and finally my dissertation on Christians who rescued Jews during the Holocaust.[19]

One of the members of my dissertation committee was Irving Greenberg, a brilliant "modern Orthodox" Jewish scholar and rabbi. Rabbi Greenberg never published much at book length, but some of his essays have been deeply influential in the Jewish community, in Jewish-Christian dialogue circles, and among those undertaking Holocaust theology.[20]

In one of these essays, Rabbi Greenberg took note of a particularly unspeakable type of atrocity that was visited upon certain Jewish children by their Nazi murderers. Anybody who studies the Holocaust knows that atrocities were so numerous that it becomes hard to focus on any one of them. But this detail stands out. It comes from the account of a Jewish Holocaust survivor.

> When the Hungarian Jews arrived, we used a music camouflage. At the time, the children were burned on big piles of wood. The crematoriums could not work at the time, and therefore, the people [after being gassed to death] were just burned in open fields with those grills, and also children were burned among them. . . .
>
> And then, on one special day they started burning them to death. The gas chambers at the time were out of order . . . and therefore the children were not gassed, but just burned alive.
>
> When one of the SS men sort of had pity on the children, he took the child and beat the head against a stone first before putting it on the pile of fire and wood, so that the child lost consciousness. However, the regular way they did it was just by throwing the children onto the pile.
>
> They used to put a sheet of wood, then the whole thing was sprinkled with gasoline, then wood again, and gasoline and wood, and gasoline—and then people were placed on them. Thereafter, the whole pile was lit.[21]

Children were sometimes burned alive at Auschwitz. People's beloved children and grandchildren were taken by their hands and feet and thrown into pits of fire, where their precious little faces and hands and bodies were incinerated as they briefly howled out their unbearable pain. It happened. Elie Wiesel testifies to the same thing in his haunting memoir, *Night*.[22]

I challenge you to read that account from Auschwitz a few times before proceeding in this chapter. Make yourself picture it. Maybe just one time picture the little face of an especially beloved child in your life. I am thinking of my grandson Jonah, my granddaughter Melody.

After describing this scene, Rabbi Greenberg put forward the following proposition: "*No statement, theological or otherwise, should be made that would not be credible in the presence of the burning children.*"[23]

Greenberg's staggering proposition became known as the burning-children test. Probably few readers will have heard of it. But it has never left me.

Test all statements (about God, theology, morality, faith, life) based on whether such statements would be credible in the kind of world in which two-year-olds have been thrown alive into pits of fire. I would hasten to add: the kind of world in which *Jewish* two-year-olds have been burned alive mainly by baptized *Christians*.[24]

My acceptance of this test for Christian theological discourse may help to explain why I am so utterly opposed to today's resurgent high Calvinism.[25] The structure of that theology, with its imperious God willing (or actively choosing to permit) all events that happen on earth, not only fails the burning-children test, it is its complete antithesis. Indeed, as Clark Pinnock argued, atheism is the logical reaction to the picture of God offered in such theology, especially after the Holocaust.[26]

Rabbi Greenberg was not saying that the burning children at Auschwitz offer the only example of evil that can test theological and ethical claims. Within the Holocaust itself there were numerous other examples that could be used. But still: burning children.

Though the uniqueness and particularity of the Holocaust must never be forgotten, Greenberg's test does offer an entry point to the concerns of theologians writing out of the experience of other historically oppressed peoples. It is not a stretch to speak of other tests: murdered and raped women; tortured and murdered indigenous peoples; enslaved, tortured, murdered, and lynched black people; tortured and murdered LGBTQ people. It's about the oppression of human beings being important to theology.

The burning-children test constrains all claims about God, Jesus, and the church that I will make in this book. One might wonder why a Christian theologian-ethicist would think that the murder of Jewish children by fire should play such a pivotal role in his theology. After all, they weren't *my* children. They weren't *my people's* children.

I am unable to draw that distinction. I consider it obscene.

GRAPPLING WITH THE NARRATIVE OF THE HEBREW BIBLE

The theological claims I wish to engage in this section of the book emerge from the biblical narrative rather than doctrinal propositions. Doctrinal claims are second-order statements, distilled from Scripture and tradition, developed over time, always filtered through human experience and shaped by human reason.

Despite having firmly rejected inerrantism, I still believe that it is better to begin with the story that the Bible itself tells. My reading of the situation is that inerrantism was a modern effort to defend Christian doctrine against modern challenges such as biblical criticism and the way liberal theology was failing to defend traditional Christian orthodoxy. Paleo-orthodoxy was an effort to defeat modernism by retreating to the premodern church. My account of post-evangelicalism is not premodern, modern, or antimodern, so I guess that makes it postmodern. It seems to dovetail to some extent with the postcritical and postliberal biblical narrative theologies most associated with George Lindbeck.[27] My primary guide to the state of that postcritical-postliberal conversation in Judaism and Christianity is Peter Ochs, a distinguished Jewish scholar at the University of Virginia.[28]

Whatever we call it, the approach I will take requires close study of the biblical narrative. I noted earlier that the Jewish tradition involves centuries of wrestling, arguing, and dialoguing with God, the texts, and other interpreters. I want to do that here, in relation to the picture of God offered in the Hebrew Bible.

Canonically, the story begins when God creates this world and all the creatures, culminating with human beings, and places them in an idyllic garden to "till it and keep it" (Gen. 2:15). Human beings succumb to mistrust, disobey their Creator, and are exiled from paradise. Humanity spirals into murderous evil. A brokenhearted God responds with massive judgment. But God starts over, dependent on the slender thread of one man, Noah, making a covenant with all creation through him (Gen. 1–11).

Already a picture of God's character is developing. God is the creator of a delightful world. God wants relationship with the creatures God has made, including human beings, but this means God gives human beings real freedom. God grieves and punishes the rebellion that follows. Yet God ultimately chooses redemption rather than annihilation. God will not give up on the world. God offers covenant structure and moral law to govern wayward human behavior.

God decides to form a special people. Abraham and his wife Sarah are promised abundant descendants and their own land as God makes a covenant with them that will eventually establish the Jewish people. They are given a miraculous child who begins the family line, about which expansive and sometimes morally problematic tales are told (Gen. 12–50). From the beginning, Israel's calling is not just for itself; as God tells Abraham, "in you all the families of the earth shall be blessed" (Gen. 12:3).

Due to famine in Canaan, the descendants of Abraham and Sarah end up in Egypt (Gen. 46–50), eventually in slavery (Exod. 1) and facing genocide (Exod. 2). God raises up the reluctant Moses to lead the embattled people out of Egypt and into freedom (Exod. 3–4). Through miraculous intervention, God engineers the liberation of the Hebrews (Exod. 5–15).

Most Jewish scholars describe the exodus event as the most formative for historic Judaism. The God pictured here is faithful to the covenant with Israel, deeply compassionate, and fiercely liberative. "I have observed the misery of my people who are in Egypt; I have heard their cry on account of their taskmasters . . . and I have come down to deliver them" (Exod. 3:7–8). This account has been central in liberation theology.

God gives Israel the Law shortly after their arrival in the Sinai desert (Exod. 19–20). The people agree to live accordingly. Massive quantities of legal material are then inserted into the narrative, some of it clearly of much later date (Exod. 21–Deuteronomy). A central biblical image of God takes shape here—God as lawgiver, with God's will as the basis of all (legitimate) human law and governance, at least in Israel. God is also depicted as a "jealous God," warning sternly about the consequences of disobedience: "I am setting before you today a blessing and a curse: the blessing, if you obey the commandments of the LORD your God . . . ; and the curse, if you do not" (Deut. 11:26–28).

After forty largely unhappy years wandering in the wilderness, Moses dies (Deut. 34). Under Joshua the Hebrews take the promised land in massive bloody conquest, ordered and blessed by God (Josh. 1–12): "The LORD has given you the city. . . . All that is in it shall be devoted to the LORD for destruction" (Josh. 6:16–17). The people distribute themselves across the conquered land according to tribe (Josh. 13–23), uniting only when external threat requires a common leader (Judges). In the Joshua narratives, God is depicted as not just permitting but ordering genocide.

Against God's wishes, the people decide to develop a kingship in order to secure themselves and their land and to be like other nations (1–2 Samuel, 1–2 Kings, 1–2 Chronicles). The kingship eventually is given to David and his family (1 Sam. 16//1 Chron. 11). Poor leadership after David and his son Solomon quickly leads to schism between a northern kingdom of Israel and a southern kingdom called Judah (1 Kgs. 12//2 Chron. 10–11).

A significant and creative part of the Hebrew Bible emerges from the royal court and reflects its concerns and interests (much of Psalms; Proverbs, Ecclesiastes, Song of Solomon). The development of a Jerusalem-based temple clearly facilitated the growth of a priestly establishment, just as an expansive royal court facilitated the development of a class of sages and court advisers.

In the royalty-related material, God is depicted initially as adjusting to Israel's preferences by giving a king, shifting the basis of governance from tribal theocratic confederation to God-ordained royal dynasty. The texts attribute the regular ups and downs, the rising and falling of various kings, mainly to divine blessing or punishment based on Israel's covenant fidelity or its lack.

But God balances the concession of giving Israel a king with the development of the prophetic calling. The prophets are those special persons raised up by God to hold Israel and its leaders accountable to their covenant with God. The prophets also interpret historical events in terms of Israel's covenant fidelity.

The prophets are *forth-tellers*, speaking painful truths about Israel's covenant infidelity and God's moral demands. Passages in these books also *fore-tell* various short-term, long-term, and eschatological futures for Israel and the world, involving judgment of Israel or judgment of Israel's (and God's) enemies, the renewal of godly leadership in Israel, and a distant future of cosmic judgment and Jewish (or global) peace, security, prosperity, and redemption.

Many of these prophecies are offered as Israel's historical journey darkens. The northern kingdom of Israel is conquered by the Assyrians in 722/721 BCE and never recovers (2 Kgs. 17). The southern kingdom of Judah is conquered by the Babylonians in 587/586 BCE (2 Kgs. 24–25; 2 Chron. 36; Jer. 52; Lamentations). Its surviving leaders are exiled to Babylon. Jews learn to live in exile and diaspora, under active assimilation efforts as well as occasional mortal, even genocidal, threats (Esther, Daniel).

The Babylonians fall to the Persians about fifty years after the conquest of Jerusalem. A new Persian imperial strategy permits the exiles to go home and rebuild a modest temple and walled city, which takes a long while (Ezra–Nehemiah; cf. Haggai). These texts reveal a grateful but wounded, insecure, and divided Jewish people.

The narrative of the (Protestant version) of the Hebrew Bible ends here. The intertestamental books, included in the Catholic Bible, describe another several hundred years of history, including events under the rule of Greece and its local clients. Some of these events seem to make their way into the latest books included in the Hebrew Bible (notably Dan. 7–12).

The Christian New Testament, to be considered in the next chapter, interprets the life of Jesus of Nazareth as the God-sent fulfillment of this history, the texts surrounding it, and the loose ends the canon leaves behind.

The Hebrew Bible is a vast compilation. Is it possible to find a consistent narrative here, a through-line from beginning to end? Any such claim is debatable, but here is one possibility: an accent on *divine love for covenant peoplehood and mission on behalf of humanity*.

In love, God chose Israel from all the nations of the world to be a special covenant people, a light to the nations, with a promise of divine care, abundant people and a fruitful land in perpetuity, and eventually, a Davidic royal dynasty.

In love, God rescued Israel from extinction more than once, beginning with Abraham and Sarah, the rescue from Egypt, the return from exile, and rescue from later genocidal threats.

In love, God offered Israel her magnificent Torah. In keeping covenant with God, Israel bears witness to the world.

In love, God anointed the courageous prophets to call the covenant people back to true obedience to Torah when they strayed.

In love, God sustained Israel when her life was fractured by war, exile, and enslavement.

The Hebrew Bible, then, is the story of a loving, creating, sustaining, liberating, rescuing, covenant-making God, and God's difficult but enduring relationship with the chosen people Israel.

THE THEOLOGICAL CRISIS AFTER 587 BCE

It is a lovely story. But it did not always cohere easily with events in the world. As of 587/586 BCE, the Jewish people had been smashed twice by imperial powers in war, had lost its land, its royal family, and its temple, and had seen massive dispersion of its population. The modest return and rebuilding effort described in Ezra–Nehemiah only partially addressed these concerns.

The Hebrew Bible clearly reveals the theological crisis created by these historical developments. In response to them, it also reveals what can only be described as numerous conflicting theological interpretations and projections of the future.

The majority interpretation of Israel's suffering was that Israel was constantly being punished by God for its covenant infidelity. Israel had to accept its punishment, renew covenant obedience, and live in hope for the future. This sin-punishment model could explain every national misery. But it did so at the cost of depicting a relentlessly punitive God.

Sometimes, though, the mood shifts. Israel's suffering is too cruel or prolonged to be viewed as divine punishment. Biblical texts shift their tone, treating the cause of Israel's suffering as more like what it would seem to be at a worldly level, which is cruel violence and oppression from ruthless foreign enemies (cf. Isa. 61:8–9). At such moments, woes are called down upon enemies, their suffering predicted (Isa. 13–23; 47; Ezek. 25–32), and Israel's vindication promised—including return from exile, renewed prosperity, and plunder of adversary nations (Isa. 43–44; 49; 55; 60–62; Ezek. 33–48).

In retrospect, it seems only natural that a people who believe they are in covenant relationship with God would need to offer interpretations of historical events. But the result tends toward incoherence and at times offers a depiction of God that is not especially appealing.

In the end, Israel was left with certain stark realities in relation to its theological self-understanding:

> Promises that God's covenant people would be protected from the physical threat posed by their enemies (Ps. 12) were not consistently fulfilled.
>
> Promises that Israel's land would be preserved for Israel (Gen. 13:14–15) were not consistently fulfilled.
>
> Promises that the Davidic line would be maintained forever (2 Sam. 7:13) were not fulfilled.
>
> Promises that the temple would stand always as the dwelling place of God (1 Kgs. 8:12–13) were not fulfilled.

The rabbis' solution was to move the center of Jewish life to Torah, family, and synagogue. Judaism became a portable faith, suitable for a politically insecure and dispersed people.

Political, royal, territorial, and cultic memories and dreams were still nurtured; indeed, they became a major part of the ultimate division between Jews and Christians. Christians interpreted Jewish hope christologically, with Israel's unfulfilled promises fulfilled in Jesus. Jews continue to wait for this world's redemption, when "no more shall the sound of weeping be heard . . . [and] they shall not hurt or destroy on all my holy mountain" (Isa. 65:19, 25).

TOWARD A POST-HOLOCAUST VOLUNTARY COVENANT

That ultimate redemption has not yet come. The Jewish people, and the world, have continued their long sojourn, a journey of many tears, of so much hurt and destruction.

The Holocaust, said Rabbi Greenberg, was the third great catastrophe in all Jewish history, an epic disaster that can only be compared to 587 BCE and the Jewish-Roman war of 66–73 CE.

Like many other Jewish thinkers, Greenberg was sure that the Holocaust posed a pivotal test to Jewish self-understanding, above all, to its understanding of God.

In response, Greenberg muted his claims about God's actions in the world and God's faithfulness to Israel. He said that Jews cannot always account for God's actions in the covenant that God made with Israel. Israel's relationship with God has been deeply wounded. Elie Wiesel also used that word: "I believe in a wounded faith. Only a wounded faith can exist after these events. Only a wounded faith is worthy of a silent God."[29]

Writing just after the Holocaust, Martin Buber had already said:

> How is a Jewish life with God still possible in a time in which there is an Oswiecim [Auschwitz]? The estrangement has become too cruel, the hiddenness [of God] too deep. One can still "believe" in Him who allowed these things to happen, but can one speak to Him? Can one still hear His words? . . . Dare we recommend to the survivors of Oswiecim, . . . "Call to Him, for He is kind, for His mercy endureth forever?"[30]

In one essay, Greenberg describes a sad breakthrough moment in his own long and painful reckoning with the Holocaust. He writes that after the burning children, "the *commanded* stage of the covenant" between God and the Jewish people "had come to an end."[31] God no longer has the right to demand covenant loyalty from his people. Obedience to divine command is no longer at the heart of the relationship.

But the Jewish people, said Greenberg, can still choose to live in covenant with God anyway—even if God is silent. And, Greenberg says, Jews are doing that.

According to Greenberg, this means the covenant between God and Israel has reached a new stage: it is now a *voluntary covenant*.[32] Jews still gather to study Scripture. Jews still seek *tikkun olam*, the healing of the world. Buber anticipated this when he suggested in the same early postwar talk just quoted: "Despite everything," Jews should still "struggle to redeem the world."[33] Greenberg said Jews are still doing that, after Auschwitz.

I would suggest that Christians can do this too. Bracketing off everything we might want to say about Jesus in the next chapter, we can join our Jewish brothers and sisters and engage the epic story told in the Hebrew Bible in this way.

We can join Jews in practicing the prophetic teachings of figures like Jeremiah, who called Israel to true obedience to Torah. We can join him in challenging rulers who place themselves above God's law and harm the innocent. We can join him in swatting away versions of religiosity that focus on rituals rather than human suffering and social injustice. We can practice what he preaches in the opening verses of Jeremiah 7:

> The word that came to Jeremiah from the LORD: Stand in the gate of the LORD's house, and proclaim there this word. . . . Thus says the LORD of hosts, the God of Israel: Amend your ways and your doings, and let me dwell with you in this place. Do not trust in these deceptive words: "This is the temple of the LORD, the temple of the LORD, the temple of the LORD."
>
> For if you truly amend your ways and your doings, if you truly act justly one with another, if you do not oppress the alien, the orphan, and the widow, or shed innocent blood in this place, and if you do not go after other gods to your own hurt, then I will dwell with you in this place, in the land that I gave of old to your ancestors forever and ever. (Jer. 7:1–7)

Jeremiah and the other prophets tell us something that both Jews and Christians can do in this kind of world: *Protect the weak and stop the killing. Create a social order in which justice and peace prevail among people at last.*

We can join in listening to the subversive prophetic book of Jonah. Jonah tells of a reluctant prophet sent by God to preach to the Assyrians, Israel's mortal enemy at the time. Jonah is given the (for him) happy news that Assyria's capital, Nineveh, is to be destroyed in divine judgment. But Jonah is given the (for him) unhappy calling to preach repentance in Nineveh and save the city.

Jonah runs away, ends up in the belly of a fish, gets spit up on the shore, preaches, gets the repentance he does not want, and sulks about it until God rebukes him (Jonah 4:11). The book of Jonah is a text aimed against any kind of religio-national ethnocentrism, including that to which the Jewish people might themselves be tempted.

Jonah tells us something that Jews and Christians can do in this kind of world: *We can care for the life, survival, and dignity of all people. We can work against disaster coming to any people, even those we think of as our enemies.*

Jews and Christians can also together revisit the amazing book of Job, so extraordinarily relevant to a post-Shoah world.

Job is a story about calamity coming to the "greatest of all the people of the east" (Job 1:3). The story is framed as following from a kind of wager between the Satan (the adversary) and God. God thinks Job is wonderfully devout and faithful and calls the Satan's attention to such a fine human specimen (Job 1:8). The Satan suggests Job's virtue is a complacent response to God's many blessings. Remove his blessings, and Job will turn on you quickly, he says (Job

1:9–11). God permits the Adversary to have at it (Job 1:12). Job rapidly loses everything and everybody other than his unhappy wife (Job 1:13–2:8).

Job's friends come to comfort him (Job 2:11–13). But he is not easily comforted. He cries out against the injustice of what has happened to him (Job 3, for example). The friends resort to some familiar pieties—the world is divinely ordered; the wicked suffer and the good are blessed; you are suffering, ergo, you must have sinned. Repent and all will be well.

Job refuses to accept this explanation. This enrages his friends, and their comfort turns to direct personal accusation (cf. Job 22). Job becomes an object of derision (Job 17, 19, 30). But he still will not relent. His last soliloquy (Job 29–31) laments not just his material and human losses, but also his loss of honor and reputation. He closes by reviewing his lifetime commitment to the very moral code offered in the Law and Prophets (Job 31).

Through the entire drama, Job protests his innocence, complains about God's unfair treatment, and pleads for God to stop hurting him or at least listen to his case. When God finally appears to speak to Job (Job 38–41), it turns out mainly to be an epic review of the wonders of creation. But Job had never questioned that. He had questioned God's justice. God says, in effect, "I am beyond your understanding, including your finite ideas of moral order and justice. The world and all that is in it are mine. Stand in awe." And Job is awed, or at least overwhelmed. He finally quiets. Maybe it's not the answer that matters to Job. Maybe it's God deigning to answer at all. Maybe.

At one level, the book of Job is a timeless treatment of the problem of why bad things happen to good people (cf. Hab. 1:1–2:5). Any human sufferer can read it and identify.

At another level, the book of Job seems a direct challenge to the punishment-blessing explanation for what happens to Israel and to many people. In that sense it challenges precisely those abundant theological explanations to be found in the rest of the canon.

At yet a third level, part of the value of Job for post-evangelicals is that the book contains multitudes. Conflicting interpretations not just of Job's experience but also of human experience and God's relationship to the world, are already embedded within the book itself. Any interpretive claim one can make about the book is itself debatable. It is not clear what the author, or the editor, wants us to take away. All this shattering of univocal biblical interpretation is very good for those of us who were not trained to read Scripture that way.

On my most recent reading, it is ultimately the spirit of the man Job that sticks. He suffers unjustly. He knows this and will not keep silent. He addresses God bluntly. He never stops seeking God's face. He swears by God's name in the same breath as assailing God's injustice to him (Job 27:1–6)—and for that matter, the injustice that afflicts others (Job 24). He never stops raising questions. But his questions are to God. His protest is his prayer.

Job tells us many things that we can affirm even in this kind of world. Evil things happen to innocent people in this world. There is no adequate explanation. Most attempted explanations fail, even the theological ones. Some are obscene. And God can seem so very silent.

In such a world, Jews and Christians can *cry out against evil. Never stop asking questions of God and neighbor about why so much is wrong. Live a life that seeks to redress as many human evils as possible.*

Pulling together everything said so far, perhaps we can humbly join Martin Buber in calling the theology offered here a post-Holocaust "biblical humanism."[34] It certainly seems akin to the Christian humanism I have named. For Buber, biblical humanism is a Jewish faith and practice rooted in the moral tradition of the Hebrew Bible, oriented toward justice, and committed to seeking *tikkun olam*—regardless of the silence of God. I believe it meets the burning-children test. It also pulls together the moral commitments of all major strands of my theology, and that of many post-evangelicals.

The God I believe in calls people to live according to a rigorous, justice-centered moral code and to seek to build a world accordingly. Much else I wish to say about God can only be said in the apophatic path—by way of negation.

Mine is not a God who determines everything that happens on earth.

Mine is not a God who overrides our freedom to decide whether to live the way God wants.

Mine is not a God who can be counted on to deliver human victims from human misdeeds, even when we pray earnestly for deliverance. Like Bonhoeffer, I believe that we must not hope for a deus ex machina God, who swoops along in the final act to save us from ourselves.[35]

Mine is not a God who favors one people or nation over others. I follow Genesis 12:3 in arguing that God made covenant with Israel ultimately to bless all the world. If God has also made covenant with the church through Jesus, as I believe, it also must ultimately be to bless all the world. And it is not necessary to teach, as Christians once did, that God can only be in one covenant relationship with one people. Surely God can make multiple covenants, and the idea seems almost directly suggested in Amos 9:7: "Are you not like the Ethiopians to me, O people of Israel? says the LORD. Did I not bring Israel up from the land of Egypt, and the Philistines from Caphtor and the Arameans from Kir?"[36] This idea has taken hold in much Jewish-Christian-Muslim dialogue, and it makes great sense to me.

Mine is not a God who needs our theological explanations for the suffering that people experience. Like Job's friends, we generally botch those explanations.

A GOD WHO SUFFERS AT HUMAN HANDS

Irving Greenberg suggested that God has chosen at this stage of history, with our massively enhanced forms of human power, to expand upon the "delegation of responsibility to humanity" for what happens on earth.[37] Part of what the Shoah has revealed is that we are fully responsible for what happens, not God. Humans did that evil, and humans allowed it—not God.

Here we touch on the perennial theological issue of divine providence, including the nature and extent of God's power in relation to the world, the creatures God has made, and the things that happen here.

Most Christian theologians appear to operate from the premise that however God related to the world, as recorded in Scripture, must always be how God relates to the world in every era.

Greenberg's novel suggestion is that God's relationship to the world is more dynamic than this, that it has movement, stages, changes. His suggestion is that full delegation of power over the world from God to humanity has clearly been made in this current era of massively expanded human power. It is a fascinating claim.

Now, the idea that humans are fully responsible for what happens on earth was already suggested in the Hebrew Bible, most clearly in this text: "The heavens are the LORD's heavens, but the earth he has given to human beings" (Ps. 115:16). More broadly, it is a premise of the entire story of creation in Genesis 1, in which humans are described as made in the image of God and given "dominion," that is, responsibility, over Earth and its creatures (Gen. 1:26–31). The Creator, the sovereign God, has delegated trusteeship to us, and we are accountable for what we do.

This would mean that from the very beginning God was constrained, or *chose* self-constraint, in relation to the world.[38] But it also suggests that God looks on as a witness to what we do, often with a great deal of sorrow and suffering (cf. Gen. 6–8).[39] This idea of a God who risks trusting us with freedom, and suffers from the choices we make, is critically important in moving us away from theologically problematic and morally disempowering understandings of divine sovereignty.[40]

But in view of the depth of God's love, and the magnitude of human suffering, "only [a] suffering God can help."[41] The only God that I can accept must necessarily be a God who weeps at the evil humans do. A God who intimately knows what it is like to be human perhaps becomes capable of fully taking in, and taking on, human suffering. And that leads us in the direction of the New Testament. . . .

I believe that God made the world, set us in responsibility over it, and chooses to communicate to us the nature of moral goodness and a rightly ordered world—even if sometimes it seems a distant dream. I believe that God has always taught humans that "true religion" is to love God by caring for creation, honoring each person's life, abiding by moral law, advocating just societies, liberating the oppressed, and even laying down our lives when necessary to do the right thing on this earth.

And I am certain that this is the path that God took in Jesus Christ.

TAKEAWAYS

- Six key theological-ethical influences on the author are named: kingdom theology, social gospel, Holocaust theology, liberation theology, Catholic social teaching, and progressive evangelical social justice.
- The burning-children test constrains my theology: "No statement, theological or otherwise, should be made that would not be credible in the presence of the burning children."
- The Hebrew Bible tells the story of a loving, creating, sustaining, liberating, rescuing, covenant-making God and God's difficult but enduring relationship with the chosen people Israel.
- The major covenant promises embedded in the Hebrew Bible—land, kingship, temple, divine protection—were unfulfilled by the close of the canon.
- Scriptural books like Jeremiah, Jonah, and Job contribute to a post-Holocaust biblical humanism accenting heightened human moral responsibility in voluntary covenant with God.
- God looks on as a witness to what we do—sometimes with a great deal of suffering.

5

Jesus

Apocalyptic Prophet, Lynched God-Man, Risen Lord

JESUS ACCORDING TO . . .

In this chapter I will offer my honest post-evangelical account of what I now make of Jesus. Even in relation to Jesus and the New Testament, I continue to assert the burning-children test. This test seems especially poignant here, in a chapter about Jesus, because one of the reasons for Auschwitz was that Christians had been taught for centuries to despise Jews in his name.

British New Testament theologian James D. G. Dunn has recently added to his distinguished publishing record a very helpful book called *Jesus according to the New Testament.*[1] In this book, based on a series of church talks, Dunn offers sketches of the different accounts of Jesus found in the New Testament. He separates for analysis eight different accounts: Jesus according to Jesus, then Jesus according to Matthew-Mark-Luke (the Synoptic Gospels), John, Acts, Paul, Hebrews, James-Peter-John-Jude, and finally Revelation.

Three things about this approach are especially interesting. One is the idea that *it is possible to identify a primal "Jesus according to Jesus" strand in the New Testament.* Dunn notes that this is certainly not a consensus view among New Testament scholars. But if Dunn is right, at least at this basic level our understanding of Jesus need not just be accounts or versions or perspectives; there's Jesus-on-Jesus, discernible underneath the various "according tos." That Jesus core ought to be of great interest to all Christians. We will consider it closely, with gratitude to James Dunn.

The second interesting thing about Dunn's approach is the way he distills all the different accounts of Jesus in the New Testament down to eight. The Synoptics are similar enough that they are covered in one chapter in Dunn's book; they have certain distinctions but major similarities and intertextual connections, and they are all closely connected to Jesus-according-to-Jesus. But other New Testament authors develop accounts that stray further from this primal core.

For example, Dunn treats the Gospel of John as a separate, late, quite distinctive theological interpretation of Jesus, more like Hebrews and 1 Peter than like Mark or Luke. I concur, and it is one reason why it will not receive further attention here.[2] Dunn gives the book of Acts a long chapter and reveals a distinctive account focusing on the preaching of Christ's resurrection. Paul gets two chapters and again emerges as the most significant theologian in the New Testament canon. Dunn describes Paul as focusing little on the life and ministry of Jesus, offering a theology of the atoning death and transformative resurrection of Jesus, developing a salvation theology of justification by faith in Jesus, and creating a mystical-participatory theology of spiritually transformative life in the Holy Spirit. And so on with other authors, the notable exception being the Epistle of James, which is deeply connected to Jesus' own teaching and the local Jewish context in which he ministered.

This leads to the third interesting thing about Dunn's approach. Ever since Jesus-according-to-Jesus, all other accounts are Jesus according to others. And the accounts vary considerably. There is not one, single picture of Jesus presented in the New Testament—a fact Dunn clearly shows. We can easily extend his observation from the New Testament era to our own. There is no single account of Jesus in church history, or in evangelicalism, or in global Christianity today. It's always *Jesus according to*.

It would be easy simply to assume that it's all chaos after that, just one opinion against another, with none better or worse. That goes too far. But it is true that even if our versions of Jesus are constrained by the New Testament accounts, as I think they should be, the latter's diversity means that Christians will always produce different accounts of Jesus, and we will undoubtedly argue about whose is best and how one knows that. Still, we must make the effort both to offer cogent accounts of Jesus and to communicate why we believe what we believe.

JESUS ACCORDING TO AMERICAN WHITE EVANGELICALISM

In this light, I believe that one of the subtle forces producing a post-evangelicalism today is discontent with Jesus-according-to-US-white-evangelicalism. I do not believe that there is only one white evangelical Jesus, but I do think that at least four inadequate Jesuses are out there. Only one of them is even remotely defensible from within a New Testament framework.

That defensible Jesus is (1) *Jesus the Crucified Savior*. His primary function is to come into this dark world to die on the cross so that we believers might be forgiven of our sins and go to heaven when we die. His character teaches us about who God is, his teachings show us how to live, but the main point of his coming to earth was to die for the sins of the world.

This was the primary version of Jesus that I was first exposed to in Southern Baptist Christianity. *Jesus loves you and died on the cross for your sins*. This Jesus can easily be rooted in the New Testament, though not mainly in the Synoptic Gospels. Paul's writings are a central source of this vision of Jesus, as is John's Gospel. It surfaces in much of evangelicalism, with different accents in terms of human choice versus divine predestination in salvation. But whether in Reformed, revivalist, or missionary circles, this Jesus who dies so that I might live forever is a central evangelical Jesus.

This is a defensible Jesus in New Testament terms, for sure. But this Jesus mainly comes to die and mainly does so for personal salvation. There is a lot missed with this version of Jesus.

But I would still take that Jesus over (2) *Hallmark-Christmas-Movie Jesus*. This is the kind, attentive, ruggedly handsome yet gentle white guy we sing about in evangelical churches sometimes. This is the Jesus whom we ask to "hold me," one who is there "when I am weak and he is strong," and "when I am down he lifts me up." This Jesus is the best (platonic) boyfriend or bro-friend I could possibly have, the one who is there for me all the time, my comfort and encourager. He also runs a really nice Christmas-related operation, so that's a plus.

I'm joking a bit, but this loving gentle Jesus depiction is not entirely foreign to the New Testament. Still, this is a sentimentalized Jesus whose main role is my emotional stabilization in a trying world. Maybe, as part of a broader New Testament account of the Christian life, this Jesus has a proper place. But there's little theology and no ethical teaching to this Jesus.

But I would still take that Jesus over (3) *Jesus Who Wants You to Succeed*. This latest Jesus is a staple megachurch evangelical Jesus. In suburban evangelicalism, this is the Jesus whose teachings can be abstracted to offer success principles for leadership and life to upwardly striving young professionals. In prosperity gospel land, this is the Jesus who wants you to be as wealthy, lovely, and thin as the well-coiffed leaders on stage, book covers, and private jets.

This version of Jesus may connect just a bit to what has been described as the wisdom tradition or dimension of Jesus' teachings. But overall, I see little contact between this Jesus and the New Testament, and little that is relevant in a world of suffering and evil.

Once we move to this point, and beyond, I think we have reached the land of what might be described as (4) *Vacant Jesus Fillable with Any Content We*

Want. This Jesus, having been distanced so profoundly from his Jewish roots, his account of himself, and any New Testament depictions, is a mere shell, symbol, or totem. This is a Jesus always available to be filled with whatever content we might like to drop in there.

In our book *Kingdom Ethics*, Glen Stassen and I essentially argue that this Vacant Jesus has predominated in much of historic Christianity. The way you get to this Jesus, we say, is by systematically ignoring the Jesus one meets in the Synoptic Gospels. Or, if he is not ignored, Christians find ways to evade what he said, to thin down his theological vision and moral demands as far as possible, to shave away anything that might make a claim on us.[3]

This Vacant Jesus is not just useless. He can be positively harmful. This can be the Jesus of the KKK, the Race God Savior of White People Only (see chap. 9). He can be the Jesus of my tribe, my class, my race, my party, my all-important self, providing ultimate religious justification for every passion I might feel like giving myself to.

Evangelical revivalism at least gave us a New Testament Jesus who wants to save people from their sins and get them to heaven. Wesleyan and Holiness traditions at least gave us a Jesus who wants to make us holy, sanctified, even morally perfect according to his own rigorous standards. Pentecostal and charismatic Christianity at least gave us a Spirit-filled Jesus who wants us to be likewise Spirit-filled and thereby totally transformed. And doctrinaire evangelical Lutherans and Calvinists at least gave us a Jesus who cares about the drama of eternal salvation and not just any old human project or vision.

I would take revivalist Jesus, Holiness Jesus, Pentecostal Jesus, or Calvinist Jesus over Vacant Jesus any day of the week.

JESUS ACCORDING TO JESUS

But better still would it be to meet Jesus-according-to-Jesus. The following is what James Dunn, distilling plenty of New Testament scholarship and a lifetime of his own study, finds as (a) the key lessons learned from Jesus, (b) distinctive features of Jesus' ministry, and (c) elements of Jesus' own self-understanding. I want to use this material as our baseline.

Dunn describes eight central lessons learned from Jesus.[4]

1. Jesus surprised his followers by creating the *Love Command* as the highest statement of moral obligation: love God with everything you have, and love your neighbor as yourself (Mark 12:28–31). In Jewish context, the first part was familiar, drawn from the daily recited Shema (Deut. 6:5); the second part was exceptional, drawn from the obscure Leviticus 19:18.

2. Jesus clearly emphasized the *priority of the poor*. This was visible in his

preaching, his parables, and his actions (Mark 12:42–44; Matt. 5:3//Luke 6:20; Matt. 11:5; Luke 4:18; 19:8).

3. Jesus offered *welcome to sinners*. He offered welcome in his own ministry, dining and meeting with many who were considered religiously defiled or unacceptable (Mark 2:16–17; Matt. 11:19; Luke 15:2). He also taught that welcoming sinners is what God does (Luke 15; 18:9–14; 19:1–10). This drew criticism because it upset the expectations of those around him; it certainly delighted those who had been excluded and were now welcomed.

4. Jesus demonstrated *openness to Gentiles*. He taught that many will come from all directions to the messianic banquet (Matt. 8:11–12), he ministered to many Gentiles, and he commissioned the disciples after his resurrection to go and make disciples of all nations (Matt. 28:19).

5. Jesus included *women among his close followers*. He surprised his culture by giving women a vital role in his ministry (Luke 8:1–3), including them among his band of followers (Mark 15:40–41), speaking and teaching and ministering to them just the same as to men (Luke 10:38–42), and appearing to them after his resurrection (Matt. 28:1–10).

6. Jesus also demonstrated *openness to children*. People brought sick kids to Jesus and he healed them. They brought their children to Jesus just to be blessed, and he blessed them (Mark 10:14), rejecting the disciples' efforts to shoo them aside. He elevated a certain kind of innocent childlikeness (Mark 10:15).

7. Jesus *relaxed Jewish food laws* and related regulations about purity. He surprised the Pharisees with his laxity in relation to handwashing regulations (Mark 7:1–23). He made the occasion an opportunity to emphasize inward rather than external cleanness. Mark comments that Jesus "declared all foods clean" (7:18–19), though we know from the rest of the New Testament that this matter remained a struggle for much of the early church.

8. Jesus *instituted the Lord's Supper*. This unforgettable last meal with Jesus became an important part of the ritual life of the early church and provides a link between the ministry of Jesus, his death, and the practice of his followers.

Dunn goes on to suggest that Jesus' own ministry was distinctively characterized by his proclamation of the kingdom of God, understood as already evident in his ministry but also with a grand consummation imminent (more on this later). He offered powerful, authoritative teaching and was notable for his striking parables. He exorcised evil spirits. (Oddly, Dunn barely mentions Jesus' healing ministry.) He focused his ministry in Galilee, though at the end he entered Jerusalem, where he knew he would die, a death he submitted himself to without resistance.

Finally, Dunn focuses on Jesus' self-understanding. His baptism at the hands of John the Baptist marked for him a moment of personal affirmation of

God's favor and commissioning for ministry. He clearly articulated a sense of being sent by God. He understood himself to be the Jewish Messiah, though especially in Mark he wants that to remain secret till the end, and he always ties his messiahship to suffering rather than triumph. He addresses God as Abba, a familiar Aramaic term not commonly used in prayer. He distinctively referred to himself as Son of Man, probably influenced by Daniel 7:13. He expected to suffer greatly and to die in Jerusalem, which he did.

Dunn sees the Synoptic Gospels as hewing rather closely to the picture just outlined, though with a handful of specific emphases. Mark adds the messianic-secret motif. Matthew focuses on Jesus as fulfilling Jewish prophecies and expectations, as a new Moses focused on redeeming Israel and reinterpreting Jewish Law. Luke highlights Jesus' anointing by the Holy Spirit and his frequent personal prayer, while heightening the notes on welcoming sinners; reaching out to Gentiles, including women; caring for the poor; and warning about the perils of wealth. That's about it.

Take a second and review the four evangelical Jesuses against the backdrop of Jesus-according-to-Jesus and the Synoptic Gospels. Might you join me in finding it a little troubling that *there are few points of contact between any of those evangelical Jesuses and the accounts of Jesus that we have just reviewed?*

The primal Jesus we have met here is deeply Jewish. He bears a kingdom-of-God message (more on this below). He cares about the poor and warns about the spiritual and moral perils of wealth. He describes God as one who welcomes outcasts, marginalized people, all those that the religious treat as sinners. He has a soft spot in his heart for children. He smashes expectations all the time, including in how he destigmatizes women and challenges purity-based religiosity.

This Jesus is a prophet in the lineage of the prophets—more than that, though exactly what is not always clear in the most primal accounts—and like many of the prophets, his authorization and commissioning come from God to him directly. This inevitably marks a challenge to authorized religious leaders, with whom he clashes. He carries himself with great intimacy with God. He has profound spiritual power. He exercises that power on behalf of others, those who need it most. He is against legalism and for an understanding of his Abba Father that leads to human welcome, healing, acceptance, and love. His teachings are authoritative, rooted in his Jewish tradition and picking up the robust global inclusivity that is part of an eschatological strand of that tradition.

This is a Jesus who knows that his calling is going to lead to his quick and terrible death in Jerusalem. He is going to die, and his death has covenantal meaning: bread and cup, body and blood, a new covenant. Elaboration of theologies about the meaning(s) of Jesus' death came later.

JESUS ACCORDING TO GUSHEE VIA MATTHEW

Now I want to go deeper. I have returned to the narratives about Jesus in the Synoptic Gospels and read them closely and receptively—without seeking to make them come out the way I want. I have made Matthew my base text and then compared from there, inspired by Dunn's claim that Matthew was "the most-used version of the ministry and teaching of Jesus in the second century."[5] Instead of worrying overmuch about historical-critical questions, I just read the texts, with one question in mind: *Who is Jesus here?* Call this next section "Jesus according to Gushee via Matthew." If we are going to commit to following a different Jesus than the evangelical ones we have received, we need to know who that Jesus is.

Born of a Virgin

Matthew and Luke start off with Jesus' birth from the Virgin Mary, offering quite different accounts of the event, with somewhat different apparent purposes. Matthew wants to link Jesus to Abraham, David, and Moses (Matt. 1:2–17; 2:13–15), and to link Mary's pregnancy to a text from Isaiah (Isa. 7:14; Matt. 1:23), as promise to fulfillment. Luke (chaps. 1–2) wants to emphasize the role of the Holy Spirit and perhaps wants to link Mary's story with that of Hannah in 1 Samuel 2. Overall, the two birth narratives strike me as grand prologue in the same way Genesis 1–11 offers a grand prologue to the Hebrew Bible.[6]

Baptism for Apocalyptic Ministry

The Synoptic Gospels all then move to John the Baptist's ministry in Judea, Jesus' baptism by John in the Jordan River, and Jesus' temptation in the wilderness.

John the Baptist/Baptizer is a known historical figure in the ancient Jewish world. He clearly preached an apocalyptic message of the imminent kingdom of God, urgently exhorting people to repent and be baptized to ready themselves for God's dramatic intervention in history (Matt. 3:1–12).[7] Jesus' kingdom message needs zeroing in on, and this is the place to begin.

We saw briefly in the last chapter that the Hebrew prophets offered many foretellings of the dramatic end that God would one day bring about. These prophecies, sometimes individually and certainly together, contain a two-sided message of coming divine action. At the end, when God finally acts to reclaim this world in a blaze of divine power, some will be punished while others will be saved. John's message is heavy with warnings on the wrath side, which motivates an awful lot of people to repent, get baptized, and ready themselves for judgment day (Matt. 3:7–12).

Scholars tell us that apocalypticism tends to flourish in extreme historical circumstances. In such times, everyday history is so awful that the human mind and spirit move to another plane. The secret of *what is really going on* is unveiled by the prophets; the justice that so urgently needs to be enacted is eagerly, imminently, envisioned; the few and the good are given hope of mercy, and the tyrants, evildoers, and compromisers are given warnings of doom. Such apocalypticism was very much in the air in Roman-occupied Palestine. It is not unfamiliar today.

Jesus starts off in the company of John the Baptist. How long he was with him is an interesting question. But eventually he seeks and receives baptism along with others. And in that baptism, two deeply important things seem to happen. He receives an anointing by the Holy Spirit, and also an affirmation of a special relationship with God as God's "Son" (Matt. 3:13–17).[8] Anointing by the Spirit was common for both rulers and prophets in Israel; Joel promised an outpouring of the Spirit in the last days (Joel 2:28–32); both could be at play here. And Jesus, the one with questioned parentage, at this pivotal moment receives a message of blessing and affirmation from God his Father.[9] The proto-Trinitarian nature of the scene was not lost on the early church.

Jesus immediately is "led up by the Spirit into the wilderness" for an extremely demanding period of testing and preparation (Matt. 4:1–11). This is apocalyptic-anointed-prophet-Son boot camp, with forty days of hunger and then three rounds of significant demonic temptation. Jesus withstands it all, learns that John has been arrested by Herod (major foreshadowing here), withdraws north to Galilee (Matt. 4:12–16), and begins his own ministry with a proclamation in exactly the same words as John—"Repent, for the kingdom of heaven has come near" (Matt. 4:17). He recruits the first four disciples (Matt. 4:18–22). He is on his way.

Jesus' overall Galilean ministry is summarized in the next section (Matt. 4:23–25):

> Jesus went throughout Galilee, teaching in their synagogues and proclaiming the good news of the kingdom and curing every disease and every sickness among the people. So his fame spread throughout all Syria, and they brought to him all the sick, those who were afflicted with various diseases and pains, demoniacs, epileptics, and paralytics, and he cured them. And great crowds followed him.

This is the work that Jesus undertakes until he chooses to go to Jerusalem at Passover, where his actions provoke the potent opposition of the authorities and result in his crucifixion, about which we will say more below.

Proclaimer of the Imminent Kingdom of God

As a Christian ethicist, I have always been so impressed by the Sermon on the Mount (Matt. 5–7) that I have routinely made it central to my exposition of Jesus' ethics. In *Kingdom Ethics*, Glen Stassen and I offer that exposition. We also situate the moral and spiritual teachings of the sermon firmly within a carefully developed account of what (we think) Jesus meant by the kingdom of God.[10]

It can be complicated, because Jesus' reported sayings about the kingdom were so numerous and not always identical in their implications. But we argue that Jesus' message of a kingdom of God has roots in the Hebrew Bible, notably in prophetic treatments of God's coming intervention in judgment and divine rule of the world, as well as in the poignant, lovely promises of what a renewed world will be like.[11]

Understanding the brutality of Roman rule and the humiliation of being dominated by pagans in the Jewish homeland also is critical for assessing what people would likely have heard, or wanted to hear, when language of the kingdom of God was used by Jesus. To claim that God, not Caesar, is king—to suggest that God is now acting to reclaim Israel (and the world)—this had dramatic political overtones. The Jewish people did have a recent history that included major revolts against foreign overlords, and rebellion was in the air in occupied Palestine. It is striking how deeply political is the language used about the newborn king, for example, in the speeches of the Lukan birth narratives (Luke 1:32–33, 46–55, 67–79). I suggest that one reason Jesus was sure he would die was because his kingdom preaching was intrinsically threatening to the Roman overlords of the Jewish people.

Stassen and I argue that Jesus developed his own understanding of the kingdom of God, rooted especially in Isaiah. We suggest that for Jesus, the kingdom has seven key marks.[12] God interrupts history, (1) unmistakably giving evidence of his presence, creating changes in human life toward (2) deliverance, (3) justice, (4) peace, (5) healing, and (6) inclusion of exiles and outcasts in community. Human beings can only respond with (7) joy—unless, that is, they prefer the world as it is, in which case they invite divine judgment.

My fresh look at the Gospels leads me now to highlight more strongly the radical apocalypticism of the Jesus we meet in the Gospels. He is offering many warnings of divine judgment. But the context for this judgment appears to be the coming Day of the Lord, when Israel and indeed the whole world will meet God's climactic judgment (cf. Matt. 25:31–46).

The radicalism, urgency, and relentlessness of Jesus are so striking. He is a young man in a hurry. He is radically God-centered, urgent in announcing the coming kingdom, and relentless in calling people to drop everything and follow him (Matt. 4:18–22; 8:18–22). His job is to prepare people for the end. And because God will come in both wrath and redemption, Jesus' message has plenty of warning and not just hope (Matt. 12:47–50; 18:6–9; 25:31–46). He is not always gentle Jesus, meek and mild, certainly not toward those whose actions are about to evoke God's judgment. He is certainly not Hallmark-Christmas-Movie Jesus.

No, this Jesus is warning of Armageddon. He is like Noah, who knows that the flood is coming in just a few days, warning people to get ready (Matt. 24:36–51; 25:1–13, 14–30), but the people just keep on doing life as usual. If you knew a massive meteor would be crashing into Earth on Wednesday, you probably would not go out surveying land on Tuesday. Jesus is telling them the meteor is coming, but they are still out surveying land. He is like the angels warning Sodom, like Jonah warning Nineveh, to repent before their cities are turned to ash. One greater than all the previous messengers is here (Matt. 12:38–42), but people aren't listening, which means they will fully merit the coming judgment (Matt. 10:5–15; 11:20–24; 16:1–4).

Amid this urgency Jesus speaks a lot about intense conflicts between people, the divisions that he will evoke, the vastly different responses to his message (Matt. 10:34–36; 13:1–43). He gathers a group of followers and tells them that theirs will be a work of conflict and hardship (Matt. 10:16–25). They will need to trust absolutely the God who commissions them, and no one else (Matt. 11:25–30). They will need to be ready to lay down their lives, to fear only God and no human being (Matt. 10:26–33; 16:24–26). They can fully expect to be opposed by many, including their very families, as Jesus himself was (Matt. 10:34–39; 13:54–58; cf. John 7:5). And they will need to leave their domestic relationships and responsibilities entirely behind (Matt. 8:21–22; 12:46–50), though not through divorce (Mark 10:2–12).

Jesus spends a remarkable amount of time telling people that the survivors on the Day of the Lord are not going to be who folks expect them to be (Matt. 9:9–13). The message of repent-and-get-ready is for everybody, but those who have the hardest time with it are those at the top of the system. The last will be first, the first last (Matt. 20:1–16). Jesus routinely suggests that those dreadful Gentiles and even Samaritans will enter the kingdom much more readily than (many) Jews (Matt. 8:5–13; 12:15–21). In Luke this theme almost gets him killed during his inaugural address in Nazareth (Luke 4:16–30).

The message is consistent—it is those notable sinners, those worthless ones like tax collectors and prostitutes and Samaritans (Matt. 21:28–32), who will catch God's eye and gain his mercy. It is the poor and poor in spirit, the abused and persecuted (Matt. 5:3–12), the lost and little (18:10–14), the humble and repentant (Matt. 18:1–5; 20:20–28; Luke 18:9–14), who demonstrate that they are ready, not those who are confident in their own rightness before God. The riffraff will get the banquet seats, while the top dogs will be in outer darkness weeping and wailing (Matt. 22:1–14). Jesus offers a message of constant and unsettling surprises, and when it comes to judgment day, people don't want to be surprised.

Albert Schweitzer (1875–1965), that amazing biblical scholar, physician, and philanthropist, was among the first to suggest that Jesus' apocalypticism was as central as I am making it here. He also suggested that this should affect how we read his moral teachings as well. He described Jesus' teachings as an "interim ethic" for apocalyptic conditions.[13] This would render their value questionable for the demands of a world that is not going to end tomorrow.

This is not how Stassen and I treat Jesus' moral teachings in *Kingdom Ethics*, nor is it the theology of the social gospel or of most peace-and-justice social teaching traditions. In *Kingdom Ethics* we acknowledge that all Jesus' teachings are framed within the kingdom context, but then we suggest an understanding of the time horizon known as *inaugurated eschatology*. That is basically the idea that the reign of God is now being *inaugurated* but will not be *consummated* until he returns some indeterminate time later. Meanwhile followers of Jesus are called to live out kingdom principles and practices in obedience to Jesus and because doing so participates in the dawning of the reign of God.

So, unlike Schweitzer, Stassen and I do develop Jesus' moral teachings into an ethical program.[14] For such a program, who can do better than the Golden Rule (Matt. 7:12), the great love commandment (Matt. 22:34–40), peacemaking (Matt. 5:7), forgiveness (Matt. 18:21–35), compassion (Luke 10:25–37), and so much more?

What if Jesus intended these teachings as a repentance-and-preparedness agenda in view of the Day of the Lord, which might be imminent? Does that invalidate the teaching for normal human living conditions? Or was this Jesus' genius, to teach that every time is an apocalyptic time, that the best way to please God is to live with taut urgency and radicalism, knowing that a just God is very soon coming to reclaim this world?

Go back to the Sermon on the Mount and read the commands, but now also pay attention to the apocalyptic notes (*italicized*). Jesus teaches: eschew anger and make peace quickly, *before judgment day comes* (Matt. 5:21–26). Turn decisively away from lust, *in view of your body possibly being thrown into hell* (Matt. 5:27–30). Tell the truth when you are speaking to people, always and without oaths (Matt. 5:33–37). Stop retaliating, turn the other cheek, respond to lawsuits by giving away more than is demanded, go a voluntary second mile when a Roman soldier demands one mile, give your stuff to people who ask for it (Matt. 5:38–42). Love not just friends but also enemies, because the goal is now to be perfect as God is perfect, it is not to be just like everyone else (Matt. 5:43–48).

Give to the poor, pray, and fast secretly so your motives can be fully purified and "*your Father who sees in secret will reward you*" (Matt. 6:1–6, 16–18). Forgive so that you will be forgiven *when it is time for God's judgment* (Matt. 6:14–15). Stop acquiring possessions (Matt. 19:16–30) and worrying about them, for God will give you what you need as you *live for the coming kingdom* (Matt. 6:19–34). Stop judging others, because "*with the judgment you make you will be judged*" (Matt. 7:1–5; 18:21–35). Stop trying to secure your life by cozying up to the Gentiles ("dogs" and "swine"). They will tear you to pieces. You can only secure your life by trusting in God the Father, like a little child (Matt. 7:6–11). Be a good tree bearing good fruit, because "every tree that does not bear good fruit *is cut down and thrown into the fire*" (Matt. 7:19). Practicing God's will in these radical ways is the only way to be ready "*on that day*" (Matt. 7:22).

In sum: with time so short, "that day" so imminent, the "gate" so narrow (Matt. 7:13), and God's approval all that matters, only moral radicalism will do. You want to be among the sheep, not among the goats (Matt. 25:31–46). You want a seat at that banquet (Matt. 22:1–14). You want to be part of the new kingdom of God more than anything. It is the pearl of greatest price (Matt. 13:45–46). There is nothing that matters more than that. Live accordingly.

The Meaning of the Miracles

As we read through the Gospels, we see that Jesus spends an awful lot of his very brief ministry exercising amazing spiritual power by healing the sick (Matt. 8:1–17; 9:2–8, 18–34), freeing the demon-possessed (Matt. 8:28–9:1; 12:22–32; 17:14–21), raising a few people from the dead (Luke 7:11–17; John 11), and even exercising such wondrous power as calming storms (Matt. 8:23–27), walking on water (Matt. 14:22–33), arranging great fish catches (Luke 5:1–11), turning water into wine (John 2:1–12), and multiplying food to feed massive crowds (Matt. 14:13–21; 15:32–39). The modern critical mind choked on the miraculous, and the literature that developed around even the possibility of miracles became massive.[15]

But if we read postcritically, this aspect of Jesus' ministry seems to have key intertextual meanings. It validates his "end times" anointing by the Holy Spirit (Joel 2:28–32). It connects him to some of the deeds of Hebrew prophets like Elijah (1 Kgs. 17) and Elisha (2 Kgs. 4–6). It ties him in an uncanny way to God's power as creator of all (Matt. 8:26–28). And it links to promises that, in the great future redemption, the Day of the Lord, illness and death shall at last be defeated (Isa. 35; 65). When John the Baptist asks whether Jesus is "the one who is to come," Jesus simply says: "Tell John what you hear and see: the blind receive their sight, the lame walk, the lepers are cleansed, the deaf hear, the dead are raised, and the poor have good news brought to them" (Matt. 11:2–6).[16] Jesus exercises supernatural powers as a sign of the dawning reign of God. Observers, of course, cannot help but wonder, "What sort of man is this, that even the winds and the sea obey him?" (Matt. 8:27).

The Path to Martyrdom

And then the end indeed comes, but only for him, not for the world. Jesus begins warning of his imminent death (and resurrection) in Jerusalem long before he and his group of disciples arrive there (Matt. 16:21–23; 17:22–23; 20:17–19; 26:1–2).

Jesus enters Jerusalem at Passover time. Not only does this link Jesus to the pivotal event and the central religious holiday in Jewish life, it also means that he arrives in a city swollen by Jewish pilgrims—with Jewish and Roman authorities on the lookout for the slightest hint of trouble.

After a dramatic demonstration of public support when he rides into Jerusalem (Matt. 21:1–11), in the Synoptic accounts Jesus immediately goes into the temple to make a shocking prophetic demonstration against it (Matt. 21:12–13). In my view, Jesus sees the temple as precisely what Jeremiah 7 describes it to be—"a den of robbers." The robber Herod built the temple to gain fake political legitimacy. The temple establishment steals from people, including poor widows (Luke 21:1–3), with the heavy temple tax (Matt. 17:24–27) and other buckraking. The temple aristocracy lives lavishly in the Jerusalem hills off these many temple fees. Rome allows these guys to take their cut as long as they compliantly serve the empire's interests. To add to this critique of the temple establishment, a few days later Jesus openly predicts that the temple will be destroyed (Matt. 24:1–2). It's like going into Washington and claiming publicly that the White House will soon be in ruins. It is a shocking statement and a sure path to trouble.

This temple business is all garden-variety corruption. It is *religious* corruption, leveraging a frustrated people's piety, linked with its sacred memories of that ancient, long-ago temple of Solomon. And it is *occupying-empire* corruption, when foreign hegemons take someone's land and subdue it by buying off a native elite. Happens all the time.

Young Jesus from Galilee comes into this powder-keg city, already with a substantial following, and then enacts a shocking antitemple demonstration. Then he returns for the better part of a week for a daily heal-in (Matt. 21:14) and teach-in (Matt. 21:23–25:46), much of it conflictual with the religious authorities. They can't arrest him because the crowds are too big (Matt. 21:15–16, 26) and his support too strong. Jesus essentially takes control of the temple for the better part of a week in what amounts to a popular movement. The situation is getting out of hand.

Lynched at the Hands of Rome

And so, Jesus' enemies arrange a murder on a Roman cross. Black liberation theologian James Cone is right in his claim that this is a lynching,[17] a political killing of a Galilean peasant preacher and disturber of the peace. Before the state executes a person, there is supposed to be an extant law violated by a crime, followed by an indictment, leading to an arrest, precipitating a legal defense, followed by a public trial governed by rules of evidence, shielded from mob passion, leading to a fair verdict. A lynching violates all these principles. Even if state authorities are involved, as they so often were in US lynchings, they are still just mob-based murders. That is essentially what happened to Jesus.

The Gospels describe the steps: Jesus' clandestine nighttime arrest, secret overnight interrogations, delivery to the Roman governor Pontius Pilate, brutal scourging (Matt. 27:26), mockery, beating, abuse, torture (Matt. 27:27–31), and crucifixion (Matt. 27:32–56). The Gospel authors are transfixed by the cruel murder of their leader, though they go light on the bloody details at the very end.

This is a Jewish prophet being murdered. Jews had seen this before.

This is a foreign potentate martyring an innocent Jew. Jews had seen this before as well.

This is a movement promising a great coming redemption, ending in the leader's murder. Jews are not the only ones who have seen this before.

The question, of course, is whether the cross is more than all these things. The church has spent its entire history thinking about that.

Resurrection

And then, a hasty entombment, and silence; an empty tomb, grieving women, angelic messengers, reports of resurrection with conflicting details, and scattered appearances by Jesus (Matt. 28; cf. Luke 24; John 20–21).

The prophet had been murdered, which was to be expected—but unlike all other murdered prophets, this one lives again. That is where the Gospels end. Jesus was dead but is now alive as the risen Lord. Those who believe in him still have work to do. The church is born, commissioned for service to the world (Matt. 28:16–20).

I believe in the bodily resurrection and ascension of Jesus, although I do not pretend to understand it. I live in the hope that if God raised Jesus from the dead, then, in the end, life triumphs over death, not just for me and mine, but for the world. The rest is mystery.

WHAT DO WE MAKE OF JESUS' MESSAGE TODAY?

Should Jesus be interpreted as an apocalyptic preacher of great power—but one who got his timeline wrong? Christians have never been too interested in that option, for obvious reasons, and it is a questionable conclusion.

Was Jesus perhaps that very rare figure who *could act as if* the Day of the Lord is coming tomorrow, even if he did not know that it would come at any particular time? After all, Jesus did say that he did not know when the end was coming (Matt. 24:36).

Is it possible to live in apocalyptic moral radicalism when you do not have a vivid belief that the apocalypse is truly imminent? To live in imminentist radicalism amid an indefinite wait has not proven easily sustainable in Christian history. But perhaps that's why we are commanded to live watchfully (Luke 12:35–36), whether it is easy or not. This is, after all, what Christians are reminded to do every Advent season, to retune our hearts with a spirit of expectancy and renewed eschatological vision.

Should Jesus be interpreted as a radical social-change teacher? Did he offer subversive practices like enemy-love and turning the other cheek as part of a strategy of moral resistance employable in many situations of injustice? This was the interpretation of Mahatma Gandhi, and of Martin Luther King Jr.[18] Here Jesus is not just a prophet but a justice strategist. It is certainly the case that many social-change movements have practiced his teachings in this spirit. But was that what he intended? Certainly, an incredible amount of good has been done in the lineage of Jesus-according-to-MLK.

Should Jesus instead be interpreted as a prophet who taught the oppressed a way to transcend their dehumanizing lives of powerlessness, fear, and domination, even when the injustices they face do not go away? This is how I read Howard Thurman, at least in his majestic *Jesus and the Disinherited*.[19] Thurman's Jesus teaches a way to rise to the majestic heights of dignity in a context of deep structural injustice. He offers a path to inner spiritual freedom and transcendence, even amid terrible and seemingly intractable oppression. *You may mistreat me, but I know who I am as a child of God, and you will never succeed in breaking my spirit.* It is this inner, transcendent spiritual freedom that then provides the moral energy needed to attack oppression in any activist program.

Should Jesus, perhaps, be seen as the most radical kind of prophet, the kind who throws himself against systemic injustice even when he surely knows that he will fail, and die? This would be a Jesus who projects a compelling prophetic-populist vision of a world of justice for the poor, peace for the violated, and dignity for the scorned, and does so *knowing that those who project such visions invariably die too soon*, their dreams left unfulfilled. But Jesus does it anyway!

To fight for justice, peace, and the dignity of the oppressed even when it is hopeless, or when the only hope is hoping-against-hope—this is the vision of contemporary Latino scholar Miguel De La Torre, who says it is realistic as an expression of the actual life circumstances and defiant hopelessness of the poorest and most oppressed of the world.[20] People who do this might well get killed—but still they are right, and they do right, and they are worthy of highest honor.

WHAT DO WE MAKE OF JESUS' DEATH TODAY?

Should Jesus' death be understood mainly as just described, as the slaying of a prophet, like Martin Luther King Jr., Oscar Romero, or Mohandas Gandhi? That certainly is true enough, and it gives us a point of contact with our modern world. But we wouldn't be Christians if the meaning of his death ended there.

Should Jesus' death be understood as a blood sacrifice to God for human sin? As Satan's apparent victory but ultimate defeat? As Christ taking the punishment for human crimes? As a ransom for human sin? As satisfying the debt we owe God for our sins? As a divine example to human beings of the true nature of love?

These are some of the theories of the cross that the church has developed over the centuries. I do not dismiss them, though some make much more sense to me than others.

When I look at the cross these days, I see an apotheosis of human and divine suffering. I see a man who has given his all for the redemption of this bloody world dying at the hands of his fellows. In this sense he symbolizes the human tragedy, all those vicious, stupid murders and other crimes done to human beings by their neighbors.

And when I look at the cross, I see God, reaching through the gap between heaven and earth to save humanity, only to end up (knowingly, willfully) suffering and dying at the hands of his own creation. This somehow sums up, at least epitomizes, God's journey of suffering in the world that God has made, alluded to in the last chapter. Dietrich Bonhoeffer put it this way: "God consents to be pushed out of the world and onto the cross; God is weak and powerless in the world and in precisely this way, and only so, is at our side and helps us. . . . Only the suffering God can help."[21]

I was reminded of the endless, paradoxical fecundity of the meanings of the cross when watching the musical *Godspell* not long ago. Here is the haunting refrain of the song that the cast sings as Jesus dies.[22] The first-person voice is Jesus; the other voice is that of the disciples, which I italicize. You just have to listen to this song:

Oh God, I'm bleeding
Oh God, I'm bleeding
Oh God, you're bleeding

Oh God, I'm dying
Oh God, you're dying
Oh God, I'm dying

Oh God, I'm dead
Oh God, you're dead
Oh God, you're dead

We kill one another. We killed our best. We killed God who came to save us. When we kill another, we kill the God who made them and loved them, who was in them and who came to save us. That is what I see these days when I look at the cross.

WHAT IS OUR GOSPEL?

I must ask one final set of questions. What do we do about the gap, or at least the pivot, between Jesus-according-to-Jesus and the Synoptics, and Jesus according to the rest of the New Testament? This is one of the oldest and hardest questions in all Christian thought.

I am fully aware of various efforts to efface the distinction, and it would be easier if it were not there. But Dunn's recent book is a reminder that New Testament scholars, at least, still see the issue. Speaking of the book of Acts, but with broader implications, Dunn says this: "It is not an idle question to ask . . . what is the continuity between Jesus' proclamation of the kingdom and the proclamation in Acts of the resurrection of Jesus?"[23]

What might be called *the religion of Jesus* is the good news of God's imminent action to bring in the kingdom of God, and the urgent call to get ready. It is also the extraordinary way in which he lived, the radical nature of his apocalyptic and prophetic ministry, his profound supernatural healing power, and his love for the poor, sinners, Gentiles, women, children, and all who are oppressed.

In contrast, *the religion about Jesus* is the good news of his atoning sacrificial death for human sin, his resurrection that signals the defeat of death and the release of the Spirit's power for transformed life, and the church as the community living in that Spirit now. This New Testament "religion about Jesus" holds a middle ground in my approach—much preferred to most of the subsequent, deeply flawed religions about Jesus that I have named, but still not the primal "religion of Jesus" that Dunn and the Synoptic Gospels offer.

I find the religion of Jesus to offer the ethics of what Buber called Hebrew/biblical humanism, though in an apocalyptic frame. This prophetic, deeply Jewish Jesus lives for God's climactic judgment and healing of the world, and he teaches followers how to participate in what is coming and get ready for it. I have always been deeply drawn to this Jesus.

I find the New Testament's religion about Jesus to be a creative theological adaptation, useful for a time horizon of indefinite duration, deeply meaningful for the individual journey through life and toward death. But it is rather substantially cut adrift from the ministry of the historical Jesus, distanced from both his own Jewishness and the earliest Palestinian Jewish church.

It is a beautiful and compelling message. It is the message that brought me to faith. But I cannot accept the common evangelical claim that this message is "the gospel." It is one version.

It is my hope for a fresh wind of study, preaching, and adoration of Jesus. To my post-evangelical friends, this is my request: please do not think that the problem with the religion you are leaving behind is Jesus. If you return to serious encounter with Jesus as we meet him in the New Testament, I do not think you will be disappointed. For me, the place to begin is in that most primal core, where we meet the prophetic, radical, just, powerful, defiant preacher of the dawning reign of God.

TAKEAWAYS

- The chapter suggests US evangelicalism features a Jesus the Crucified Savior, a Hallmark-Christmas-Movie Jesus, a Jesus Who Wants You to Succeed, and a Vacant Jesus Fillable with Any Content We Want. None is adequate.
- The chapter reviews the findings of James Dunn related to Jesus-according-to-Jesus and Jesus according to the Synoptic Gospels.

- The author then offers an account of Jesus based on a close reading of the Synoptics, focusing on Jesus as apocalyptic prophet, lynched God-Man, and risen Lord.
- The contemporary significance of the message and death of Jesus are considered, together with the pivotal question, what is our gospel?
- Post-evangelical Christianity needs at least to redress the imbalance between the heavily Pauline-magisterial Reformation gospel and a focus on Jesus and his kingdom ministry.

6

Church

Finding Christ's People

LEAVING CHURCH

Lots of people are abandoning church, and many local churches are declining, in crisis, or closing altogether. The statistics are staggering, with substantial drops in church membership and attendance and a rise in those who never attend any religious services.[1] Post-evangelicals are clearly among the refugees. This is a chapter about how post-evangelicals might think about, and what we should do about, church.

Let's begin by zooming out, considering different types of church "leavers."

People leave churches *to go to other churches* for a variety of reasons. In our free-market church environment, lots of people flow in and out the doors of various churches, hoping for higher levels of religious meaning and satisfaction.

Pastors are not thrilled by the revolving door. In ministerial ethics classes we address pastors with the old-school instruction not to go out "stealing sheep" from other struggling pastors.[2] But you don't have to go out to steal sheep. The rotating sheep—colloquially known as church hoppers—eventually come to you.

But this is not the same problem as people *leaving church altogether*.[3] Some leave because their faith in Christ has faded or lost salience. Some walk away because they are burned out from too many years of service. Some drift off to other weekend pursuits. Some leave because they got their feelings hurt. Some quit because they must work all the time or have complicated personal lives. Some abandon ship because they are tired of church conflict. Some leave for silly reasons.

Post-evangelicals are abandoning church too. Some are leaving for reasons that overlap with why others are abandoning church—but others leave *for reasons peculiar to the American evangelical experience.*

Those reasons begin with disillusionment over teachings that are viewed as harmful to the vulnerable. Some leave over the harm LGBTQ people and their families have experienced (see chap. 7). Others leave over patriarchal teachings. Some leave over the damaging effects of purity culture (see also chap. 7). Others leave over white evangelical racism (chap. 9). Some say: all of the above.

People are also leaving evangelical churches over reactionary attitudes toward science and liberal learning, over anti-intellectualism and theological rigidity, over the inability to deal with honest questions or anything other than all-happy-all-the-time faith, and over the identification of evangelical faith with conservative/Republican/Trumpist politics (chap. 8).[4]

The most embittered are leaving evangelicalism in a state of trauma, reporting their evangelical experience as one of abuse or violation.[5] These include people abused by ministers, especially those ministers protected by their churches rather than held accountable. But one sees today a broader sense of religious trauma and abuse.

I believe that church, properly understood and practiced, remains valuable, constructive, and even indispensable for following Jesus over the long term. As a pastor, I want to encourage post-evangelicals not to give up on church. But I know that the hurts are many, the obstacles grave.

I will first sketch a theology of church that builds on the theological work done in the previous chapters. I will tell about the two church communities that are an essential part of my life. Finally, I will survey the broader post-evangelical church landscape.

TOWARD A BIBLICAL THEOLOGY OF CHURCH

If we take both Old Testament and New Testament together, one composite way to define church is this: *The church is the community of people who stand in covenant relationship with God through Jesus Christ and seek to fulfill his kingdom mission.*

The church consists of those persons who have responded to Jesus by entering into the new covenant (Luke 22:20; 1 Cor. 11:24–26; 2 Cor. 3:1–6; Heb. 8) that he established in order to pursue his mission (Mark 6:7–9; Matt. 28:16–20). Local churches consist of those believers who covenant together in a specific congregation with its specific understanding of how to order its life and pursue Christ's mission.

The fact that the church has access to God through Jesus Christ does not, in my view, invalidate the Jewish covenant with God, nor does it rule out the possibility that God has made or could make covenant with other peoples in other ways toward the same broad ends (Amos 9:7). God is free to covenant with whom God wishes (see chaps. 4–5). The church consists of those who covenant with God through Jesus Christ. We ought to feel a sense of sacred kinship with the Jewish people—and all other people who bear a similar sense of covenant with God and share a redemptive mission in this world.

The Nicene Creed declares the church to be one, holy, catholic, and apostolic. These are theological assertions about what the church is—expressions of faith. These claims can also be pivoted to serve as imperatives concerning what the church should be. Let's consider both dimensions.

The church is one (John 17:10–12, 20–23; Eph. 4:1–3; 1 Pet. 3:8) in the sense that Jesus founded one church and prayed for its unity (John 17). While there are millions of local expressions of the church around the world, all Christians everywhere are part of one church, the church universal. This we should affirm even as we recognize, mainly with sadness, the schisms among the churches that we see.

The church is holy (Rom. 12:1–2; Eph. 1:3–5; 5:25–27; Col. 1:21–23; 1 Pet. 1:13–16; 2:8–10) on account of Christ's holiness and in the sense of being set apart for a holy purpose by Christ.

The church is catholic (meaning universal; Acts 2:1–21; 8; 10; Rom. 4:17–19; Rev. 5:9; 7:9–10; 15:3–5) in the sense that the whole Christian faith is proclaimed to all persons, and the church's membership is open on equal terms to every tribe, tongue, and nation.

The church is apostolic (Matt. 16:18; 1 Cor. 4:1–13; Eph. 2:19–21; 2 Pet. 3:1–2; Rev. 21:14) in the sense that it was established by Jesus with and through the apostles, and that it moves forward from the apostolic generation to our own.[6]

This creedal declaration does create certain moral imperatives for those who claim identification with the church:

Members of the church *should seek unity* in their local congregations and with all other Christians, however difficult that quest can sometimes be.

Members of the church *should seek to live in holiness*, with the help of the Holy Spirit, in obedience to Christ's commands, and seek to protect the holiness and spiritual health of the church.

Members of the church *should recognize the catholicity of the church*, honor our covenantal fellowship with Christians of every type, and reject any ideology that would narrow the bonds of Christian fellowship—including racism, homophobia, and xenophobia.

Members of the church *should seek to keep their churches and themselves tethered in covenant fidelity to the apostolic witness to Jesus*. While the shape of faithfulness to Christ is a matter of discernment, we are not free just to make it up as we go along.

I want to look at three widely cited New Testament images of the church and then two other concepts that I think critically important.

The church is *the body of Christ* (Rom. 12:5; 1 Cor. 12:27; Eph. 4:12; Col. 1:24). This is to affirm that since the resurrection and ascension of Jesus, he is present bodily in the world through his people. The church is where Christ can be met bodily in the world. I follow Dietrich Bonhoeffer in suggesting that we need an expansive and even literal understanding of that idea.[7] The church as body of Christ is where Jesus can be experienced corporeally in the world.

This implies the moral imperative that the church, and Christians, must do everything possible to learn how to embody Christ's presence faithfully in the world. Everything we see in the life and ministry of Jesus—his mercy, justice, love, healing, passion, courage, sacrificial spirit—should be visibly incarnated in his body, the church.

The church is *the temple of the Holy Spirit* (1 Cor. 3:16–17; 2 Cor. 6:14–16; Eph. 2:21). This is to affirm that the church, collectively and in its people, is a holy place, a place in this world where God dwells. While Christians may gather corporately in a sacred space that we might call a sanctuary or even a temple, the New Testament says that the church is itself a temple, a place where God dwells. This move desacralizes geographical or built space and elevates the mystical presence of God's Spirit in God's people.

This idea suggests the moral imperative that the church must seek to be holy and to be a context where God's Spirit can be encountered. We must live in such a way that it is plausible for people to believe that we are a place where God dwells.

The church is *a new creation* (2 Cor. 5:16–21; Gal. 6:14–16), in which human enmities and divisions are overcome, in which the groaning old creation begins to give way to a world made new. This gets pretty close to what Jesus meant by talking about the kingdom of God, and so:

The church is *a people devoted to the kingdom of God* (Matt. 6:33; Mark 12:28–34; Luke 9:1–3; Acts 8:11–13; 19:8–10). The church's mission is to continue Christ's mission until he returns. Here I am continuing my kingdom-centered account and suggesting that Christian mission should reflect Jesus' mission, even if the apocalyptic spirit is not sustained. The church as kingdom people works for the manifestation of God's reign among us and in the world.

The church is *a covenant people trained through worship, Word, and sacrament* (1 Cor. 11:23–32; 14; Col. 3:15–17; Heb. 13:15–16; Jas. 5:13–14). The church gathers collectively to worship God, to study Scripture, and to practice its sacramental life. We do these things because we are commanded to and because they are goods in themselves. But we also do so as training in covenant faithfulness.

It is possible—indeed, it is sadly well documented—that groups of people claiming to be churches can become negations of the church. Churches can become divided and divisive, unholy and hateful, racist and xenophobic, alienated and alienating from the apostolic witness to Jesus Christ.

Some people leave churches like that, thinking mistakenly that they have left the church. Instead, they have left negations of what Christ intended the church to be. Fleeing such communities may not be a sign of wavering faith in Jesus; it may be an affirmation of it.

The reality is that not every place claiming to be a church is part of the church universal, that many churches fail their calling. This fact forces us toward something like the old distinction between the churches that we see (the church visible) and the church that Jesus recognizes as his people (the church invisible). We may not be able to find Christ's people where we thought to look. But I am convinced that we *can* find them.

A SECOND LOOK AT THE EVANGELICAL CHURCH CRISIS

D. G. Hart was cited earlier as an Orthodox Presbyterian critic of modern evangelicalism. A major focus of his critique has to do with evangelical ecclesiology. Hart argues that modern evangelicalism sacrificed any meaningful theology of the church.[8]

It did this in two ways. One was through its elevation of parachurch (rather than church) institutions and leaders as paragons of evangelicalism. It did this from the very beginning, as its top ranks and most visible "products" included radio evangelists like Charles Fuller, itinerant preachers like Billy Graham, and institutions like Youth for Christ, the Billy Graham Evangelistic Association, *Christianity Today* magazine, Fuller Seminary, and even the National Association of Evangelicals itself. One could self-identify as an evangelical simply through loyalty to one or another of these individuals or institutions. Evangelicalism remains filled with, even dominated by, parachurch organizations.

The second path to weakening evangelical ecclesiology was through the intentional building of a denomination-transcending coalition. The new evangelicals of the 1940s wanted to build a big evangelical tent, and they did not want "sectarian" differences to stand in the way. They scooped up, or attempted to scoop up, every kind of vaguely conservative Protestant church group.

Many of these groups, however, had long argued over core aspects of ecclesiology—including the nature of church membership, structure of church leadership, goals of Christian mission, and meaning of baptism. Hart argues that there is no meaningful shared theology of church across the entire evangelical "family," and this is unmistakably correct. The quest for "evangelical unity" and political clout through strength in numbers had the unintended consequence of weakening Christian ecclesiology and loosening people's ties to real churches in the world. It also made authority problems chronic and insurmountable.

Kristin Kobes DuMez, a church historian at Calvin College, is working on the thesis that evangelicalism is a consumer culture.[9] Having been a part of that evangelical culture for forty years, I know she is right. What many heavily consumerized evangelicals understand church to mean has been taught to them through the most successfully marketed musicians, authors, trinket salesmen, and parachurch groups. Evangelicalism is also a *brand* (and collection of brands), a kind of proprietary product that those at the top defend for a variety of reasons, including the fact that they and their institutions have vested financial interests in doing so.

All of this threatens the humble local congregation. Why go to some mediocre worship service at the little church on the corner when you can consume glittery evangelical products?

Finally, evangelical political fixations since the 1970s have often substituted a political vision for an ecclesial one. Where evangelicalism, and evangelical churches, have become little more than outposts of a political party, they have abandoned any connection to the historic identity and mission of the church. This issue will be revisited in chapter 8.

MY CHURCHES: LOOKING INSIDE THE DOORS

Seeking the Kingdom Class, First Baptist Church of Decatur

The church is both universal and local. My most intimate and important experience of local church meets at ten o'clock every Sunday morning in room E-210 of First Baptist Church of Decatur, at the corner of Clairemont and Commerce. It is a community of about fifty people called Seeking the Kingdom. This is a small group that I started more than a decade ago. I want to tell you about it and reflect on lessons I have learned from it.

First Baptist Church of Decatur (FBCD) is more than 150 years old. Founded during the Civil War, it sits in historic downtown Decatur, just east of Atlanta.

FBCD was a Southern Baptist congregation for most of its history. But in the great sundering that tore apart the Southern Baptist Convention (SBC), the congregation chose the moderate Baptist side. This choice was both ratified and finalized when the church selected Julie Pennington-Russell as its senior pastor in the summer of 2007. Because Southern Baptists have joined many other evangelicals in banning women as senior pastors, FBCD was pushed out of the SBC.

My family joined FBCD the same summer Julie started as pastor, just after we moved to Atlanta for me to start work at Mercer. You join FBCD by presenting yourself publicly for membership, to be approved by a congregational vote.

We joined, and within about six months I started this class called Seeking the Kingdom. It has been, from the beginning, an intergenerational group, open to all who are interested. Our numerical high was about sixty attendees on the average Sunday several years ago. Today we average around thirty. The family members who attend with me are my mother-in-law, Lynnie, and sister Kate.

The class is called Seeking the Kingdom because I wanted to signal from the beginning that my understanding of the gospel, and of the mission of the church, centers on Jesus and the kingdom he proclaimed.

We meet for one hour each week. I try to do just two things during that time: lead study of some portion of Scripture and provide opportunity for people to share their prayer concerns, which are then addressed in prayer one by one. This hour supplements the worship services, so my class does not need to meet all spiritual needs. But I do firmly believe that a deeper dive into Scripture and an extended time for prayer concerns is the best use of our precious hour. The meaningfulness of that experience, and the community that has been fostered, is borne out time and again.

As an expression of the church universal, our little community is one, holy, catholic, and apostolic. We protect our unity and that of the congregation in which we are embedded, we seek to encourage one another in godly living, we welcome everyone, and we remain tethered to Scripture, with a focus on Jesus and the Gospels. It has not always been easy to do this.

Many times, we have experienced breakthrough moments—either in class, or in relationships outside of class time—in which we sense God's Spirit moving and the moment becoming sacred. These times often happen as we experience fresh insights on Scripture, share our hearts with one another, pray for each other, and find ways to offer problem solving and direct help to each other, as well as to those outside our group whose needs are brought to our attention.

Our group went on a shared journey toward broadened catholicity from about 2008 forward when it comes to LGBTQ inclusion. Decatur is both an old small town and a modern magnet suburb, and one community magnetically attracted to Decatur is LGBTQ Christians. Some of them began making their way into our congregation and into my small group.

It was the community experience in the Seeking the Kingdom class over many months that most contributed to changing my mind and heart on gay inclusion. I will say more about the substance of that issue in the next chapter. But, for now, I must say that studying, praying, and living in community with LGBTQ Christians was transformative for me. Some say I lost contact with a faithful reading of Scripture. I, and my community, would say that we gained in practicing Jesus' mission and embracing the catholicity of the church.

I never "had an agenda" to pursue LGBTQ inclusion in the class, nor did the people who came my way. They were Christians who had found their way to FBCD and then from there selected my small group because it suited them. Once in the community, they gradually made themselves known, as we all do. In both class times and private occasions, I learned transformative truths through these encounters. I gradually came to a place of readiness to do the biblical and theological work required to rethink "the gay issue." But it was the context of the Seeking the Kingdom class and the lovely community being built there that created that readiness and, indeed, that urgency. We made the transition together and helped the broader congregation do the same.

Having made the transition to full inclusion some years ago, we do not need to discuss it very often now. We are just doing church together, with people's sexuality incidental unless someone tells us otherwise.

Seeking the Kingdom reminds me of some of the virtues of Baptist church life, at least in our kind of Baptist church. Local church autonomy allows us to become who we are, to follow Jesus as we believe he is leading us, without anyone from outside telling us what is or is not acceptable. Believer's baptism makes it easier to emphasize our shared, voluntary covenant commitment. An emphasis on lay leadership and on making good use of everyone's gifts makes it easy for new ventures, like my small group, to be started. A strong pietist tradition helps us take seriously the humanity, suffering, and religious experiences of one another—and makes us less likely to allow any kind of doctrinaire posture to harm the vulnerable or block community. If someone comes into our kind of Baptist church and gives evidence of the Spirit's work in their life, we take that seriously. I am so grateful that no pressures from any external evangelical power players can affect the life of our church or our class.

The Seeking the Kingdom group also helps me understand better the wisdom of the apostle Paul's focus on the local church as a site where the kingdom of God advances. I want social transformation, and I believe Jesus wanted it. Indeed, I want *tikkun olam*, the perfecting of the world. I work for that. I pray for that. "Your kingdom come. Your will be done, on earth as it is in heaven" (Matt. 6:10). This is Jesus' own kingdom prayer.

But while we pray and work for world transformation, there is this little community that meets weekly, prays for each other, takes care of each other, eats together, and serves together. There are people in that little group who stayed away from church for decades because of what some church or Christian did to them or their loved ones. They cautiously make their way to our class, and they find church again. They find safety, wholeness, and love. They find inclusion in community, one of the marks of the kingdom. And they stay. In this sense even a local congregation's small group can be an incubator of God's reign.

There is another aspect of covenantalism that needs addressing. When we make a covenant, as opposed to a contract, there is a level of permanence about it. At least, there should be. Part of what has made Seeking the Kingdom so meaningful to many of us is the durability of the group, the length of time we have been in community, and our deep, shared sense of commitment. Somehow, over time, the consumer mentality that so dominates American church life has given way to a sense of covenantal bondedness and permanence.

A few times in the twelve years that I have been at First Baptist, and the eleven-plus years that I have led this class, I have felt inclined to flee. Church conflicts account for a few of those times. I have also sometimes felt a bit weary of the leadership commitment and of the way I am tied down most Sundays to this particular spot on earth.

The last time I felt that way, the most remarkable thing happened. I entered the room that Sunday planning to tell the group that I needed to step away to pursue a road ministry. I was going to initiate a conversation about who would lead after me. After I had said enough to signal my intention, one of our dear, hilarious, most committed saints said something like this: "You can travel and speak as much as you need to, but if you try to leave us, I know where you live, and I will hunt you down. This is your group, your community, and you belong here."

Everybody nodded their heads matter-of-factly. Yep, Randall was right. You're staying, David. In that moment, the covenant community held me and would not let me drift away. I was surprised. This was so, well, un-American. How dare someone tell me I was not allowed to leave!

But Randall was right, a deep covenantal rightness. There is a community that requires my presence. I am not allowed to walk away. I wonder if there is anything, deep in our hearts, that we need more than this?

What are you going to do about church? I could do a lot worse than saying this: find a small group like Seeking the Kingdom. It does not have to be in a local church if that is not something you can handle right now. Find some people and get together every week. Study, pray, eat, worship, and do kingdom work together. The Christian life does not thrive in isolation, and podcasts are not enough. Find flesh-and-blood kingdom people in a real physical space somewhere and do life together as far as you can manage it.

Holy Cross Catholic Church

So that was Sunday morning. Now it is Sunday night at 5:30. Traveling with me to nearby Tucker for Catholic Mass are my wife, Jeanie, and my father, Dave, both devotedly Catholic.

I have given you a glimpse now of the embodied split in the religious life of my family—some family members Baptist, some family members Catholic, with myself as the only crossover. You will recall that I was raised Catholic and became Southern Baptist by conversion. My dear wife, Jeanie, was raised Southern Baptist and joined the Catholic Church almost twenty years ago. Many post-evangelicals find themselves in a similarly odd place. As evangelicals become disillusioned, we begin a new spiritual search. Sometimes couples do not end up in exactly the same place. In our case, Jeanie became Catholic, I became moderate Baptist, our parents stayed where they started, and, more recently, I reconnected with the Catholic faith of my childhood and my bride.

I have already indicated (chap. 2) my appreciation for significant elements of the Mass. Overall, I view the design of the Catholic Mass as something like a polished gem, refined over time to a state of great beauty—if you know what you are looking at, which I certainly did not when I left the Catholic Church at thirteen. The movement of the Mass manages to accomplish so much in something like an hour—processional, with the cross held high; greetings in the name of the triune God; early confession of sin, brief but compelling; an Old Testament passage read by a layperson; a sung psalm; an Epistle reading by a layperson; the Gospel reading by the priest, and the ceremony around it; a brief homily; the centering moment provided by the creed and the prayers of the people. An offertory and music. Then right to the Table—the people offer gifts that are then offered to God and come back to the people as Christ's body and blood; the kneeling, in humility; the Lord's Prayer as an important part of the eucharistic rite; the precious chance to pass the peace with neighbors just before the Supper; more kneeling; the chance to watch the people come up to Communion and pray for them, or instead to be quiet with God; that final Trinitarian blessing and recessional.

The universality of the Mass means that a Catholic anywhere can have roughly the same experience. Jeanie and I attended Mass in Rouen, France, last summer on a Sunday. My French is limited indeed, but the Mass is the Mass. A visitor from anywhere can follow the main lines of what is going on. We did so happily that day, as on many other Sundays in Europe.

The Catholic Church itself is so richly global. It embodies the ethnic catholicity of the church.[10] Our congregation has people from all over the world—not just a massive number of Spanish-speaking immigrants, but also a substantial number of congregants from Asia and Africa. Masses are conducted each week in Spanish, the congregation has a Spanish-speaking priest on staff, and special occasions bring out other language-trained priests.

The US Catholic Church has a massive head start on US Protestant churches in serving a multiracial society with many immigrants. Yes, the Catholic hierarchy was historically dominated by Italians, but that has faded dramatically and is not felt in our local parish. It is striking how difficult it is, for example, for Baptist churches in the South to move beyond their ethnic enclaves, while around the corner people from every continent are praying at Catholic Mass. This global reach also makes it easier—but certainly not inevitable—for Catholic congregations to be trained away from nativism, xenophobia, and racism. All they need to do is look around. A timely pastoral word helps as well.

The Catholic Church has other appealing resources and practices. These include the substantial theological and ethical teaching tradition and its accessibility through the catechism, the social encyclicals, and other resources.[11] Catholic Charities, St. Vincent de Paul, and other ministries have long-standing traditions of effective service to the poor.[12] Catholic issue advocacy at its best is nonpartisan and challenges the blind spots of a divided Washington. And no religious leader in the world has a bigger platform than the pope. I have not even mentioned the aesthetic beauty of most Catholic churches, in comparison with . . . well, you know. Let's just say evangelicals have not built a lot of beautiful churches.

Everyone knows that all is not well in US and global Catholicism. Left-right divisions up to the level of the magisterium now plague Catholics like everyone else.[13] The sex abuse scandals have harmed thousands and deeply damaged the church's reputation. The fixedness of Catholic teaching and practice on women, LGBTQ people, birth control, and other issues is a problem, and the same struggles for identity and inclusion are happening in the Catholic Church as in evangelical churches. Many parishes lack meaningful small-group contexts such as the one I described above. I am seeking to find the treasures in the Catholic Church even as I am a quiet conscientious objector to the elements that mirror problems on the evangelical side. And I go, in part, to build spiritual unity with my wife. I love her and want to be in church with her.

WHERE SHALL POST-EVANGELICALS FIND CHRIST'S PEOPLE?

I am fortunate—blessed—that I have found the two local expressions of the church that are likely to sustain me for the rest of my life. I am also fortunate that I get to travel around and catch glimpses of what other congregations are doing. I see plenty of good examples of what the local church can be and do.

I urge post-evangelicals to be open to church options of many types. You will recall that the postwar neo-evangelicals tried to carve out a third way between fundamentalists to their right and mainliners to their left. Those groups are still there. Post-evangelicals likely will not be interested in a fundamentalist turn, but I hope that many will give the mainline a look. The old caricatures should be set aside for actual exploration. You might be surprised by what you find. Mainline churches vary dramatically, and they are also evolving in response to their own challenges and the new landscape of American religion.

I know for a fact that it is a cultural adjustment when lifetime evangelicals venture into mainline churches. Everything is different, it seems—the buildings, worship services, church calendar, robes, music, prayer books. I remember trying to figure out for the first time how to juggle the Episcopal hymnbook, printed order of worship, and *Book of Common Prayer*, all with just two hands. You can feel like an alien, or even an impostor. You're not. You're a visitor, and won't always be.

I am seeing interesting efforts to welcome and serve post-evangelicals in a variety of mainline church settings. University towns have a lot of Methodist, Presbyterian, Episcopal, Lutheran, Disciples, Baptist, UCC, nondenominational, and other churches that are happy to welcome evangelical refugees. I have spoken at a progressive Baptist congregation in Virginia (Williamsburg Baptist Church) that is intentionally and successfully reaching out to college-age questioning/post-evangelicals.[14] Other events at churches like this are on my calendar. It looks to me like post-evangelicals will be a welcome source of renewal and new energy in many mainline churches.

I expect university towns will be seedbeds of many such efforts, because universities are filled with such evangelical exiles—who will either find another church option *right then* or may be lost entirely to Christian faith. I remember talking with a college freshman who told me that her parents required her to take a bus to attend the local Calvinist congregation every week. But she told me this in a mainline congregation after I gave a talk about post-evangelical Christianity. She was defying her parents by being there. Maybe she will find a new church home. I hope so.

For those post-evangelicals open to high liturgy together with LGBTQ inclusion and theological toleration, the Episcopal Church beckons as an especially attractive option. I now have gotten to know one Episcopal congregation (St. Luke's in Atlanta) and a cathedral and diocese (Christ Church in Cincinnati, the diocese covering much of Ohio) that are making intentional efforts to reach post-evangelicals.[15] Surely there are others. There was a time when my wife and I considered becoming Episcopalians. Maybe today I can be an honorary one.

I am also seeing congregations that once identified as evangelical and have now transitioned into post-evangelical churches. Some of these made the transition a few years ago over the LGBTQ inclusion issue when they revised their policies, lost many members, had to reconsider their identities, and finally became post-evangelical. And there are cases, such as Ken Wilson and Emily Swan of Blue Ocean Faith in Ann Arbor,[16] in which pastors are forced out of their evangelical-identifying communities and have had to start afresh and plant new churches. These are harrowing experiences, but there can be new life on the other side.

There are also new church planting efforts that strike me as post-evangelical, like the very promising multisite Urban Village in Chicago, a United Methodist Church plant.[17] My visit there several years ago filled me with hope. As long as majoritarian evangelicalism blocks LGBTQ inclusion and other needed reforms, smart young progressive-minded church planters are going to create new alternatives that smell and feel like evangelical churches, without the theological and ethical rigidity. They will keep the praise and worship music, the devotional warmth, and the blue jeans, and jettison the rest.

I expect that as evangelical congregations increasingly find they must fight out LGBTQ inclusion, especially those with many young members, some congregations will transition to post-evangelicalism. In other cases, individuals will seek new (or old) church options as their evangelical congregations won't move forward to full inclusion or other changes. It is an interesting, even painful question that many who might be described as "on the post-evangelical spectrum" are already facing—how long do we stay in semi-appealing evangelical churches, hoping to be a voice for change? There is no single answer to this question, but I am encountering it everywhere.

My counsel to my fellow post-evangelicals is simply this: keep looking until you find the group of Christ's people that is a good fit for you. You will have your own set of nonnegotiables that you might be looking for; here is mine. Seek out a flesh-and-blood local community of covenanted believers who are seriously committed to following Jesus and seeking his kingdom together, who reflect and seek Christian unity, holiness, catholicity (for all, including LGBTQ people), and apostolicity. Seek out a community where you can experience the love of God and people, Christ alive and active on the earth, the loving presence of God's Spirit, people doing kingdom work, support for your journey, and serious nourishment through Scripture, worship, and sacrament. Look for a place where you can make a covenant commitment to real people for the long term. Then do that.

TAKEAWAYS

- Post-evangelicals are abandoning church for reasons peculiar to the American evangelical experience, including disillusionment over harmful teachings, reactionary attitudes toward science and liberal learning, right-wing politics, and having been violated or traumatized.
- The church is the community of people who stand in covenant relationship with God through Jesus Christ and seek to fulfill his kingdom mission.
- The church is and must seek to be one, holy, catholic, and apostolic.
- The church is Christ's body, the temple of the Holy Spirit, the new creation, a people devoted to God's kingdom, and a covenant people trained through worship, Word, and sacrament.
- Modern evangelicalism sacrificed any meaningful theology of the church.
- I describe the strengths of my two local church communities in the Atlanta area—Seeking the Kingdom of First Baptist Church of Decatur and Holy Cross Catholic Church.
- Post-evangelical church options include older mainline churches, evangelical churches becoming post-evangelical, and new church plants for post-evangelicals.
- Several nonnegotiables for post-evangelical church life are proposed.

PART III

Ethics: Being and Behaving

7

Sex

From Sexual Purity to Covenant Realism

Evangelicals have been known for a very definite sexual ethic that could be summarized as *no sex for no body outside straight marriage*. They didn't just say it. They meant it. And they were evangelistic about this belief, wanting it not just for themselves but for everyone, by law if possible. Evangelicals were the ones who mostly led antigay legal campaigns beginning in the 1970s. We also led anti–premarital sex campaigns, as we enlisted government to fund and use our abstinence-only and sometimes purity-and-shame-based approach in public-school sex-education classes. We advanced those campaigns aggressively inside our families and churches, with considerable effect.

Today, the fallout of evangelicalism's sexual campaigns is seen in many ways, including numerous statements by post-evangelicals who deeply resent what they were told and the damage that they say it did to them. Books lamenting the suffering of LGBTQ (ex-)evangelicals are everywhere; some of the most important include the memoirs by Justin Lee, Amber Cantorna, Jeff Chu, and Jennifer Knapp.[1] Now there are also books, such as Linda Kay Klein's *Pure*, about the damage, especially to women, caused by "purity culture."[2] And, of course, if one was both female and nonheterosexual, as is Amber Cantorna, the full force of both campaigns was available for deep, intersecting, painful internalization.

This chapter offers my diagnosis of where evangelicalism went wrong in relation to premarital sexual purity and rejection of gay and lesbian relationships (and persons). Both were forms of a purity ethic. For straight people, the only pure sex was in marriage; for gay people, there could be no pure sex at all, ever. I will propose a sexual ethic that sets enthusiastic mutual consent as a floor and covenant marriage as its main norm. I believe this approach is good for human beings, draws from the wisdom available in Christian tradition, and is realistic in relation to culture today.

THE BIBLE ON SEXUALITY

Evangelicals developed their belief that sex belongs only in heterosexual marriage mainly from reading Scripture, primarily New Testament texts attributed to the apostle Paul. Passages like this one from Colossians received a great deal of preaching:

> Put to death, therefore, whatever in you is earthly: fornication, impurity, passion, evil desire, and greed (which is idolatry). On account of these the wrath of God is coming on those who are disobedient. These are the ways you also once followed, when you were living that life. But now you must get rid of all such things. (Col. 3:5–8; cf. 1 Cor. 6:12–20; Gal. 5:19–20; Eph. 5:1–5; 1 Thess. 4:2–4)

Other passages positively affirm that sex belongs (only) in the marriage bed and should be honored there: "Let marriage be held in honor by all, and let the marriage bed be kept undefiled; for God will judge fornicators and adulterers" (Heb. 13:4).

Yet Paul also teaches that singleness is preferable to marriage, and that marriage is a concession to lust. Paul clearly offers this teaching in the context of his belief in the imminent return of Christ, but the teaching stuck even when the return did not happen:

> To the unmarried and the widows I say that it is well for them to remain unmarried as I am. But if they are not practicing self-control, they should marry. For it is better to marry than to be aflame with passion. (1 Cor. 7:8–9)

Paul's frequent vice lists illustrate the immoral pagan life out of which Gentile believers have been rescued by Jesus, contrasted always with the moral purity expected of Christian converts. Those lists often highlight sex-related vices, painting a hyperbolic picture of a Greco-Roman world awash in sexual excess. (Romans 1:18–32 is a good example of such a text, and it proved especially important in its vivid condemnation of same-sex activity.) This probably reflected what Paul understood Greco-Roman culture to be like. His stereotype of pagan sexual perversity had enough truth to it to be plausible, especially if one considers the behavior of upper-class men and those in the imperial court.[3] But reading these texts in a late-twentieth-century evangelical church easily intensified the shaming associated with sexual desire.

Beyond Paul, Jesus' teaching about adultery in the Sermon on the Mount reinforced a kind of sexual perfectionism, as it was understood to mean that a single sexual thought about another person was the moral equivalent of the very act of adultery.

> You have heard that it was said, "You shall not commit adultery." But I say to you that everyone who looks at a woman with lust has already committed adultery with her in his heart. (Matt. 5:27–28)

This text famously led evangelical presidential candidate Jimmy Carter to tell *Playboy* in 1976 that he had committed adultery in his heart many times.[4] In *Kingdom Ethics*, Glen Stassen and I counter that in this teaching Jesus is addressing not the stray spark of attraction but instead a pattern of lustful coveting. We also argue that Jesus is here placing responsibility for men's lust on men rather than on women, thus reversing a harmful paradigm that has contributed to women's subordination, shaming, and cloistering in many contexts.[5]

Taken together, the most widely read New Testament passages about sex did more than ban sex outside of marriage. They associated it with lust, adultery, paganism, and shamefulness, nowhere more so than in relation to homosexuality. As well, the fact that both Jesus and Paul apparently were celibate and could be fairly read to prefer celibacy (Matt. 19:10–12) also left a very deep impact. The Christian moral tradition developed an antisex thread that weaves through the whole of Christian history. It manifested in the association of sex with original sin, diatribes against women's seductiveness, the elevation of celibacy as the highest spiritual path, and the treatment of sex within marriage as for childbearing only, and as a utilitarian duty (especially for women)—which prevailed until the sexual revolution led to a culturally driven change in approach.

Close reading of the Hebrew Bible could have helped the church avoid these mistakes. The Old Testament never manifests an antisexuality posture. The texts depict a wide variety of sexual patterns. Polygamy, arranged marriages, and concubinage all show up in the Hebrew Bible—though the problems associated with these approaches are also realistically depicted, and they are not endorsed in the New Testament.

The staggeringly erotic Song of Solomon offers a remarkably positive vision about sex.[6] Both male and female sexual desire are clearly portrayed in this smoking-hot book, even if veiled (a bit) in poetic mist. How many times is sexual attraction, longing, and encounter celebrated in any Christian churches as in a text like this one from Song of Solomon 4:1–7?

> How beautiful you are, my love,
>   how very beautiful!

Your eyes are doves
behind your veil.
Your hair is like a flock of goats,
moving down the slopes of Gilead.
Your teeth are like a flock of shorn ewes
that have come up from the washing,
all of which bear twins,
and not one among them is bereaved.
Your lips are like a crimson thread,
and your mouth is lovely.
Your cheeks are like halves of a pomegranate
behind your veil.
Your neck is like the tower of David,
built in courses;
on it hang a thousand bucklers,
all of them shields of warriors.
Your two breasts are like two fawns,
twins of a gazelle,
that feed among the lilies.
Until the day breathes
and the shadows flee,
I will hasten to the mountain of myrrh
and the hill of frankincense.
You are altogether beautiful, my love;
there is no flaw in you.

By being cut off from the development of Jewish life and thought, most Christians never found out that such attitudes became embedded in the Jewish tradition. How many evangelicals know that one of the things Jews are allowed—and encouraged—to do on Shabbat is to make love with their spouses?[7] It is hard to imagine typical Christian Sabbath observance offering any parallel expectations. We have tended toward too much Paul and not enough Song of Solomon, too much "spirit" and not enough "body." It is an enduring problem in our tradition, eased only somewhat by greater recent acceptance of the role of sexual pleasure in marriage—after complete sexual restraint beforehand.

PURITY, GENDER, AND SEX

Something that went terribly wrong in many evangelical contexts was the turn to sexual purity as the main way to state the moral norm, and the gendering of responsibility for it.

As Linda Kay Klein's stunning book shows, in an effort by evangelical elders to prevent premarital sex, young women were taught that they were fully responsible for any arousal of male desire and also responsible for keeping wolfish young men at bay. The main strategy used to motivate women to accept these responsibilities was shame. This shaming has deeply traumatized many women, and it has certainly driven many out of the churches. It also utterly failed to accomplish its goals. As Klein argues:

> Researchers are finding that purity teachings do *not* meaningfully delay sex. . . . They *do* increase shame, especially among females. . . . This increased shame is leading to higher levels of sexual anxiety, lower levels of sexual pleasure, and the feeling among those experiencing shame that they are stuck feeling this way forever.[8]

In summary, then, studies show that purity culture and abstinence-only sex education *do not* raise the age of first sexual experience. They *do not* decrease the number of sexual partners. They *do*, however, increase the experience of sexual guilt and anxiety and decrease sexual efficacy and satisfaction, especially among women.[9]

Purity culture also had an odd effect on family relations. The purity movement was linked to evangelical patriarchalism. This regularly was expressed in a "father protects daughter's virginity" move, including Daddy-Daughter purity balls and faux wedding rings. I am all for fathers being very close to their daughters. But this approach was oddly incestuous, an Electra-complex theology that reinforced patriarchy, undercut the development of young women's moral agency, and yuckily superimposed Daddy into every tentative sexual exploration.

Overwhelmingly, evangelical theology and practice is governed by men. Men decided that sexual purity was the best name for the norm, and men decided that this overall approach was the best way to protect sexual purity. Evangelical patriarchalism deeply distorted and damaged the message communicated to both boys and girls about sex. If adult Christian women had been equally involved in crafting formation efforts about sex, it is hard to imagine that it all would have come out the way it did.

Recent years have witnessed the uncovering of horrific sexual abuse and sexual assault in some evangelical church contexts.[10] The places where "complementarity," purity, and patriarchy were the guiding norms have hosted massive abuses of power, and the reckoning is only just beginning. Linda Klein's book is crystal clear in linking clergy sexual abuse and other male sexual misconduct to purity culture—her work joins that of others in efforts to advance the Christian version of the #MeToo movement.[11] Egalitarian pastors and churches can commit sexual abuse and assault, for sure. But it should be taken as a truism that *any context of patriarchy, clergy dominance, and sexual perfectionism will prove an especially fertile breeding ground for male sexual misconduct.*

It is true that New Testament authors often use the language of purity and impurity when describing moral expectations of Christians (Rom. 1:24; 6:19; 2 Cor. 6:6; 12:21; Eph. 4:19; 5:3; Phil. 1:10; Col. 3:5; 1 Thess. 4:7; 1 Tim. 4:12; 5:2; 2 Tim. 2:22; Titus 1:15; Heb. 10:22; 1 Pet. 3:2; 1 John 3:3). Purity language was certainly an aspect of the Hebrew Bible and Jewish tradition, especially expressed in the Holiness Code in Leviticus and tied to efforts to keep Israel untainted by neighboring idolatry and immorality. Purity language is about what is morally right and wrong, but it deploys a language more visceral than customary ethics-talk; it lives in the neighborhood of dirt, disgust, pollution, and revulsion, not merely objective wrongdoing. As used in the evangelical subculture, it brought sexual shame to a whole new level.

If a person commits an objective sin against God's moral law, presumably the remedy is confession followed by God's forgiveness, and the slate is wiped clean. But the language of purity resonates with pollution, taint, corruption, and stain. This is powerfully charged language to use in relation to sex, and it has had consequences that go beyond feeling guilty to feeling ruined.

The relationship of sexuality to purity needs serious interrogation. If purity consists of having unmixed motives, when is human sexual activity truly pure?[12] Sexual desire is driven by many motivations, usually related to seeking personal pleasure and affection, hopefully also related to offering it. At the motivational level, sex is rarely if ever pure. And whether someone is married or not has little to do with that. There is plenty of mixed-motive marital sex.

If we make the natural bodily association with the word "purity," terms like fresh, clean, clear, untainted, unpolluted, and uncontaminated come to mind. But nothing about sex feels pure in that way. It is messy, wet, bodily. Some people never quite get used to the earthy, dirty messiness of sex. It is perhaps especially shocking when one is inexperienced with it.

To tell adolescents that their purity will be tainted forever by one sex act outside of marriage (or one kiss, or one sexual thought, or one masturbatory act—no, I am not making this up) connects with all that unspoken but very real embodied ambivalent experience around sexuality. Here is how Klein describes this disturbing dimension of purity culture, in her experience:

> Virgins are described as a shiny new car that everyone wants to buy, and all those who have had sex are described as used cars that nobody wants. . . . Then there is the unused tissue versus the "used" tissue full of snot, mucus, and phlegm, which is said to represent a girl or woman who has had sex; . . . [and] the untouched cookie or candy bar versus the one that has been chomped into; the unwrapped lollipop versus one that decreases in size and desirability after being licked for the first time . . .[13]

To then teach that once you say "I do" all that shame and impurity dissolves into mind-blowing pure marital sex simply did not work for everybody. One researcher quoted by Linda Klein says this:

> I've heard about numerous tragic wedding nights that often don't get any better. . . . Inability to be sexual is a big problem for both men and women coming out of the church. They've practiced turning themselves off so much that when they have a sexual occasion, they can't turn themselves back on again. Human beings don't have a switch.[14]

Much human wreckage has been left behind by purity culture. Indeed, one of the evangelical Christians most associated with it, Joshua Harris, in 2019 renounced his *I Kissed Dating Goodbye* work (and his Christian faith) and asked for forgiveness for the harm done.[15] Some of his former readers do not appear ready to grant it; their wounds are too deep.

AT THE INTERSECTION OF NATURE AND CULTURE

Human behavior in relation to sex is always tied to both nature and culture. The nature of human sexual development is such that puberty not only gradually transforms children's bodies into adult bodies but also releases hormones triggering heightened sexual desire. This desire forcefully impels people toward sexual encounters, many of which produce pregnancies, some of which produce babies, which is how the species moves forward.

Cultures have always felt it necessary to regulate these powerful natural drives, usually also connected to the natural emotional desire for love. The main way cultures regulate sex is by creating approved kinship, courtship, marriage, and family structures and practices. Each culture must figure out a way to solve a certain kind of riddle—how do we regulate sexual behavior so that children are indeed produced, but are produced in a context in which they will be adequately cared for? Cultures need (heterosexual) sex for baby-making, but they need sexual restraint for children's well-being.

Obviously, one way to solve this riddle is through elevating marriage as a socially recognized commitment that for the couple creates unique duties and privileges in relation to each other, their children, and the community. A marriage-based culture holds marriage in respect; encourages responsible, sexually interested adults in the direction of marriage; and reinforces the value of permanence in marriage. Religious traditions, of course, add to this picture their distinctive accounts of the purposes and value of marriage and proper conduct within marriage, and offer their spiritual resources to enable couples to achieve success in marriage.

I submit that the United States used to have a marriage-based culture like this, but today it is in tatters, for a variety of reasons.

One crucial problem has arisen at the intersection of nature and culture. Puberty is happening earlier, and marriage, if undertaken at all, is happening later.

Puberty starts a kind of ticking clock. It unlocks the sexuality that is latent in every human body and begins the hormone flow impelling people into each other's arms.

The power of sexual desire is not to be trifled with. From a cultural systems perspective, if this sexual power is going to be tied to marriage, then marriage had best not be delayed too long past puberty. That gap—between puberty and culturally approved sex in marriage—is a perilous one. Moral restraints imposed by parents and even by young people themselves are not impervious to the power of sexual and romantic drives. The longer the gap between puberty and marriage in a marriage-based sexual system, the more problems will be created for people as they succumb and have sex—which can produce heartbreak and pregnancies and abortions and babies.

There is an economic dimension here as well. Many millennials today are putting off the whole marriage-family-kids project because they simply cannot afford it. In their defense, then, there is an argument to be made that delaying those things is in fact a responsible choice due to their inability to reliably finance a family. And yet the hormones keep flowing.

When I was a young evangelical, puberty happened around 13 and the average age of first marriage around 24.[16] I married at 22. Today puberty onset has moved to 10 to 12, and the average age of first marriage is now 30 for men and 28 for women.[17] That eighteen- to twenty-year gap is far too long. Religious and cultural constraints cannot be expected to prevail over nature for twenty years, not even for devout Christians. And the rate of marriage itself is declining, so that there is certainly no expectation on the part of today's young people that a wedding ring is inevitable at the end of their long chaste journeys.[18]

There is a flip side to this as well, and it has to do with those good evangelical kids who get married at a young age simply to be able to have sex without feeling guilty; or who marry the first person they have sex with *because* they feel guilty; or who are not straight but marry a person of the opposite sex because they think that is the only option they have. I've known a lot of folks who have gotten married in college, for instance, when in terms of maturity they had no business making that kind of decision. This means that the subcultural evangelical ethic also ends up pressing people into marriage when they should in fact probably wait. Evangelical culture sometimes results, in other words, in children getting married before they have even grown up.

All of this was already beginning to happen during the True Love Waits heyday. But evangelicals, who always quote Scripture and rarely quote sociologists or anthropologists, did not respond with any kind of realism. Instead they doubled down on purity and shame. No wonder they failed. No wonder that failure is one of the major forces impelling people out of evangelicalism, or Christianity.

We need a sexual ethic that makes sense amid today's cultural circumstances but that still pays attention to the real problems that the Christian sex-in-marriage-alone ethic was trying to solve.

EVANGELICALS AND LGBTQ PEOPLE: WHAT WENT WRONG

It is easy for today's evangelicals conveniently to forget that our coreligionists made quite the cultural splash by being on the leading edge of antigay advocacy from the very beginning of the gay-rights movement in the late 1960s.

Fundamentalists sometimes argued for the death penalty for gay sex, based on Leviticus 20:13. I vividly remember being the next guest on a Christian radio station and hearing someone make that case on the air.[19] Every so often even today some fundamentalist preacher is found on YouTube doing the same thing.[20] And that's here in the United States—it is commonplace in parts of the global south, not just from preachers but also in legislative proposals. Some of that fierce antigay animus has arguably come from US fundamentalist and evangelical missionary work.[21]

Evangelical Christian activists like Anita Bryant in Florida responded to the gay-rights movement with every kind of demagoguery and scare tactic.[22] Gays were spoken of as pedophiles coming to seduce and destroy children. This rhetoric was not confined to the 1970s or to Anita Bryant. The AIDS crisis that began in the 1980s evoked similarly hateful rhetoric.[23] The gay community noticed and certainly knew who their enemies were. I have met gay people all over America for whom Christians and "the church" were literally their most dangerous enemies. I have also known gay people who stood vigil over their dead friends when those friends' Christian families would not even deign to bury them.

Sometime in the 1990s, the cultural tide began shifting. Moving just a bit with the times, some evangelicals adopted a kinder, gentler rhetoric of "love the sinner, hate the sin." But, in the end, this was not that much kinder or gentler—hating the sin involved plenty of disgust-producing rhetoric that inevitably, and sometimes literally, bled into gay and lesbian people's lives. The role of disgust in dehumanizing people must never be underestimated.

As the Christian Right lost battle after battle in the "family values" culture wars (over divorce, premarital sex, women working outside the home, the loss of the patriarchal family), stopping the acceptance of LGBTQ people and their relationships became the Last Stand. The evangelical establishment threw pretty much everything it had into preventing legalization of gay marriage. That failed in 2015 with the US Supreme Court decision in *Obergefell v. Hodges*.[24] But the resistance mainly retreated, to evangelical families, churches, and schools, and it continues to this day.

What evangelical leaders never seemed to realize was that their every anti-LGBTQ sermon, book, post, video, and doctrinal statement was also heard by a closeted population of suffering LGBTQ persons in their own families, churches, and schools. They did not know this because these people were closeted—or interiorly so conflicted as to not even know yet that they were closeted. Terrorized, the fundamentalist/evangelical LGBTQ population was invisible to those who were making the authoritative declarations.

That is, until they became visible, in immensely brave coming-out-only-to-be-kicked-out family meetings; in bans from church, choir, leadership, and school; in suicide attempts and completions; and finally in every kind of survivor storytelling.[25]

These moments forced a reckoning. Would evangelicals be able to listen to *their own loved ones*—their children, siblings, parents, colleagues, teachers, and students? Would their reading of the sources of Christian morality, especially the Bible, be at all penetrable by the evidence presented by their own suffering family members and friends?

My own effort to work through that challenge is probably known to most who are reading this book. It is found in some speeches of mine on YouTube, and in my 2014 book *Changing Our Mind*.[26]

I will not rehearse the arguments here. We can all pause while you go read that book, then get back together and continue our chapter.

Ready? Good.

I want to offer here more of a meta-reflection. I ask in this chapter what went wrong with evangelical sexual ethics. I want to think here about what specifically went wrong in relation to LGBTQ people.

What went wrong with evangelical sexual ethics in relation to LGBTQ people is not that different from what went wrong in relation to purity culture—*an inability to deal with reality because the Bible did not appear to permit it*.

In this case, the unassimilable reality is that a small but persistent percentage of the human population feels no attraction to members of the opposite sex. They are drawn to members of the same sex. I know that sexual orientation is more complicated than this in many instances, but this is the baseline case that must first be addressed.

Evangelicals were unable to face this fact. They tried an immense number of evasions of reality: Same-sex attraction was a delusion. It was temporary. It was demon possession. It was willful. It was changeable. The delusion could be cured, the temporary feeling could be made to pass, the demons could be exorcised, the will could be changed. Gay people could be "repaired."[27]

And if the patient did not respond to the cures so generously made available, the moral judgment heaped upon them in their personhood deepened—both *within* LGBTQ Christian persons, in their own stricken consciences, and from the moral authorities in their worlds, in their harsh rejection.

The sheer facticity of homosexuality was not just reported by millions of people. By the 1970s it was also backed by every major professional association of psychologists and sexologists. All described homosexuality as a routinely occurring variation reported in all times and cultures.[28] All said that by far the primary harm associated with it is in the stigma (and persecution) inflicted upon this population. What needed to change was not gay and lesbian people, but the cultural worldviews that stigmatized and harmed them.[29]

But this would require a historic shift in Christian belief. It would require new ways of interpreting the Bible, ways that reinterpreted the handful of condemnatory passages and elevated the many passages potentially leading to better treatment and full inclusion. It would require abandoning traditional Christian condemnations, grouping these with other examples of previously mistaken Christian condemnations that were later abandoned. It would require being willing to allow experience and other sources to affect the interpretation of Scripture and tradition. It would require seeing this as the latest example of a need to adjust faith to the legitimate discoveries of science.

It was a heavy lift. It *is* a heavy lift.

Fundamentalism is not able to make this move. And because, as noted earlier, evangelicalism tends to be just as biblicist in its method as fundamentalism, evangelicalism also has not been able to make the changes necessary to accept sexual minorities. Indeed, the LGBTQ issue has helped clarify that there is no real difference in theological method between fundamentalism and evangelicalism.

When faced with a choice between human experience, reason, science, and suffering, and traditional readings of scriptural texts, it chose the latter. In doing so it continued to ask of its gay and lesbian people that they either alter their sexual orientation or permanently choose celibacy, whether they had any readiness or call for that life or not. It could not see the human beings in front of them as they were, in all their dignity and suffering. It saw categories of persons needing to be repaired or repressed.

The harm caused by this choice of tradition over reality, of dogma over persons, is one of the main reasons for a substantial exodus out of evangelicalism.

The exiles know that a religion that systemically harms vulnerable groups of people is not a good thing in the world. It is the opposite of Christian humanism; it is inhumanity in the name of Christ.

> And [Jesus] said, "Woe also to you lawyers! For you load people with burdens hard to bear, and you yourselves do not lift a finger to ease them." (Luke 11:46)

TOWARD POST-EVANGELICAL SEXUAL ETHICS

Where do we go from here? I suggest that a renewed vision of the concept of covenantal marriage, applied to all followers of Jesus, is the best way forward. I have argued this elsewhere at greater length.[30] But meanwhile, as we head into the breach we find in today's culture, we also need to help post-evangelicals strengthen their commitment to a baseline of mutual enthusiastic consent and noncoercive, nonexploitative sex, as well as other dimensions of sexual responsibility.

Here's my proposal.

We need to accept that human sexuality is a very powerful drive for most people, combining in one awesome package desires for pleasure, connection, touch, love, and sometimes procreation. Once the puberty clock starts ticking, for the great majority of people, sexuality is an immensely powerful force—and it is only a matter of time, maturity, and opportunity before it is expressed bodily.

We need to accept that for something like 3 to 5 percent of the population, their given version of sexuality is lesbian, gay, or bisexual. It is past time to drop all stigma associated with this natural variation in the human family, which our faith has done so much to worsen. I personally affirm that full acceptance of LGBTQ people is a nonnegotiable dimension of post-evangelical Christianity, and most others in this terrain seem to feel the same way.

Transgender persons vary from the norm in relation to gender identity, not sexual orientation. They also suffer and are stigmatized for varying from the norm. They also must be treated with full dignity, equality, and justice.

Properly expressed, sexuality is very good, in the pleasures it brings and in the consequences it creates. It gives joy, love, and life. It is one of the things that makes life worth living. Post-evangelicals should be positive about the good gift of sex.

But we must also acknowledge that irresponsible, exploitative, and sadistic sexuality is extremely dangerous. It can deeply harm others and self.

We should recognize that for good reasons *cultures have always stepped in to provide moral regulation of sex*. Most cultures have developed an approach that is marriage-centered. In Western Christian cultures, this marital norm finally evolved to include an expectation of personal freedom to select a mate based primarily on romantic love and to enter into a permanent dyadic, sexually exclusive relationship, and for marriage to be the context in which children, vulnerable and dependent, are born and raised to adulthood.

Modern Western marriage, sometimes dated to the nineteenth century, was an ultimately unstable combination of older Christian religious commitments and economic considerations, together with newer concerns about mutual choice, shared values, and the prospect of enduring marital love, all of it undercut by the lack of an egalitarian vision between the sexes, and all of it excluding gay and lesbian people.[31]

Since the 1960s, this religious-romantic mating system has largely unraveled. The norm against sex outside of marriage collapsed first, in tandem with the availability of effective birth control. Divorce rates exploded in the 1960s and 1970s, then they settled down a bit, but partly because marriage rates dropped. Courtship and what used to be called "dating" became confused and then incoherent. Economic factors began extending adolescence and young adulthood, delaying marriage, and making many people unmarriageable in terms of current expectations.

And so, we find ourselves in a vast social experiment about sex in a postmarital, or half-postmarital, society.

Anyone who works on a college campus knows that the prevailing norm is that bodies and sex are good, people having sex should exercise responsibility and use birth control, and all parties must be certain that everyone is sober and consenting.

Is this a sexual ethic? Well, it is a bare minimum. Still, that bare minimum needs to be endorsed.

Because of the human connection and potential vulnerability of sex, sex is always a matter of moral significance.

Because moral responsibilities are always heightened in proportion to the number and vulnerability of people affected, the possibility of pregnancy is always a relevant consideration in sexual ethics. Pregnancy and the choices that follow are among the most significant moral events in most people's lives.

Because exploitative, nonconsensual, and criminal sexual acts against others are among the gravest harms one person can do to another, protecting the baseline of mutual enthusiastic consent and noncoercive, nonexploitative sex is critically important.

Besotted with purity and perfectionism, our evangelical tradition has rarely endorsed these norms. I have never personally come across an American evangelical school or church in which young people are taught about the need for enthusiastic mutual consent and fulfillment—and they are certainly not taught about birth control.

The result, I fear, besides lots of unwanted pregnancies, is a hidden sexual assault epidemic within Christian spaces—with assault not being called assault, and women being blamed for provoking whatever we are not calling assault.[32] The combination of deeply ingrained patriarchy—after all, the teaching is that God wants men to *take charge* and women to *submit*—and a lack of any sexual-ethical norm other than marriage makes for a dangerous sexual Wild West for the evangelical millions attempting to enter this normless space.

Post-evangelical kids who came up with abstinence-only or fear-based sex education need at least to be taught that sex that is coerced or not enthusiastically consented to is not OK. This will require teaching both men and women that the only good sex is mutual and egalitarian.

As for randomly arranged hookups, it is still true that *persons* have sex. Persons are implicated in the connections that are made, or half made, or never attempted. Participating in kinds of sex that require disconnecting body and soul is a form of self-inflicted spiritual violence. Popular magazines have been full of storytelling related to this latest form of body/soul dualism.[33] It isn't good for people. And it may help account for why so many people are simply not having any kind of sex at all—nearly 25 percent of adults, in one recent study.[34]

Both in terms of consent standards, and in terms of hookup culture, entrenched male power continues to prevail. We all know the stories—men assaulting women, men getting women drunk in order to have sex with them, women enduring unsatisfying hookup sex because that is all that is available. These are commonplace accounts in our era. What they have in common is male selfishness through the abuse, use, and abandonment of women. Is this progress over the old-school marital ethic? I don't think so.

In this context, I would like to renew my long-standing and perhaps unfashionable proposal that a particular vision of covenantal marriage remains the best aspirational sexual ethics norm.

One major theme of historic Christian ethics is covenant. As we have seen, covenant is a major theological and moral theme in Scripture. Marriage is one of the contexts in which the church has often emphasized a covenantal approach. Most wedding services to this day retain a covenantal structure, as a couple articulate vows to behave in a certain fashion toward their new spouse, for life, as God is their witness.

Covenants are *possible* because human beings have the potential to bind our actions in advance based on our deepest commitments and goals, and then to keep the promises we make. Covenants are *necessary* because human beings easily drift away from our deepest commitments or lose heart in times of frustration.

The covenant promises traditionally exchanged in a Christian wedding include sexual fidelity in a lifetime covenant that the spouses promise is to endure despite varying circumstances (in sickness and in health, for richer, for poorer . . .). They also include deeply moving language about loving, honoring, and cherishing one another.

It is still my view that post-evangelical sexual ethics should elevate marriage as the central institution for structuring adult sexual relationships, that marriage should be understood as a covenant, and that the promises made on the wedding day are binding. By binding, I mean that they bind our actions regardless of our fleeting preferences or feelings. Love, passion, desire, and choice bring us into adult sexual and romantic relationships. But especially over today's long life spans, marriages tend to tumble into ruin, one after the other, due to unresolved conflicts, offenses against one another, drifting apart, or countless other problems. Covenantal marriage involves both parties imposing a moral structure on their behavior and their relationship that is aimed at ensuring its permanence. Covenant says we are just not free to leave when we feel like it.

The end of one marriage after another may not seem like the worst thing in the world, but it has real costs: relationships constantly shadowed by uncertainty, pain, drama, and suffering for the adults when marriages break down, financial distress (if not crisis) amid marital breakup, the need for government involvement in family matters, and most importantly, the potential for tremendous suffering and dislocation for children.[35] It remains my view that while love and passion draw us into adult erotic relationships, covenant commitments stabilize them, and everyone who depends on us depends on that stability.

This is not to say that the covenants that adults make in marriage will not sometimes be breached or come to an end. It is to say that a society—and a church—in which marriages routinely end is not good for anyone, especially the most vulnerable. We need a renewal of the norm, and practice, of permanence in marriage. This is not a conservative or a liberal cause. It is about human well-being. It also happens to be what Jesus taught (Matt. 19:3–9// Mark 10:2–9), and it seems clear that he did so to protect those most vulnerable when marriages are abandoned.

I believe that in today's cultural context, the paradigm of covenant is by far the best way to structure adult sexual relationships for those who choose to enter into them but are not in a position to marry. The idea would be to structure long-term romantic-sexual relationships in a covenantal fashion even if legal marriage is unreachable or unwise. The couple would bind their behavior with truthful shared promises as to the nature, depth, and extent of the commitment that their sexual relationship signals. Then they would keep their promises. If their commitment changed or ended, they would be honest about it. I offer this as a concession to reality; it is better than a sexual Wild West. Still, in my view, the religious, moral, cultural, and legal meaning of covenantal marriage makes it the norm.

The general direction of progressive sexual ethics in the last generation has been to deemphasize marriage and heighten a focus on pleasure, mutuality, equality, and interpersonal connection. Why can we not seek both? Marriage covenants, with mutuality, equality, pleasure, and fully shared commitment, are the better path. We very much need a renewal of marriage as a social institution. Post-evangelicals could make a real contribution to our culture, and to human well-being, by making a realistic, non–shame-based case for such a renewal.

A few final thoughts:

Post-evangelical efforts to address sexuality sometimes seem to succumb to an overreaction to puritan perfectionism. Pastor-writer and blogger Nadia Bolz-Weber, in her kindhearted recent book on sex, summarizes her ethical stand in this way:

> Whatever sexual flourishing looks like for you, that's what I would love to see happen in your life. Let us seek to be stewards of our bodies, to live in the joy of our createdness, honest about our shortcomings. . . . Let us find beauty and pleasure in our individual human bodies, trusting each other to use our gifts of sexuality according to . . . our strength and capacity. Let us treat ourselves and others, no matter what our talents, as if we are all holy.[36]

Bolz-Weber specifies her ethical norm a bit further in this statement:

> Unless your sexual desires are for minors or animals, or your sexual choices are hurting you or those you love, those desires are not something that you need to "struggle with." They are something to listen to, make decisions about, explore, perhaps have caution about. But struggle with? . . . No.[37]

I deeply admire the pastoral sensitivity here, but I do believe that a post-evangelical vision in the area of sexuality needs to go beyond sexual flourishing and do-no-harm ethics.

In short, we need covenant, not just flourishing.

This is one reason to throw the brakes on the current embrace of polyamory. I think Brandan Robertson is a fantastic advocate for LGBTQ inclusion.[38] But I noted in his recent book an unequivocal endorsement of polyamory:

> At the heart of a Christian relational ethic should be the value of commitment and covenant, and many non-monogamous relationships are centered on a deep and enduring commitment of more than three people to walk in relationship throughout life. . . . I can see no reason to deem such relationships to be unethical or sinful.[39]

Robertson seems to suggest that polyamory should be viewed as something like a sexual orientation or identity, that polyamorists are yet another small minority that is differently "relationally wired."[40] With the weary wisdom of my advanced years, I would counter that embracing polyamory on this basis will weaken the case for LGBTQ equality. I would also suggest that polyamory is not likely to be a realistic option for sustainable, long-term covenant relationships. If children are involved or even possible, polyamory risks destabilizing their always-vulnerable lives.

We do need to temper evangelical perfectionism with a loving realism about human nature and today's cultural realities. But we must not entirely lose contact with the wisdom of Scripture, history, and tradition.

Sexual-ethical perfectionism errs on the one side. Sexual libertinism errs on the other. Evangelicalism erred on the one side to avoid erring on the other. I hope that the covenant realism proposed here manages to find a middle way.

TAKEAWAYS

- The negative fallout of evangelicalism's sexual ethics is seen especially in critiques related to purity culture and LGBTQ exclusion.
- The most widely read New Testament passages about sex associated illicit sex with lust, adultery, paganism, and shamefulness. An antisex thread was woven into Christian tradition.
- Close reading of the Hebrew Bible could have helped the church. The Song of Solomon offers a joyful celebration of sex.
- Something that went wrong in many evangelical contexts was the turn to sexual purity as the main way to state the ethical norm, and the gendering of responsibility for it.
- Any context of patriarchy, clergy dominance, and sexual perfectionism will prove an especially fertile breeding ground for sexual misconduct.
- What went wrong with evangelical sexual ethics in relation to LGBTQ people was an inability to deal with reality because the Bible did not appear to permit it.
- A recovery of the concept of covenant and a renewal of marriage, applied to all followers of Jesus, is the best way forward.
- We also need to help (post-)evangelicals strengthen their commitment to a baseline of mutual enthusiastic consent and noncoercive, nonexploitative sex.

8

Politics

Starting Over after White Evangelicalism's Embrace of Trumpism

THE DIFFICULTY AND COMPLEXITY OF CHRISTIAN POLITICAL ETHICS

The question of how Christians and the church should relate to the worldly political arena has perplexed Christian thinkers from the very beginning of Christianity. The issues are extremely complex and have tested the most gifted leaders and most brilliant minds in our history.[1]

The complexity begins with Scripture. Most of the canon centers around the varying stages of a Jewish theocracy, including those later stages when it was shattered by imperial invasion, cataclysmic war, and bitter exile. The New Testament was written in the context of the Roman Empire—first as it manifested in the Palestine of Jesus' time and then in the diaspora church environment of Paul and most of the other writing apostles.

If Protestants read the Catholic or Orthodox Bible, we would also encounter Maccabees, historical books that describe intense religious pressure to compromise Judaism placed upon occupied Jews in their homeland, fierce resistance unto death, and finally revolution and a new Jewish regime. Maccabees could then link with the book of Revelation to provide resources for periods of persecution and even, with Maccabees, an ethic of violent revolution.

None of these materials were written in the context of anything like modern democracy. Everything that one must say about how the Bible should be interpreted in historical context applies to forming Christian political ethics. The lack of a democratic context in the writing of Scripture—other than, perhaps, what one can glimpse in the inner dynamics of early church life, and the principles one can draw from biblical theology—has deeply affected Christian public ethics. Much of that impact has been antidemocratic, and this tendency surfaces routinely in US evangelicalism.[2] This is bad news if one believes, as I do, that democracy is the best form of government that good-yet-fallen humans have ever devised, and that Christians need to join other Americans in working for the best possible version of US constitutional democracy.[3]

Nowhere are the limits of evangelical biblicism clearer than in the political arena. There is no way that the Bible can be said to produce a single, coherent political vision or ethic. It has proven to be usable for endless alternative politics: theocratic, royalist, authoritarian, fascist, ethno-nationalist, slavocratic, colonialist, Christian democrat, revolutionary, reformist, liberal, libertarian, socialist, communist, anarchist, quietist, millenarian, and even today's social-conservative white evangelical Republicanism.

Even to understand these options and how Christians have gotten there requires access to the entire history and tradition of the church, including both our lived history and teaching tradition. Knowing this history and accessing this teaching tradition certainly would not resolve all questions of political ethics. But it could help set some boundaries and prevent some mistakes. Unfortunately, popular American evangelicalism has not proved especially interested in this history, and today it is blowing past those boundaries and making those mistakes.

I have already noted that discomfort over the direction of (mainly white) evangelical politics is one of the major factors driving people out of evangelicalism today.[4] This is not a new phenomenon. I have been writing about dissenters leaving white evangelicalism over its lockstep political conservativism since the 1990s. But like everything else since the presidency of Donald Trump began, this long-standing concern has intensified dramatically in our time. I do not know how long Americans shall find themselves under the shadow of this individual, and I can hardly bear to spill more ink on Donald Trump. But the issues that we are facing in this period require the best reflection that we can offer, with a plan for a course correction. That is my hope for this chapter—to describe how we got here and to point toward a post–white-evangelical democratic politics.

THE POLITICAL TRAJECTORY OF WHITE US EVANGELICALS

As far back as the 1970s, dissident evangelical historian Donald Dayton was expressing concern that white evangelical politics was so deeply conservative. That was not just because he dissented from that politics, but because he knew that evangelicals had sometimes expressed a very different political vision. He was a scholar of reformist nineteenth-century evangelicals, people like evangelist Charles Finney, who were abolitionist, antiracist, suffragist, deeply concerned for workers and the poor; people who were, overall, profoundly transformationist in this-worldly terms.[5] No one could therefore plausibly claim that being evangelical just intrinsically meant being politically conservative. Dayton wanted to help us rediscover *that* (in his view, much better, much more faithful-to-Jesus) evangelical political heritage. Progressive evangelicals such as Ron Sider explicitly drew on that heritage when grounding their own political engagement.

Dayton recalled that when he was a Christian college student in the 1960s the reflexive social and political conservatism of school leadership and most of his fellow students was quite striking.[6] At a time when the campuses of the nation were abuzz with social-change ferment, resistance to the draft, opposition to the Vietnam War, concern for the environment, and support for feminism and the civil rights movement, white evangelicals were still focusing on personal moral vices and resisting all progressive social movements. Jim Wallis noticed the same thing in his Detroit-area evangelical church and at Trinity Evangelical Divinity School, and it was one of the factors that pushed him toward the ministry with Sojourners that he has been pursuing for fifty years.[7]

But the tendency did not begin in the 1960s. We need to go back one further generation. In his recent dissertation, Union Seminary doctoral graduate Isaac Sharp documents that the 1940s neo-evangelical movement was already producing the kind of socially conservative politics that we have now come to expect of white evangelicals.[8] Two other dissertations by my graduates—Justin Phillips and Jacob Cook—also trace the same pattern, though Phillips's goal is to examine key exceptions in the South.[9] Cook unveils the reactionary politics of neo-evangelical founder Harold John Ockenga throughout his career, with plenty of head-spinning quotes from the turbulent 1960s.[10]

Sharp shows that the main responses of white evangelical leaders to the civil rights movement ranged along a spectrum running between full-blown segregationism, strident calls for the police or military to protect "law and order," and requests that civil rights leaders slow down and let individual hearts change at their own pace.[11] These postures deeply offended most black Christians. Some black Christians who had identified as evangelicals in the neo-evangelical stream that we have featured here moved into passionate dissent or abandoned that identity.[12] After this period, evangelicalism became much more clearly a "white" term, connoting or denoting the religion and politics of conservative white US Protestants only, even though the theology of many black, Latino/a, and Asian American Christians was just as conservative. The deep alienation of many nonwhite Christians from white evangelicalism will be considered further in chapter 9.

Another interesting feature with direct links to our own moment has been white evangelicalism's attraction to power—and the relative ease with which evangelicals have proved seducible by politicians if given direct access to them.

One of the very purposes of the National Association of Evangelicals was to challenge the liberal mainline leaders in their role as the establishment voice of Protestantism. They wanted to show that the country was full of good Bible-believing Christians who were not a bunch of religious *and* political liberals. And soon enough, young evangelist Billy Graham was in meetings with President Eisenhower, which was cool until he was heard on tape sharing racist jokes with President Richard Nixon, which was not so cool. Few today would argue that Billy Graham's engagement with American presidents was his best work, and yet it was certainly thrilling to many of his followers at the time.[13] Today, easy evangelical access to (Republican) presidents continues to thrill evangelical leaders and their constituents.

The more we dig, the further back we need to go. Early-twentieth-century US fundamentalism exhibited a strong current of antiliberal politics, and not just the reactionary separatism that became their hunkered-down position after 1925. Recall that one of the triggers for fundamentalist reaction was the liberal politics of the social gospel movement, which was opposed by fundamentalists not just because of worries about its theological orthodoxy but also because of its Christian democratic socialist politics. As Matthew Avery Sutton shows, fundamentalists opposed the labor movement and the Progressive movement during the early part of the twentieth century, and went on to oppose the New Deal, Social Security, the United Nations, the welfare state, Medicare, Medicaid, and pretty much all other progressive reforms. They were also gung-ho Cold War anticommunists, and they deeply identified America with Christianity.[14]

In a fantastic new book, Paul McGlasson joins Sutton in highlighting the pivotal role played by dispensationalism, with its effort to extract from scriptural texts exact scenarios of a coming end of days.[15] Though unfortunately McGlasson seems to identify evangelicalism with dispensationalism, his account is helpful in reminding us how steadily each generation of dispensationalists has managed to read the signs of the times in the same way. He calls it "a kind of futurism attached most directly to a conservative political and cultural vision of good and evil."[16] This does indeed resonate with those of us who actually read both Hal Lindsey in the 1970s and Tim LaHaye a generation later.[17] Who can forget that the antichrist for LaHaye is the UN secretary-general in his novels, Nicolae Carpathia? Priceless.

But our digging needs to go still further, back to the mid-nineteenth century. This takes us into the pre–Civil War period and the question of what happened to all that great evangelical religion that supposedly suffused the land after it was swept by revivalist conversions. What happened, of course, was that the transforming power of Jesus Christ met the entrenched power of American racism, and for the most part racism won (see chap. 9).

We must dig further still. Joel Goza's new book, *America's Unholy Ghosts*, closely studies the writings of Thomas Hobbes, John Locke, and Adam Smith.[18]

> Goza argues that Hobbes (1588–1679) "provided a modern imagination formed by the slave master's myth." Locke (1632–1704) "provided a tangible way for government and religion to partner in institutionalizing that imagination in democratic and religiously 'tolerant' societies." Smith (1723–1790) "articulated a morality of indifference to the gross inequalities our institutions fostered, ingraining the slave master's myth into society's soul." [33]
>
> Together, Goza claims, this unholy trinity laid the foundations for Americans to believe that government is about protecting property rights rather than advancing the common good, that economics is a morality-free zone, that race-based inequity is fully acceptable because of the worthlessness of nonwhite lives, and that justice is about retribution for crime rather than a prophetic vision of dignity, equality, fairness, or basic fellow humanity. [33]
>
> Goza also argues that these philosophers, in the often overlooked religious parts of their writings, helped distort American Christianity. They taught Christians to believe that intimacy with God does not require intimacy with broken and abused people, that true religion is about "soul salvation," and that indifference to injustice is irrelevant to a personal relationship with God. [34]
>
> I am not convinced that these philosophers are the primary source of these distortions of Christianity. But they may well have contributed to them.

What Goza is saying is that white American politics, economics, and religion are all poisoned *at their root* (for more, see chap. 9).

THE BIRTH OF THE 1970S CHRISTIAN RIGHT

Did you notice that I have not even mentioned the birth of the Christian Right in the late 1970s? That's intentional, because especially after the review just offered, it is a grave mistake to suggest that the problems we see today began then. I myself have made that mistake in more superficial past analysis.

We do need to engage the modern Christian Right, so here goes.

One way to begin the story is through its dissenters, as Sharp does. Scholars of the modern evangelical left have noted that it was born in the context of the 1960s. This was when what might be called the peace-and-justice evangelical left took the rebels' side in the street battles of that era. Some supported the Democrat George McGovern for president in 1972, including Ron Sider, who led Evangelicals for McGovern. Some of these evangelicals were hugely media savvy and attracted considerable attention.[19]

But evangelical-left partisan political activity was utterly dwarfed two elections later when a conservative coalition involving figures such as Jerry Falwell became engaged in Christian Right politics, which included strong and public endorsements of Republican candidate Ronald Reagan over the born-again Democratic President Jimmy Carter.[20] This inaugurated a now forty-year entanglement of white evangelical leaders and their people with the modern Republican Party, an entanglement that has resulted in the GOP–white evangelical identity fusion that we see today.

It is at least arguable that in the beginning, this was a marriage of convenience. Evangelicals would support the GOP in its hawkish foreign policy and libertarian economics. The GOP would protect segregationist evangelicals from government civil-rights legislation, especially in their schools and churches,[21] and would support evangelicals in their "family values" agenda, such as opposition to abortion, feminism, and homosexuality. The fact that militaristic foreign policy involving weapons of mass destruction, as well as libertarian laissez-faire capitalism, are not easily defended through close study of Jesus' teaching was left to the side.[22]

Falwell, televangelist Pat Robertson, and the like spoke often of a return to God and a Christian revival in America. They were not interested in Republican victory for its own sake, at least not at first. They supported Reagan and eventually Republicans in general because these politicians promised certain policies that the Christian Right pastors believed important for the national return to God and Christian morality that they sought. At least, that is my generous reading of what stood at the core of their concern.[23] These Republicans also promised, and delivered, direct access to their offices.

This was the period when the America we now know, a country split inexorably along "red" and "blue" lines, started to become visible. White evangelicals and fundamentalists were deep "red," disproportionately unsympathetic to every "blue" social reform and social protest movement of this period. Black Christians leaned blue politically, as did most Jews, the liberal part of the white Catholic and mainline Protestant populations, and a dissenting minority of white evangelicals, which used to include me.

CURRENT DEVELOPMENTS

As the Democratic Party has become more secular and less sympathetic to evangelical concerns, and as court rulings increasingly have gone against their convictions, the evangelical embrace of the GOP has deepened. It is not just evangelicals—other traditionalist religious groups making the same move include the conservative part of US Catholicism, Mormons, conservative Jews, many Muslims, and others. The more Democrats become known as the aggressively secular party, the pro-abortion (not just pro-choice) party, and the pro-LGBTQ party, the less appealing they are to conservative believers of all types.

Religious liberty for conservative religious folks has moved to the center of recent discussions. Liberals often just dismiss these concerns, but it is not as simple as that. Evangelicals fear that aggressive liberals and secularists want to stamp out their institutions through government power—such as, for example, denying 501(c)(3) tax-exempt status or access to federal dollars for schools that hold onto traditional bans on LGBTQ faculty or same-sex relationships. When this position was explicitly articulated by Democratic presidential candidate Beto O'Rourke in 2019, evangelical anxiety soared. It wasn't just conservative evangelicals. Longtime evangelical progressives like Ron Sider also protested.[24]

These fears have only deepened the tendency of evangelicals to look to GOP administrations to secure their interests. Donald Trump was not the only Republican candidate and president to promise to protect evangelical institutions, but he certainly delivered on that promise, intensifying the relationship between him, his party, and evangelicals.

Today, to be (white) evangelical just equates to being Republican, and the Republican coalition increasingly depends on a massive white evangelical base. The symbiosis is complete and fully mutual. Eighty-one percent of white evangelicals voted for Trump in 2016.[25]

Especially with some of the most visible pro-Trump evangelical leaders, garden-variety political preference transformed into full-blown religious celebration: Donald Trump as fulfillment of biblical prophecy (Trump #POTUS45 as King Cyrus #Isaiah45); as avatar for "godly moral principles"; as one who helps America "uphold truth [and] stand for the way of our God."[26] It was quite an endorsement for the thrice-married reality-TV host, serial liar, serial abuser of women, serial conspiracy theorist, serial race-bomb-thrower whom we elected president. Because that celebration was so over the top, it became one of the reasons many dissenting evangelicals abandoned the label and the community.

From within their worldview, there *are* plausible reasons why white evangelicals supported Donald Trump. Most of these reasons would apply to most any GOP president in this era, including antiabortion policies, the appointment of conservative judges, business-friendly tax and regulatory policies, efforts to protect American jobs, efforts to secure US borders, support for Israel, and that friendliness to conservative Christians and their religious liberty concerns just mentioned.

But in historical perspective we can see that the worst parts of Trumpism track closely with the worst parts of the long evangelical political heritage: racism, sexism, nationalism, xenophobia, and indifference to ecology and the poor. It is not a stretch to follow Ta-Nehisi Coates in seeing Trump as the "first white president," that is, as a white backlash response to Barack Obama as the first black president.[27] The Trump presidency further tempted white evangelicals (= Republicans) to excuse his assaults on civility, on truth, on people of color, on dissenters, and on the rule of law—all due to the promises he made and kept on the matters that concern them. A corrupt man, and a corrupting one, his presidency represents a low moment indeed.

SEVEN MARKS OF HEALTHY CHRISTIAN POLITICS

What in the world do we do now? What I will try to do here is simply to distill seven marks of what I believe to be a healthy Christian political engagement. The five primary streams of Christian thought and practice that influence this vision are (Ana)Baptist separatism, the prophetic black church tradition, the social gospel movement, post-Vatican II Catholic social teaching, and the witness of modern progressive evangelical leaders. Notice that all accept a post-Christendom world, with a disestablished church and the separation of church and state. The principles offered here apply to the United States but could also speak to other countries. Post-evangelical politics will have to set aside most of what white US evangelicals have been doing, but there are plenty of resources for reconstruction.

A Distinctive Christian Identity—Not a Civil Religion

A healthy Christian politics is contingent upon Christians and the church being *utterly clear about the distinctness and primacy of our identity as Christians*, as followers of Jesus Christ, over against all other identities and loyalties. Christians are those whose solemn promise is to follow Jesus in all contexts and circumstances. Churches are communities of baptized Christians. Christians and churches live in various nations, under various regimes, but our primary communal identity must be as the church, and our primary personal identity must be as a Christ-follower. Any engagement that we offer with politics must come from this clear identity core. This is much easier to say than to accomplish and maintain, because human identity is multifaceted and many competing identities tug at the loyalties of Christian people.[28]

Especially in lands where Christians have had numerical majorities, and most especially in nations where Christianity has been the official state religion, Christian identity has often been hopelessly merged and confused with national identity. To be born in 1820s England was to be Anglican Christian. It wasn't much different from being born in 1950 Jackson, Tennessee, where the unofficial official religion was Southern Protestant. Christianity in many places was or is the civil religion of the nation, and people often have not really known the difference between being a Christian and being a Brit or American or German or Serb. This is routinely disastrous for Christian witness, because Christians who are confused about their core identity often abandon the teachings of Jesus for the demands of other lords, notably, the nation itself—without knowing they are doing so.

Such identity confusion is a major problem for white evangelicals, whose identity is mingled with Americanism, whiteness, capitalism, Republicanism, and now Trumpism. Post-evangelicals, for the most part, already see the problem. We must learn how to protect the primacy and independence of our identity as followers of Jesus.

A Politics of Hope, Not Fear

A healthy Christian politics is driven by hope and not fear. This is hope in God, not in the state, political parties, or politicians. The hope we should adopt is Jesus' hope of the kingdom of God. This kingdom of God sets a moral agenda of peace, justice, deliverance of the oppressed, healing, and restoration of people to community. Meanwhile, the church affirms that Jesus is Lord and Christ is King, even as we wait for the full consummation of his rule. The church is that community of people who obey Jesus and work toward his reign, until Christ returns.[29]

Christians can and often do choose to engage in earthly political activities as one aspect of obedience and one arena in which kingdom advances can be achieved. But hard experience teaches the church to be very careful about identifying specific policy gains or losses with the kingdom of God. We have also learned that political engagement always involves making some compromises and being willing to accept half wins or two-thirds losses, and that over-investing hope in the political arena leads to a wide variety of temptations and seductions. It also can weaken the church's distinctive identity and attention to its own lived faithfulness to the way of Jesus.

White US evangelicals have vacillated between hope when a Republican wins and despair when a Democrat wins. (The exact opposite is also true on the left.) God's action in history has been confidently interpreted as blessing when our side wins and punishment or imminent Armageddon when our side loses. Post-evangelicals will need a chastened theology of history and a form of hope that extends further than the next election.

Critical Distance from All Earthly Powers—Not Partisanship, Partnership, or Surrender

A healthy Christian politics learns from Scripture and church history that the church must remain at a critical distance from all earthly powers. The church is not a partner to the state, the church is not to become identified with a political party, and the church must never offer uncritical loyalty or moral surrender to any ruler or politician. These are lessons that have often been learned through disastrous Christian failures—as in our time.

God is sovereign, and Christ is Lord over all. The state's role under God is to advance the common good and protect innocent life (Rom. 13:1–7). The church's role under God is to preach and live the gospel, and to love God and neighbor. Church and state have overlapping arenas of concern but different responsibilities. When they meet, both need to remember who they are, and what their respective roles are, and to respect the boundaries.

I picture the ideal relationship between Christians and earthly politicians with a spatial image. The church is in one place, the ruler is somewhere else. If given the opportunity, the church sends its representatives to speak to the ruler or other officials of the state. When in the presence of state officials, church leaders articulate the relevant convictions of the church and then withdraw. They do not strategize with politicians, form partisan alliances with political parties, make partnerships with the state or its officials, or surrender their independence and convictions in order to retain access. By the way, this applies to Christians on all sides of the political spectrum.

Politicians are generally far less interested in hearing Christian moral convictions stated in their presence than in co-opting Christian influencers for their own political purposes. They feign interest in the former while pursuing the latter. And, of course, at times states turn directly hostile to faithful Christian witness, blocking access to rulers or even turning on the churches in persecution. Keeping that possibility always in mind helps discipline a healthy Christian politics. Given the church's routine capitulation to secular powers when granted access to them, it is easy to conclude that the best situation of the church in relation to the state is a distant and wary one—at least if a central concern is protecting the moral integrity of the church.

A Discipline Provided by a Christian Social Teaching Tradition—Not Ideology or Improv

A healthy Christian politics brings a rich social teaching tradition rather than ideology or improvisation into its public engagement. The church has a profound body of teachings to bring to bear on nearly every social-ethical-political issue that might arise in contemporary life, as well as on the broader meta-issues of how Christians should engage politics. This tradition is too good, too rich, and too constructive to be left behind.[30]

Any church group of any substantial history has made some contributions to this epic library. The oldest, hoariest traditions—Orthodox, Catholic, and mainline Protestant—have produced the most resources for it. In my experience, the most extensive and accessible body of Christian social teaching available today is found in the Catholic Church, including the modern papal encyclicals, Vatican II documents, and the catechism.[31]

Not coincidentally, when Catholic leaders are called upon to address state officials on various issues, generally they draw from this social teaching tradition and do not improvise. They are disciplined by their official doctrine and the political ethics in which they have been trained. Perhaps because they have such a long and mixed history of relating to the state, high officials of the Catholic Church seem to know how to keep their distance these days—much better than our evangelical brethren. They are far less naive about how political power works.

Because no source in Christian life is infallible, these resources from the library of Christian political thought are not infallible, nor are the scholars and leaders who represent them—in large part because of the voices they have never adequately consulted. But they are indispensable as part of the treasury of our shared experience. Consulting them can prevent a multitude of sins and stupidities. In the spirit of openness and ecumenicity, a healthy post-evangelical politics today will involve consulting widely and looking for resources in diverse places.

A Global Perspective—Not Parochial or Nationalist

A healthy Christian politics takes a global rather than parochial or nationalist perspective. This is so in three senses.

First, as noted in chapter 6, we are a part of the global church (as confessed in the creeds), we are responsible for our connection to that global church, and we humbly and gratefully draw on the resources of the global church.

Second, those about whom we are concerned in our public engagement include all the world's citizens and creation. The Christian social teaching tradition itself continually directs us to a globalized rather than localized concern. The biblical teachings that all are made in God's image, that God loves the peoples of the entire world, and that Christ lived and served and died for all discipline us away from narrower and more parochial visions.[32]

Third, based on hard-earned lessons of history, we explicitly reject a political vision damaged by racism, xenophobia, or nationalism. We repentantly recall the numerous times that the church has fallen prey to such ideologies, and we hope to do better in our own day. Honest repentance for past sins is an important part of a healthy Christian politics, as Jennifer McBride so powerfully has argued in her study of Dietrich Bonhoeffer's social ethics.[33]

For all these reasons, the evangelical Christian embrace of American nationalism is a disastrous mistake. A post-evangelical politics must utterly repudiate it.

A Vision for the Common Good— Not the Church's Self-Interest

A healthy Christian politics concerns itself with the common good rather than the church's self-interest narrowly conceived.[34] This is an aspect of the modern Christian social teaching tradition that becomes obvious upon even the most limited inspection. But it is also a matter in which the church has routinely fallen short, because the church, and churches, are also human institutions susceptible to selfishness and narrow visions of the good.

Imagine again the church sending its representatives into the lair of the state. The church does so, or ought to do so, with a message that is primarily governed by kingdom purposes and directed toward the common good. Thus, the bishop tells the ruler, please attend to the poor more generously. The pastor tells the president, please look after the sick who cannot pay for doctors. The denominational executive tells the Department of Homeland Security, please provide humane provisions for migrants who are coming to our shores. No cages, please. No family separations.

Why all of this? Because the church exists to follow Jesus and to advance his kingdom. The church in its public-facing witness scans the horizon, near and far, looking for those whose needs for justice, peace, deliverance, healing, and merciful welcome are most acute. When it seems human needs in these arenas fall under the responsibilities of the state, the church advocates for appropriate state action when it has an audience with the state.[35]

Now contrast this vision for Christian politics with, let's just say, a different one. Imagine a church that uses its access to rulers to advocate for its own self-interest. Give us, we say, better and broader tax exemptions. Go easy on our pastors when they are accused of molesting children. Interpret religious liberty laws so that we can discriminate against certain people in our businesses and charities. Give us the best seats at the table when you convene religious leaders. Tell everyone that our religion is the preferred national religion.[36] This is a hopeless corruption of Christian political engagement. The church's public witness must be about the common good, not special pleading.

A People Who Practice What They Preach— Not Hypocrites or Load-Shifters

A healthy Christian politics emerges from faith communities of holistic integrity that practice what they preach. Everything that these churches ask the state to do, we ourselves are already doing within the range of our own mission. Thus when we leave our spaces to go to government spaces, when we ask the state to serve the poor better, to care for refugees better, to support families better, we are able to point to all kinds of things we are doing and lessons we have learned in the very same enterprises related to the common good.

We are not approaching the state to ask it to do what we should be doing but are not. Knowing the difference between the missions of the church and the state, we do not ask the state to advance Christianity. We do not ask the state to prefer Christianity either formally or informally. We do not ask the state to silence the church's critics. If we live in a country that sets limits on state support of religion, as the United States does via its Constitution, we support those provisions.[37]

We do ask the state to advance the common good. We are aware of overlapping concerns, and these overlaps are sometimes a bit difficult to negotiate. The church serves the poor in soup kitchens and homes, while the state serves the poor in tax policy and food vouchers. We do not ask the state to do our job, but neither do we discourage sufficient tax collections for the state to do its job, a common problem on the libertarian American evangelical side. Just because we can serve a few poor doesn't mean the state is off the hook for its share. Just because we can create small-scale health-care operations doesn't mean the state can evade its larger systemic responsibilities. If the state chooses to contract out some of its health care or poverty relief efforts to church-run entities because we are very good at it, we *may* accept such contracted funds but must consider the entanglement costs very carefully.[38]

The church's public witness is hollow if we are not practicing in our life and on our scale what we are asking the state to do on its turf and its proper scale. The integrity of Christian political ethics is directly related to the integrity of church life and Christian discipleship.

For a long time, I have called for various versions of these seven marks of healthy Christian politics: a distinctive Christian identity, action based on hope and not fear, critical distance from earthly powers, grounding in the broad Christian social teaching tradition, global perspective, orientation toward serving God's kingdom and the common good, and efforts to practice what we preach. Today, that might just amount to a call to repentance for those coming out of white evangelicalism. We have much to repent. Will we do so?

TAKEAWAYS

- The complex question of how the church should relate to the worldly political arena has always perplexed Christian thinkers.
- The Bible does not produce a single, coherent political ethic and has been cited for many very different political approaches.
- Though white fundamentalism and evangelicalism have sometimes been politically progressive and reformist, the predominant strand has been conservative.
- The Christian Right, born in the late 1970s, worked with Republican leaders to engineer a partnership between white evangelicals and the GOP, which holds to this day.
- Strong white evangelical support, and even theological celebration, of the Trump presidency continues to trouble many observers, including this author.
- Seven commitments of a post-evangelical politics are proposed: a distinctive Christian identity, action based on hope and not fear, critical distance from earthly powers, grounding in the broad Christian social teaching tradition, global perspective, orientation toward serving God's kingdom and the common good, and efforts to practice what we preach.

9

Race

Unveiling and Ending White-Supremacist Christianity

"White Christianity in America was born in heresy."

Yale University theologian Eboni Marshall Turman made this statement before a large audience in plenary session at the American Academy of Religion meeting in November 2019.[1]

Marshall Turman, a formidably talented leader in African American theology, did not explain her meaning. In that room, she did not need to do so. But as I heard her, I thought dolefully about how very long it took me as a white American Christian ethicist to be ready to engage or even to understand such a statement. I wondered doubtfully how many white American Christians today would be prepared to discuss it rationally.

And I thought it might just make a sobering text for my final "sermon" in this book. Because part of what is so deeply wrong with white evangelicalism has to do with race. If what comes after evangelicalism does not address our racism at its roots, we shouldn't bother.

WESTERN CHRISTIAN RACISM: A HERESY VISIBLE IN FIFTEENTH-CENTURY EUROPE

To say that *white Christianity in America was born in heresy* is to make a theological statement about racism prior to any moral evaluation. It is to suggest that our local racism problem is ultimately rooted in heresy, a violation of central tenets of Christian doctrine. It is also to say that this heresy was present from the birth of American Christianity. There was no original innocence; the heresy and its resulting sins were there from the beginning.

This raises the question of whether the ultimate historical source of such heresy can be identified. I noted in the last chapter that scholars today are pressing forward in a great diagnostic project trying to figure out when and how racism became so deeply ingrained in Western civilization.

It seems to me that a compelling starting point is fifteenth-century Europe as it began conquering and colonizing the world in the name of Christ. The story begins with those first imperial powers, Spain and Portugal, but soon after extends to all the European colonial nations, including England, Holland, France, Belgium, and so on. These were empire-building nations on the cusp of their grand adventures. They confidently believed themselves to be the center of the world, superior to all other cultures, entitled to conquer and colonize, in doing so actively advancing God's will. The European powers believed this for many centuries. Some would say that they, and their descendants, believe it still.

These European conquerors, and the church officials who blessed and authorized them, had fourteen hundred years in which to learn key elements of Christian theology that might have affected their plans. Just to pick three of the most relevant items, these would include the doctrine that all humans are made in the image of God and thus are of equal worth to God (Gen. 1:26–27), the doctrine that all human beings are kin because all are descendants from Adam and Eve (Gen. 2:4–25; 3:20), and the doctrine that God is the author of moral law, which includes universal bans on murder, adultery, theft, and covetousness (Exod. 20:1–17).

But the European imperial powers decided to believe heresies instead. They believed in the unequal worth and value of, and the ontological differences between, persons based on their "race" and "color," and they came to believe that God's moral law against murder, adultery, theft, and covetousness did not apply in the relation between European conquerors and those they conquered.

Christian faith taught that people should be humble, aware of their mortality, sinfulness, and dependence on God. But the European conquerors instead succumbed to the deadly sin of pride. They believed they were the best people on earth, the most advanced, the agents of civilization, the bearers of faith. Their church told them that they had the right and duty to conquer, colonize, and enslave non-European populations. As Willie Jennings has put it, these Europeans developed a "diseased social imagination."[2] It infected the entire world.

Christian faith should have served as a brake on this pride and the wicked behaviors that it spawned. But Christianity had long since been fatally compromised by nationalism and proximity to political power. Rather than speaking with the prophetic voice of an Isaiah or Jesus, European Christianity became a cheerleader for colonial conquest and enslavement, in the name of Jesus.

One could possibly imagine an imperialist, conquering, enslaving world power that is not also racist. But I cannot recall having ever read about one. Certainly, the fifteenth-century European imperial mind racialized and colorized its prideful vision. It wasn't just that colonial Europeans were better because they were Christian, more technologically advanced, and militarily superior. They were also better because they were persons of the "race" and "color" called "white," by contrast with lesser persons of other colors and races. The terms get scare quotes because they are all social constructions. But their effects are real enough.

There were many pivotal moments in the racializing and colorizing of the European Christian mind. Certainly, the direct encounter between light-skinned Europeans and darker-skinned peoples whom they conquered and enslaved played a significant role. *We* were white and Christian and European and better; *they* were "red" and "brown" and "black," and heathen and native and worse. We were normal humans, or peak humans, and they were less-than-that humans. We were entitled to rule. They were slated to suffer, serve, and die. All of this with God's supervision and blessing.

The single best term to describe this kind of vision is white supremacism. Whiteness confers supremacy. And that, even a child in Sunday school ought to be able to tell you, is nothing but heresy. Yet it came to dominate the European and colonial mind.

I do suspect that theologian J. Kameron Carter is right that the ultimate origin of a racialized European Christian mind is traceable to historic Christian anti-Judaism.[3] Born from biblical Judaism, born as a messianic-apocalyptic Jewish movement, in its childhood a diaspora Jewish-Gentile Christian movement, the church gradually became a largely Gentile community that structured theological anti-Judaism into its teachings. All it took was for this theology of rejection to become an anthropology of rejection based on "race" or even "blood." Once it was adapted to classify and reject a people based on race and blood, the paradigm was available for other uses.

The racializing of Christian anti-Judaism definitely occurred in mid-fifteenth-century Spain. Jews who had been forcibly converted to Catholicism beginning in the late fourteenth century (called *conversos*), and their descendants, were sometimes suspected of still secretly practicing Judaism and not being true Catholics. Eventually the nobility decided that *limpieza de sangre*, "cleanliness of blood" or "blood purity," should be a status marker to delineate between the so-called Old Christians and New Christians such as these. This was a way to discriminate using a blood purity test even if true religious sentiments could not be divined. This racializing of anti-Judaism (also employed against Muslims in Spain) was a fateful move that ever after was available for deployment.

The bottom line is that over many centuries white Europeans and their colonial offspring developed what theologian Reggie Williams calls a *racialized humanity*, and inevitably a *racialized divinity* as well.[4] In technical terms, both theological anthropology and Christology were compromised by heresy.

Despite all biblical texts to the contrary, humanity was now viewed not as one, but as many. Human diversity is real. But a human racial hierarchy is fictional—indeed, heretical. That is what white Europeans built: a perverted anthropology in which white people occupy the peak of the hierarchy, the highest in goodness and value. Then down, down, down it goes from there. The darker the body of the person, the lesser the value. Black bodies, especially, became associated with sin, pollution, and degradation.[5] Racism specifically as *antiblackness* was written into Christian theology and practice.[6]

God, and Jesus, became white too. God's whiteness was seen not just in art, though white God/Jesus was common in stained glass and painting. Jesus, as the best and highest of human beings, became a white man in the white imagination. This was white racist Europe making a god in our own image. In biblical terms, when people create gods in their own image, that is called idolatry. Jesus as white, as our white guy, our white Savior, our white God—this became taken for granted. You might not notice it until someone challenges it with a different image.

This begins to communicate why Eboni Marshall Turman could say: *White Christianity in America was born in heresy.*

WHITE AMERICAN CHRISTIANS EMBRACE THE SIN OF BLACK SLAVERY

The Portuguese began enslaving Africans in the mid-fifteenth century. More than 150 years later, the twenty or so Africans who arrived in the new Jamestown settlement were treated as indentured servants, as were some white Europeans. But over the succeeding decades only African servitude became chattel slavery, with slave status inheritable. This development is highly significant, because it showed that antiblack racism was required to institutionalize a mass system of chattel slavery. Somehow, white bodies could not be enslaved en masse and forever, but black bodies could be. White-supremacist heresy began to bear its sinful fruit on our soil.

Most human beings *need to believe that what they are doing is morally justifiable*. I think this very much helps to account for what developed in slaveholding

America. White European racism before 1619 was sufficiently strong to help people justify the beginnings of African slavery. But the growing practice of African slavery here after 1619, with all its intrinsic and visible moral wrongs, required an intensification of white racism. It also required an intentional deformation of other aspects of Christian belief and practice so that Christian people could accommodate themselves to slavery. Christianity would need to be made amenable to building a state on the backs of black slaves.

There were plenty of motivations to maintain slavery. The economy of an entire region gradually depended upon it. The most powerful people in the South built their lives, prosperity, families, and culture upon slavery. Financial interests well outside the South also benefited from the profits derived from slavery. Slavery was wired into the arrangements concluded in Philadelphia in 1776 and then in the Constitution in 1789. The shape of American politics from the beginning was affected by slavery.

But we still had a choice. Despite it all, we could have followed the British lead and abolished slavery. Instead, we deepened our excuses, weakened our ethics, and denied biblical theology.

From the very beginning, there were voices proclaiming that slavery was sin—including but not limited to black people who protested it. All honor goes to those like the Quakers who opposed slavery quite early. Somewhere deep inside themselves, many white Americans, including direct participants in the slave system, knew that what they were doing was sin. But they went on doing it.

One thing led to another, one step led to the next, and an entire country gave in to heresy and sin. It makes me think of that fateful line from Genesis 4, when God addresses Cain, who is on the brink of murdering his brother: "Sin is lurking at the door; its desire is for you, but you must master it" (Gen. 4:7b). Disregarding God's warning, "Cain rose up against his brother Abel, and killed him" (Gen. 4:8b). Cain did not master sin; it mastered him. And like a lion, sin devoured both Cain and Abel. The sin of slavery devoured us in the same way.

WICKEDNESS FLOURISHING IN WHITE RACIST CHRISTIANITY

In Romans 1:18–32, the apostle Paul attempts to account for the moral chaos and degradation of humanity. His argument begins with the claim that all human beings have plenty of access to knowledge about God and morality because God has plainly revealed it. But "ungodliness and wickedness" flourish when people "by their wickedness suppress the truth" (Rom. 1:18). Paul is saying that people actively suppress the truth "by their wickedness"—as an expression of their wickedness, and to enable further wickedness.

Paul argues that as a result, "God gave them up to a debased mind and to things that should not be done. They were filled with every kind of wickedness" (Rom. 1:28–29a). The suggestion is that God sometimes punishes people by allowing them to spiral downward, reap what they sow, and sink into ever greater debasement. The result is "every kind of wickedness," including "covetousness, malice, . . . murder, strife, deceit, craftiness," and slander; as a way of life in which people feel free to be "insolent, haughty, boastful, inventors of evil, . . . foolish, faithless, heartless, ruthless" (Rom. 1:29–31).

Paul could almost be describing a way of life in which, coveting ever-greater wealth, and filled with pride in their own superior value, people set up a heartless, ruthless slave system in which they are free to covet, buy, sell, rape, steal, enslave, abuse, slander, deceive, and murder people; that is, a slave state.

That similarity may not be coincidental. Paul was writing to Christian communities in Rome. Let us not forget that Rome was the capital of a massive slaveholding empire. Rome's new Christians included many slaves and former slaves, who knew all too well the degradations of slavery.

The difference is that the Roman slaveholding empire was pagan. The colonial and Southern US slaveholding empire was largely run by Christians. The first who made me see a connection between European colonialism and Romans 1:18–32 was the Spanish colonial cleric Bartolomé de Las Casas, who made the point explicitly in describing the horrors he witnessed.[7] He saw firsthand that expression of absolute power over others, that spiral downward into ever-crueler forms of torture and more wicked forms of evil.[8]

So it was that the moral degradation sank in deeply and spiraled fiercely, all while white slaveholding Christians found a way to live with themselves.

BLACK OBSERVERS HAVE ALWAYS NAMED THE HERESY

Maybe some white readers are surprised by some of what I am saying in this chapter. But the realities I am describing are certainly embedded in the collective memory of African Americans. Black observers have been telling this story for four hundred years.

Slave narratives, ex-slave memoirs, protest documents, and other materials primarily read by historians offer access to this collective memory even today. One place to find it easily is in novels written by African Americans. In 2017–18, for my American Academy of Religion presidential address,[9] I decided to read as many classic and contemporary novels by black Americans as I could manage, with one main question in mind—what do these novels tell us about white Americans' values, behaviors, and religion?

The novels, written over a hundred-year period, describe the general pattern of white behavior as morally debased, unconstrained by meaningful religion, and accompanied by astonishing white blindness and moral obtuseness. White people act toward black people with pride, greed, slander, arbitrary use of power, and unchecked anger and violence. This makes honest friendship across the races very difficult, if it is ever sought. White people should know better, because the Bible could easily tell them so. But they are blind to their wrongs. Notice the similarity to Romans 1.

In case it is not perfectly clear, black novelists of various periods do *not* say that white Americans, their morality, and their Christianity were debased way back then, but OK now. They instead say that the moral degradation baked into white American Christian culture is still quite palpable today, even where improvements have occurred. Dealing with what white (mainly Christian) people might do is still a factor that affects everyday lives for black and brown people. The damage to the morality of white Christian people is at the foundation, and it has never been repaired.

That has certainly been the consistent judgment of the most significant black intellectuals of the last 150 years. The depth and steadiness of this kind of critique is just staggering when you first meet it. I have compiled a few choice comments, representative of many others:

> Frederick Douglass: "There is the Christianity of this land, and the Christianity of Christ. To be the friend of the one, is of necessity to be the enemy of the other."[10]
>
> Ida B. Wells: "Our American Christians are too busy saving the souls of white Christians from burning in hellfire to save the lives of black ones from present burning in fires kindled by white Christians."[11]
>
> W. E. B. DuBois: "A nation's religion is its life, and as such white Christianity is a miserable failure."[12]
>
> James Cone: "Black people did not need to go to seminary and study theology to know that white Christianity was fraudulent. As a teenager in the South where whites treated blacks with contempt, I and other blacks knew that the Christian identity of whites was not a true expression of what it meant to follow Jesus. . . . We wondered how whites could live with their hypocrisy—such a blatant contradiction of the man from Nazareth."[13]
>
> Malcolm X: "If the so-called Christianity now being practiced in America displays the best that world Christianity has to offer—no one in his right mind should need any much greater proof that very close at hand is the *end* of Christianity."[14]

WE MISSED EVERY OPPORTUNITY TO REPENT

James Baldwin once wrote: "Go back to where you started, or as far as you can, examine all of it, travel your road again and tell the truth about it. Sing or shout or testify or keep it to yourself: but know when you came."[15]

When I think about the stages of American history in terms of the intersection of race and religion, I now mainly see a refusal of white Christians to repent. Let us consider the roads not taken.

Consider the evangelical revivals of the late eighteenth and early nineteenth centuries.[16] These revivals swept the land, including the South, with the good news that God loves sinners and died for us all in Jesus Christ. Millions, both black and white, were saved in ecstatic experiences of divine grace.

It was an opportunity to follow Jesus all the way from personal salvation to repentance of slavery and racism. Populist and antislavery Christian egalitarianism was originally quite strong. But as Christine Heyrman, Paul Harvey, and others have shown, eventually southern evangelical leaders and culture compromised that egalitarianism and assimilated to local values.[17] The tragedy of the South is that *passionate evangelicalism and passionate racism grew simultaneously, becoming as painfully intertwined as the white and black Christians of the region.*

The heightening of political tensions over the moral legitimacy of slavery by the mid-nineteenth century, and the rise of an aggressive abolitionist movement, provided another opportunity for white Christians to repent of slavery. Of course, some did indeed repent—many abolitionists were reform-minded Christians who could fairly be described as evangelical.

But the South's white evangelical Christians were not persuaded. Instead their leaders published learned biblical defenses of slavery, their preachers proclaimed texts that supported slavery, and their piety was no obstacle to eternal acceptance of slavery.

For nearly forty years I was a Southern Baptist. Thus, it is especially important for me to acknowledge that the Southern Baptist Convention was formed in 1845 in a dispute over whether a slaveholder should be appointed as a missionary. All four of the founding faculty of Southern Baptist Theological Seminary, where I both studied and taught, owned slaves and offered theological defenses of slavery.[18] This was never publicly discussed during the six years I was a student or faculty member at that school.

The period immediately after the Civil War was another huge missed opportunity. By the end of his life, President Abraham Lincoln had offered a religious way forward in a series of remarkable addresses. He suggested an interpretation of the Civil War as a punishment from God on the entire nation for the sin of slavery. He proposed a postwar renewal of American democracy that would finally include all of the nation's people. He communicated a sense of the tragedy of the whole society's enmeshment with slavery rather than a punitive vision toward the South. Together, he said, all of us could bind up our wounds and build a better democracy.[19] And then he was murdered in Ford's Theatre.

The Reconstruction period (1865–77) is receiving considerable attention by historians these days.[20] It is increasingly seen as an abortive (forcibly aborted) experiment in building a multiracial democracy in this country—as well as a brief period of economic reform that brought poor blacks and whites together in common cause. Blacks were now free, voted in large numbers, and helped elect numerous black state and national representatives, including black governors and senators.

But the white South was deeply resistant, and there was no true national or racial reconciliation. The unwillingness of white people to live on equal political and social terms with black people was the most fundamental reason. When federal troops were withdrawn in 1877, and the South was left to its own devices, a reign of terror fell upon black Southerners. "Redemption" was the cruelly ironic term given to the period after Reconstruction, which involved the creation of the Jim Crow South, the suppression of black political rights, the rise of the KKK, and the expansion of a lynching regime that terrorized black people and took at least five thousand lives.[21]

Reconstruction had been a signal opportunity for white repentance. Imagine the South's churches, clergy, and people deciding that this was exactly the time to shake free of racial hatred and the morally damaging sense of white racial superiority. But this opportunity also was missed.

The turn of the twentieth century saw two more missed opportunities.

The rise of the social gospel movement on the activist liberal side of the Protestant divide was one of the most remarkable developments of the late nineteenth and early twentieth centuries. Guided by energetic and gifted scholars, preachers, and activists like Washington Gladden and Walter Rauschenbusch, the energies of much of the vast white Protestant establishment were turned in the direction of social reform, notably in economic and urban life.[22]

But for the most part, the white social gospelers paid little attention to the plight of their black Christian sisters and brothers. When lynching ran rampant, and brave black leaders like Ida B. Wells risked their lives to tell the truth about what was happening,[23] the white social gospelers stayed quiet.

Meanwhile, the black social gospel was developing.[24] Leaders like Wells, W. E. B. DuBois, Alexander Crummell, Mordecai Wyatt Johnson, and Reverdy Ransom were offering social reform messages very similar to the white social gospel, though centering on the even more acute injustices experienced by black people. The black social gospel leaders were aware of what Rauschenbusch and his group were writing and doing, but the attention was not returned. Segregation prevailed, energies were divided rather than united, and Jim Crow survived another half century. It was another missed opportunity.

There was a second major opportunity from the same period. In 1906, on Azusa Street in Los Angeles, an outpouring of the Holy Spirit transformed thousands. People of all races came to faith in Christ in the three-year Azusa Street Revival.[25] Unexpectedly, their experience continued into tongue-speaking (glossolalia), healing, and other supernatural expressions that most Christians thought had ended with the New Testament period.

This smashing breakthrough of the Holy Spirit came to a richly interracial group, which by its very nature challenged American segregation. For a while, the interracial character of what became known as the Pentecostal movement—still sweeping the globe today—was one of its most remarkable characteristics. Overcoming racial segregation through the power of the Holy Spirit became part of the core agenda of Pentecostalism. But the Holy Spirit was not invited to defeat American segregation, and Pentecostals for the most part retreated into customary racial divisions.

In the 1940s, the birth of the movement that gave us modern evangelicalism was another opportunity to repent of racism and build a truly egalitarian, multiracial Christian movement. But the leaders of the new evangelicals were all white men. The institutions they led were largely segregated. The felt need for separate adjunctive organizations such as the National Black Evangelical Association and the National Hispanic Christian Leadership Conference tells the tale.[26]

As noted earlier, when the casual segregationism of the evangelical establishment was challenged by leaders such as William Pannell, Tom Skinner, and John Perkins beginning in the late 1960s, the response of the white evangelical power structure was woefully inadequate.[27]

On the integration of white churches, the answer was *go slow*. On civil rights legislation, the answer was *go slow*. On the elevation of black and brown leaders, voices, ideas, and priorities in mainstream evangelicalism, the answer was *no thank you*. And on the development of a truly multiracial evangelical movement with fully shared power and the decentering of white men, the answer was, basically, *when hell freezes over*. In recent decades, black Christians attempting to work in white evangelical spaces, such as Ed Gilbreath at *Christianity Today*, have reported their deep, continuing frustration.[28] It is a pattern, not an exception.

The civil rights movement, more broadly, was its own missed opportunity. Despite the participation of some white people, mainly northern clergy and volunteers, the white evangelical South largely stood silent or worse. The nonviolent, love-your-white-neighbor civil rights movement led by Dr. King was met with his 1968 assassination.

America's white politicians and people could have responded to this disaster by a commitment to King's cause. But instead one of our two major political parties chose a commitment to the politics of inflaming white racial fears. Rather than leading to principled Christian resistance, this so-called Southern Strategy helped the Republican Party gain the undying support of the South's white voters, massive numbers of whom were and are evangelical Christians.

Every election season has seen racist signaling by candidates. At the presidential level this has included "law and order," "young bucks," "welfare queens," Willie Horton, birtherism, drug mules, Mexican invasion, and the list goes on. You can look it up.

Compare the stated public policy agenda of the NAACP or the Southern Christian Leadership Conference with that of the (white evangelical) Family Research Council or American Family Association to see the vast political gulf between white and black Christians in this country.[29]

The election of Barack Obama as America's first black president was another opportunity. America's white Christians could have responded with celebration of this racial breakthrough and with serious effort at further progress. Some did. In general, however, the election of Obama led not just to white evangelical policy resistance, which might have come to any Democrat, but to a great deal of racially loaded rhetoric and a rise in what is now being called white nationalism.[30]

To succeed Obama, Republicans could have nominated a candidate who celebrated the fact that America had made the breakthrough of having a black president, even while proposing very different policies for her or his own administration.

Instead, given seventeen choices, the Republicans chose the most extreme white backlash candidate.[31]

Whatever reasons white Christians might give for their support of Trumpism, they must account for why Trump's consistent race-baiting did not prevent them from supporting him. The lack of salience for white evangelicals of concerns that are fundamental to most people of color helps explain the deep, relationship-breaking, even enraging resentment felt by a great many black and brown Christians, as well as the abandonment of evangelicalism by many of its own young people. It's a basic question: *How is this behavior not disqualifying?* The radical nature of this failure is leading to the radicalization of resistance to white evangelicalism in America.

This moment we are living through isn't just a missed opportunity. In terms of the four-hundred-year-old heresy and sin of white Christian racism in this land, it is a definite movement backward.

RETHINKING EVERYTHING BY LISTENING TO PEOPLE OF COLOR

Everything discussed in this book so far—every single topic—intersects with and has been discussed by scholars and clergy of color. Focusing on African American Christian perspectives on some of the topics we have considered is how I will end this chapter.

Evangelicalism, Scripture, Authority, God, and Jesus

African American religion began during slave days. It was a distinctive combination of African beliefs and practices (sometimes including Christian and Muslim faiths) transformed in the context of the horrors of slavery and through exposure to the religion of the slaveholder. Christian belief gradually came to dominate among slaves and free blacks, with much heightened allegiance after the great revivals of the early nineteenth century.

Especially after that, every theological test that one could offer of what counts as evangelical religion would include the religion of most black Protestants. Any history that says evangelicalism goes back to the eighteenth or nineteenth century must include the religion of most black Protestants. But this was not a lineage that the new evangelicals claimed in the 1940s.

So black and white Christians often shared an evangelical faith. But it is also true, as womanist theologian Stacey Floyd-Thomas has written, that "black and white Christians did not worship the same God."[32] White Christians worshiped a God who imposed slavery upon black people and demanded their obedience. Black Christians, not all but many, worshiped a God who viewed slavery as oppression, sided with the slaves, and would one day act to bring them freedom. It is a staggering example of failure in the unity of Christ's church.

"Both read the same Bible," said Abraham Lincoln in his second inaugural address. It is true that slaveholder Christians and slave Christians shared the same canonical text. But black Christians tended to read the Scriptures through specific lenses: the creation story in which all are God's children and all matter; the exodus narrative in which God frees the groaning slaves; the prophetic tradition in which the Hebrew prophets demand social justice; and the Gospel stories in which Jesus sides with and dies as the godforsaken one, suffering as and for the oppressed.[33]

Slaveholder Christianity viewed God as the author of all that is, the creator of slavery and social hierarchy, the upholder of the unjust law and wicked social order. White Jesus became the Savior of souls for heaven, the gentle friend, the prototype of white manhood—anything other than the prophet who proclaimed a reign of God's justice for all people, who was thrown up on a cross as a lynching victim.

Black biblical scholars such as Renita Weems have shown that black Christians during slave days certainly knew that there were plenty of passages in the Bible that sanctioned slavery and enjoined obedience to masters. The texts had been used against them time and again.

But over time, as Kelly Brown Douglas says, enslaved blacks learned to "appropriate particular scriptural texts through the lens of their own experience," or as Weems puts it, they "rehearsed and interpreted the contents of the Bible as they saw fit."[34] This was pivotal, and instructive to anyone thinking about Scripture today.

Resistant black Christians learned to subordinate slave obedience passages to the grand dignity, liberation, and justice themes that could be found through the whole of Scripture.[35] They needed to make this move for their own psychic survival. They felt authorized to make this move by the blazing witness of their own experience. And they learned a visceral "hermeneutic of suspicion" toward any powerful white person claiming the right to mistreat them based on the teachings of an inerrant Bible.

This subversive, prophetic, liberative black Christianity fed every kind of resistance to slavery and racism. It nourished the black social gospel movement, which in turn nourished the civil rights movement, and the tradition continues today.[36] It is this tradition that has sustained much of the magnificent moral resistance offered by black Americans to white racism. And this same tradition has influenced some resistant white Christians. It is sad that few of these have been US evangelicals.

It should be noted that not all black Protestants stand in the prophetic tradition. Raphael Warnock, pastor of the legendary Ebenezer Baptist Church in Atlanta and at this writing a candidate for Senate in Georgia, is among the latest to describe the competing church approaches.[37] Black literature, both historical and novelistic, is full of often angry, sometimes humorous, depictions of fundamentalist, evangelical, quietist, and subordinationist black preachers. James Baldwin offers some of the most pungent examples in both his essays and his novels.[38] Nonprophetic, unjust white evangelical churches and their leaders could use a similarly robust dissenting literature.

Critique of much of the mostly male-led black church is also a central theme in womanist thought. Womanists have insistently addressed the authorities question engaged in chapter 3. It was womanist ethics, created by the late Katie Cannon, that first argued that novels by black women authors such as Zora Neale Hurston should be considered significant authorities for theological and moral reflection.[39] Stacey Floyd-Thomas has proposed that along with the black women's literary tradition, womanist sociology and historiography are important sources for theology.[40]

The more a group has been denied access to traditional religious leadership, the more their most acute theological and moral reflections will occur in other venues. This denial of access to religious leadership must end, and meanwhile the sources to which marginalized voices have had access must be engaged. Nowhere in historic white evangelicalism were we ever encouraged to engage sources like the novels of black women writers.

Today's black humanism movement, such as the work of Anthony Pinn, reflects an interesting twist. African American humanism, partly based on the critiques already noted, seeks to decenter the black churches and emphasize the pursuit of black people's well-being through reason, science, education, and critical thinking.[41] In some ways, African American humanism connects with the Christian humanism I have discussed here, though it is more resolutely secular. It marks yet another reminder that bad religion produces the rejection of religion, a major feature in our post-evangelical moment.

Sex, Marriage, and Family

That last point is a reminder that the rich African American religious and literary tradition offers considerable internal protest and not just external protest. Prophetic black religion may be evangelical by many definitions, but it has always protested versions of black Christianity that do not liberate. Womanist theology and biblical interpretation have been especially clear in their protest not just against white Christianity and culture but also against oppressive black church and family beliefs and practices.[42]

Women's subordination in the name of Jesus is a problem in many black fundamentalist and evangelical churches, as in white ones. So is the sometimes-cruel repression of black LGBTQ Christians. Post-evangelicals of all colors can find considerable common ground by engaging the growing literature offered by black thinkers like Kelly Brown Douglas, Traci West, Pamela Lightsey, Thelathia Nikki Young, and Horace Griffin, works demanding an end to homophobia in black churches and families. These works parallel similar literature coming out of white Christian contexts.[43]

The background context for black Christian sexual ethics is different from white sexual ethics, and the literature in black sexual ethics reflects this. African American attitudes toward sex are deeply affected by the entire sordid history of how black people's bodies have been viewed and treated in this country.

The main story line is that the white gaze, the slaveholder gaze in particular, viewed black male bodies as objects to be feared, mastered, subjugated, exploited, and routinely humiliated, castrated, and destroyed to reassert white dominance. The same white gaze viewed and treated black female bodies as objects to be subjugated and exploited for sexual assault, forbidden pleasures, and the production of more slaves.

Some scholars today argue that from the period of slavery forward, white people have exhibited a simultaneous attraction and repulsion, fascination and fear, in relation to a hypersexualized image of black people. Kelly Brown Douglas argues that "the exploitation of Black sexuality" has been and remains fundamental to maintaining white power.[44]

Some 250 years of this experience under slavery, and the often-terrifying conditions that have followed, have deeply affected embodiment and sexuality for black people.

The objectification and humiliation of black men, at least according to many womanist authors, has contributed to a tendency among some black men toward hypermasculinity, homophobia, and mistreatment of women. Victimization and subjugation have caused intense trauma to black women and have deeply affected black women's self-concept, body image, and ability to trust men.[45]

Overall, the despicable abuse and subjugation of black people's bodies by white people has never been forgotten by black people, and it makes black-white relations far more complex than the rational adjudication of historical claims of wrongdoing. *Your people castrated and raped my ancestors*—that's a whole different level of alienation and hurt than white people tend to think about. We cannot begin to repair relations between white and black people without going directly toward the pain at its deepest level.

Black Christian thinkers who write about sexual ethics must overlay on top of all that trauma the biblical materials about sexuality discussed in chapter 7, and the long history of the sex-in-marriage-only ethic discussed there as well. But they do so while remembering that some of those pious white Christians who were so serious about sex belonging in marriage were the same ones who were raping and impregnating black women both during and after slavery—or looking the other way when other white men did so. These were the same men who routinely prevented, refused to recognize, or broke up marriages between slaves, and after slavery didn't mind depriving black families of their members via lynching.

This same society continues to routinely accept economic conditions for black people that white people would find appalling, thus making marriage all the more difficult to obtain and sustain in many cases. Perhaps all of this makes more sense of the suspicion that many black people have about the historically proclaimed sexual ethics of white Christians, though many black evangelical Christians still express adherence to those same norms. In a post-evangelical discussion of sexual ethics, this similar-yet-different history will need to be kept fully in view.

Politics

Black Christian political ethics is almost uniformly reformist or radical. Black political writers know that nearly 90 percent of America's political history has involved official, institutionalized, state racism. They also know that every effort to weaken white supremacism and advance black rights has involved massive struggle, bloodshed, and white resistance, and that every substantial gain for black people has evoked fierce white backlash. Few if any black political thinkers are sanguine about American democracy, though most have wanted to improve it rather than abandon it.[46]

Today, a movement known as Afro-pessimism is growing quickly. The hope that America can be reformed is fading. One reason for the very deep pessimism is, of course, Donald Trump. The collapse of significant resistance to Trump in the Republican Party deepened the revulsion among most blacks against the GOP and also deepened their historic connection with the Democratic Party. Earlier I warned against any fusion of Christian and partisan identity, and the connection is very strong in this case—but for very good reasons.

On the other hand, black political thinkers and activists know all about the limits and blind spots of white liberals. They do not need to be disabused of any illusions. The sense that America, including white liberals, has offered only limited, spotty, and always partial black participation in our purported democracy runs very deep.

White post-evangelicals will need to entirely rethink our vision of politics. As Richard Hughes so well put it, we have many "myths that we live by."[47] Black political thought can help disabuse us of our myths.

Finally: Church

Chanequa Walker-Barnes is a womanist theologian, pastoral care scholar, and valued colleague of mine at Mercer University. Her recent book *I Bring the Voices of My People* is a most important new addition to the racism and Christianity conversation.[48]

Walker-Barnes is finished with white Christians talking vaguely about racial reconciliation, on their own terms and without seriously dealing with white supremacism. She is done with supposedly interracial churches that never quite become spaces of shared power and leadership. She has studied, and experienced, what white US evangelicals have been able to offer, and it is not enough.

Her work reflects a new stage in the discussion of religion and race, especially in what remains of the Christian South. It is a more radical time, an unveiling of the continued power of the heresy built into white America and white evangelical Christianity. Radical times call for radical truth-telling. Polite prayer breakfasts will not do.

Her witness challenges white post-evangelicals with this question: how serious are we about overcoming white supremacism?

It may not be quite enough to find a nice inclusive Episcopal church led by Progressive White Cleric to replace the lily-white rocking megachurch led by Conservative White Guy in Jeans on Stage.

Are we committed to moving toward a fully antiracist way of life?[49] Are we ready to give up what has probably been a full-immersion bath in Christian whiteness?

In our break with white evangelicalism, how radical are we prepared to be? Are we willing to lay down everything, even white Christianity, at the foot of the cross?

I am so very late in saying all this.

I am appalled at my lateness.

As a doctoral student I saw the anti-Semitism of historic Christianity contribute to the Holocaust, and I became a fierce opponent of anti-Semitism.

As a junior scholar I saw fundamentalist Southern Baptists drive women out of their teaching and ministry posts, and I became a fierce opponent of Christian patriarchalism.

As a midlevel evangelical ethicist, I saw our country descend into authorized torture, and I became a fierce opponent of the degradation of Muslim men's bodies in the name of national security.

As a seasoned scholar, I saw the harm that my own teaching had done to gay Christians, and I repented to become a fierce opponent of antigay traditionalist faith.

And when exactly did I see that white American Christianity was born in heresy, and that my polite center-left self has been complicit in it? About five minutes ago. More precisely, about the day after Donald Trump's election and the great reveal of the evangelical 81 percent.

It must be that dealing with white European American Christian racism is the most threatening challenge of all. It must be that the horror is too great, the shame too awful, for many of us white guys to want to look over in that direction if we can avoid it.

I am sorry. So very sorry. I believe that I have begun to repent. Whether I have succeeded in doing so will be judged by others, and by Christ himself.

TAKEAWAYS

- White supremacism is a heresy and a sin, a violation of core Christian theology.
- White American Christianity, flowing from European imperial colonialism and justifying slavery, was born in racist heresy and the sin that it caused.
- The degradation of slavery and its justifying racism sank in deeply and spiraled fiercely, all while white slaveholding Christians still found a way to live with themselves and their version of Jesus.
- Black novelists, theologians, and other leaders have been consistent in their depiction of the damage caused by white supremacism to white Christian integrity.
- There have been many pivotal moments in US history when opportunities existed for the abandonment of white supremacism, but these have mainly been missed.
- Close attention to black scholars leads to a rethinking of every category of what we thought we knew, including all the themes of this book.

Epilogue

I moved my little family to inner-city Philadelphia in the bleak November of 1990. I was a midcourse doctoral student at Union Seminary, having completed the course work and comprehensive exams but not having begun my dissertation. I needed a job, and Ron Sider of Evangelicals for Social Action was offering one. I was to edit his magazine and work on other projects as needed. The pay was slight, the neighborhood gritty, the weather cold, and sundown in winter seemed to happen at about four o'clock in the afternoon. Oh well.

I didn't just need a job. I needed some clarity. I had not worked out the theological whiplash incurred in moving between Southern Baptist Theological Seminary and Union Theological Seminary. I didn't really know who I was anymore in a theological sense. Southern Baptist? Liberal Protestant? Academic ethicist with vague religious interests? The concept of "evangelicalism" had not really entered my mind until this move to Philadelphia.

I remember taking long walks with Ron Sider around our Germantown neighborhood. We talked about all kinds of things. I don't know how many of these talks we had, but I do remember with deep gratitude one specific conversation.

Ron asked me who my main theological influences were. I believe I listed Reinhold Niebuhr, Dietrich Bonhoeffer, Paul Tillich, and Rudolf Bultmann. Tillich and Bultmann were quite a stretch, because I had read little of either. When you are a grad student sometimes you make stuff up to sound like you know what you are talking about.

Ron said, in essence—those are liberal Protestants. They have good things to say. But you need to engage the evangelical world. You need deeper theological grounding if you are going to be a useful Christian ethicist, which I think is what you truly want.

During my thirty months on his staff, Ron exposed me to some of these evangelicals directly—it seemed that everyone came through Philly and met with him or participated in his magazine or programs: Nicholas Wolterstorff, JoAnne Lyon, Tony Campolo, Jim Wallis, Gretchen Gaebelein Hull, Wes Granberg-Michaelson, John Perkins, George Barna, J. H. Yoder (before his scandals), Richard Lovelace, Jim Skillen, Steve Mott, Vinay Samuel, and so many others. You may not know their names, but they became the architects of my house on solid ground.

I did indeed gradually find that solid ground under my feet. I was going to be a progressive evangelical Christian, grounded in Scripture, personally devoted to Jesus, with a justice-oriented moral vision and an activist concern for the world's problems.

Everyone needs solid ground under their feet.

No one wants to hang in midair . . . at least not for long.

I have written this book not mainly so that I can dissect what I believe to be the failures of white evangelicalism, but so that I can clarify for myself, and maybe for others, where some solid ground might be found. I am at least provisionally satisfied that there is some solid ground here for building a Christ-honoring life as a post-evangelical.

And that is so very much my goal. I want to live for Jesus till I die. And I want to help other people find a way to do that too, if they are willing.

This I know: many millions of young people got lost in that evangelical maze. They couldn't get past inerrancy, indifference to the environment, deterministic Calvinism, purity culture, divine violence, Hallmark-Christmas-Movie Jesus, rejection of gay people, male dominance, racism, God = GOP, or whatever else.

If I have helped to provide, even for a few people, a way out of this lost place and a way ahead in the direction of Jesus, then all I can say is: *thanks be to God*.

Appendix

Toward a Post-evangelical Typology

A Who's Who of the Post-Evangelicals

BY ISAIAH RITZMANN

Not all "post-evangelicals" have the same experience or share the same beliefs and feelings in relationship to their evangelical background.* To talk about different kinds of post-evangelicals is to help people name their experience, with both its burdens and its gifts. To not represent such differences, to assume the post-evangelical experience is all of a piece, is a kind of injustice. I have discerned nine different types of post-evangelicals in three main categories.

1. Still-Vangelicals

This group of folks—theologically, spiritually, and culturally—are 70 to 80 percent still evangelical. However, since evangelicalism often defines itself in such stark, black-and-white, "you are all in or you are out" ways, these people feel emotionally pressured into an identity crisis: Am I really evangelical? This crisis is very real emotionally, but it conceals the theological/cultural reality that the people are still basically evangelical.

1.1 The in-denial type. These people are in denial about their relationship

*Isaiah Ritzmann read an early draft of this book and in response offered this typology of post-evangelicals. Having found it helpful, I asked his permission to include it in the book, which he was kind enough to grant.

Ritzmann holds a master's degree in theological studies from the University of Waterloo in Ontario, Canada. He works for a nonprofit in Kitchener, Ontario, where he facilitates community education initiatives. Inspired by the Catholic Worker Movement, he is passionate about the intersections of Christian faith, personal hospitality, intentional community, and economic and ecological justice.

to evangelicalism once they get to the 70–80 percent shared identity. One in-denial type are those who say they are no longer evangelical, even though they share so much of the same theology and spirituality that the claim is basically untrue. The other in-denial type say they are still evangelical but aren't fully honest—to themselves or others—that they've shifted sufficiently to be in another category.

1.2 The Anabaptist/Reformed/Methodist type. These are people who, recognizing some of the flaws of evangelicalism, retreat into the identity of another Protestant tradition. In doing so they do not recognize that (a) they are still mostly evangelical, theologically and spiritually, and (b) there are reasons that their part of their Anabaptist/Reformed/Methodist tradition chose to ally themselves within evangelicalism. In other words, this type is perhaps overly optimistic or naive about modernist/liberal expressions of their tradition.

1.3 The irresistibly hungover type. People of this type, often young evangelical millennials, were formed and energized by the progressive evangelical theology of people like N. T. Wright and the progressive social ethics of people like Shane Claiborne. Theologically and spiritually, they are basically evangelical. Politically and socially, however, as far as east is from the west, so far is their politics and ethics from evangelicalism, and especially the religious right. They were once inebriated with the idea of an evangelical left of some sort, but with the election of Donald Trump they are mainly filled with headaches and constant nausea.

2. Still Christians

Folks in this group are still Christians but have moved so far away from evangelicalism—theologically, spiritually, and culturally—that they are no longer evangelicals either in how they identify themselves or in how we can identify them.

2.1 The high-church type. This type consists of folks who have converted to Roman Catholicism, Eastern Orthodoxy, or some form of high-church Anglicanism. They are attracted by the orthodoxy without anti-intellectualism and the deep spirituality without kitschy emotionalism.

2.2 The liberal Protestant type. People in this type are still Christian and have joined a mainline Protestant group. They have become broadly tolerant theologically—both of their own beliefs and of the beliefs of other Christians, to the point of accepting beliefs once considered heretical or perhaps un-Christian. They themselves might hold traditional Christian beliefs on some subjects but feel no qualms about members or leaders of their community who have a low Christology or even border on agnosticism or atheism.

2.3 The exiles. While still Christian, they are substantially no longer evangelical, but for ethical and theological reasons rooted in their evangelicalism do not feel they can either be high church or liberal Protestant with integrity. They likely feel stuck and confused.

3. Still People

These folks have left Christianity entirely and have a range of thoughts and feelings toward both Christianity and evangelicalism.

3.1 The Jesus-rocks type. This group of people have joined another faith or have become self-identifying agnostics or atheists. However, they still identify with the person of Jesus and celebrate him as someone who inspires them and had a good message for the world.

3.2 The no-looking-back type. This group have joined another faith or have become self-identifying agnostics or atheists. They aren't looking back and don't much consider their evangelical or Christian background.

3.3 The traumatized type. These people have various affiliations religiously; some may even still go to church of some kind. What they have in common is that their experience within evangelicalism has traumatized them, and they experience legitimate mental health symptoms because of their experience in evangelical churches. Their needs must be acknowledged, respected, and understood by the other types, no matter their affiliations. Whatever post-evangelicals do, as individuals and as a group, they must take this trauma into account in what they decide.

Notes

Introduction

1. I am placing the term "evangelical" in quotation marks this first time because everything about it is contested, including whether it describes anything real. I will enter into that conversation in chap. 1.
2. Pew Research Center, "America's Changing Religious Landscape," May 12, 2015, https://www.pewforum.org/2015/05/12/americas-changing-religious-landscape/.
3. Daniel Cox, "Are White Evangelicals Sacrificing the Future in Search of the Past?" FiveThirtyEight, January 24, 2018, https://fivethirtyeight.com/features/are-white-evangelicals-sacrificing-the-future-in-search-of-the-past/.
4. "Dissident" is the term I will use for those who still claim the evangelical identity/community but critique it vigorously, while "post-evangelicals" are those who have definitely left; for some individuals the situation is ambiguous.
5. Michael Gerson, "Why White Evangelicals Should Panic," *Washington Post*, August 29, 2019, https://www.washingtonpost.com/opinions/evangelical-leaders-are-tidying-the-kitchen-while-the-house-burns-down/2019/08/29/49d09a14-ca95-11e9-a4f3-c081a126de70_story.html.
6. "In Pew Research Center telephone surveys conducted in 2018 and 2019, 65% of American adults describe themselves as Christians . . . , down 12 percentage points over the past decade. Meanwhile, the religiously unaffiliated share of the population, consisting of people who describe their religious identity as atheist, agnostic or 'nothing in particular,' now stands at 26%, up from 17% in 2009." Pew Research Center, "In U.S., Decline of Christianity Continues at Rapid Pace," October 17, 2019, https://www.pewforum.org/wp-content/uploads/sites/7/2019/10/Trends-in-Religious-Identity-and-Attendance-FOR-WEB-1.pdf, 3.
7. "Only about one-in-three Millennials say they attend religious services at least once or twice a month. Roughly two-thirds of Millennials (64%) attend worship services a few times a year or less often, including about four-in-ten who say they seldom or never go. Indeed, there are as many Millennials who say they 'never' attend religious services (22%) as there are who say they go at least once a week (22%)." Pew Research Center, 8.

8. From Public Religion Research Institute: "The reasons Americans leave their childhood religion are varied, but a lack of belief in teaching of religion was the most commonly cited reason for disaffiliation. Among the reasons Americans identified as important motivations in leaving their childhood religion are: they stopped believing in the religion's teachings (60%), their family was never that religious when they were growing up (32%), and their experience of negative religious teachings about or treatment of gay and lesbian people (29%). Fewer than one in five Americans who left their childhood religion point to the clergy sexual-abuse scandal (19%), a traumatic event in their life (18%), or their congregation becoming too focused on politics (16%) as an important reason for disaffiliating. Among those who left their childhood religion, women are twice as likely as men to say negative religious teachings about or treatment of gay and lesbian individuals was a major reason they chose to leave their religion (40% vs. 20%, respectively). Women are also about twice as likely as men to cite the clergy sexual-abuse scandal as an important reason they left their childhood faith (26% vs. 13%, respectively)." Robert P. Jones, Daniel Cox, Betsy Cooper, and Rachel Lienesch, "Exodus: Why Americans Are Leaving Religion—and Why They're Unlikely to Come Back," PRRI, September 22, 2016, http://www.prri.org/research/prri-rns-poll-nones-atheist-leaving-religion/, 6.
9. David P. Gushee, *Still Christian: Following Jesus Out of American Evangelicalism* (Louisville, KY: Westminster John Knox Press, 2017).
10. David P. Gushee, *The Righteous Gentiles of the Holocaust: A Christian Interpretation* (Minneapolis: Fortress Press, 1994).
11. See Ronald J. Sider, ed., *The Chicago Declaration* (Carol Stream, IL: Creation House, 1974); Sider, *Rich Christians in an Age of Hunger: A Biblical Study* (New York: Paulist Press, 1977); Sider and Richard K. Taylor, *Nuclear Holocaust and Christian Hope: A Book for Christian Peacemakers* (New York: Paulist Press, 1982); Sider, *The Scandal of Evangelical Politics: Why Are Christians Missing the Chance to Really Change the World?* (Grand Rapids: Baker Books, 2008).
12. Founded in the mid-1970s in South Barrington, IL, by Bill Hybels, Willow Creek Community Church became one of the largest and most influential megachurches in the late-twentieth-century US evangelical world. In 1992, Hybels founded the Willow Creek Association, which eventually grew to include a membership of more than eleven thousand churches. In April 2018, in the wake of articles reporting that former church members and staff had come forward with accusations against him of sexual harassment and misconduct that spanned decades, Hybels "accelerated" his planned October retirement and stepped down as senior pastor of the church that he founded more than forty years earlier. Lyman A. Kellstedt and John C. Green, "Willow Creek Association," in *Pulpit and Politics: Clergy in American Politics at the Advent of the Millennium*, ed. Corwin Smidt (Waco, TX: Baylor University Press, 2004), 285–97; Manya Brachear Pashman and Jeff Coen, "After Years of Inquiries, Willow Creek Pastor Denies Misconduct Allegations," *Chicago Tribune*, March 23, 2018, https://www.chicagotribune.com/news/breaking/ct-met-willow-creek-pastor-20171220-story.html; Bob Smietana, "Bill Hybels Resigns from Willow Creek," *Christianity Today*, April 10, 2018, https://www.christianitytoday.com/news/2018/april/bill-hybels-resigns-willow-creek-misconduct-allegations.html; Laurie Goodstein, "How the Willow Creek Church Scandal Has Stunned the Evangelical World," *New York Times*,

August 9, 2018, https://www.nytimes.com/2018/08/09/us/evangelicals-willow-creek-scandal.html.

13. David P. Gushee, "Five Reasons Torture Is Always Wrong," *Christianity Today*, February 2006, 33–37; Gushee, "What the Torture Debate Reveals about American Evangelical Christianity," *Journal of the Society of Christian Ethics* 30, no. 1 (Spring–Summer 2010): 79–97; Gushee, Jillian Hickman Zimmer, and J. Drew Zimmer, eds., *Religious Faith, Torture, and Our National Soul* (Macon, GA: Mercer University Press, 2010); Gushee, "Faith, Science, and Climate Change," in *In the Fray: Contesting Christian Public Ethics, 1994–2013* (Eugene, OR: Cascade Books, 2014), 127–40.
14. David P. Gushee, *Changing Our Mind* (Canton, MI: Read the Spirit Books, 2014).
15. As a professional organization for religious scholars and scholars of religion, the mission of the American Academy of Religion (AAR) "is to foster excellence in the academic study of religion and enhance the public understanding of religion." As explained in its mission statement, "the Academy welcomes all disciplined reflection on religion—both from within and outside of communities of belief and practice—and seeks to enhance its broad public understanding." American Academy of Religion, "Mission Statement," accessed September 7, 2019, https://www.aarweb.org/about#MissionPurposeValues.
16. "AAR Presidential Address: David Gushee, In the Ruins of White Evangelicalism," 2018 Annual Meeting of the American Academy of Religion, November 17, 2018, https://www.youtube.com/watch?v=KPkl-sBFzdQ&t=7s.
17. Tony Jones, *The New Christians: Dispatches from the Emergent Frontier* (San Francisco: Jossey-Bass, 2008); Doug Pagitt, *A Christianity Worth Believing* (San Francisco: Jossey-Bass, 2008); Ray S. Anderson, *An Emergent Theology for Emerging Churches* (Downers Grove, IL: IVP Books, 2006); Brian D. McLaren, *A New Kind of Christianity: Ten Questions That Are Transforming the Faith* (New York: HarperOne, 2010).
18. Rob Bell, *Love Wins* (New York: HarperOne, 2012); Nadia Bolz-Weber, *Pastrix* (New York: Jericho Books, 2014); David Dark, *The Sacredness of Questioning Everything* (Grand Rapids: Zondervan, 2009); Jennifer Crumpton, *Femmevangelical* (St. Louis: Chalice Press, 2015); Deborah Jian Lee, *Rescuing Jesus* (Boston: Beacon Press, 2015); Peter Rollins, *The Orthodox Heretic* (Brewster, MA: Paraclete Press, 2010); Rachel Held Evans, *Faith Unraveled* (Grand Rapids: Zondervan, 2010). Many other books by these authors, and other authors, could be named.
19. Evolving Faith Conference, https://www.evolvingfaithconference.com/home; Liberating Evangelicalism Conference, http://liberatingevangelicalism.org/speakers/.
20. "Liberation theology" generally describes those theologians who argue that the mission of God in the world, and therefore of the church, is the liberation of this world's most oppressed people. "Womanist theology" is the term given to a movement led by black women theologians, based on a term ("womanism") introduced by novelist Alice Walker. For specific authors, see especially chap. 9 in this volume.
21. Keith Mascord, *A Restless Faith: Leaving Fundamentalism in a Quest for God* (2012; repr., Eugene, OR: Wipf & Stock, 2016); *Faith without Fear: Risky Choices Facing Contemporary Christians* (Eugene, OR: Wipf & Stock, 2016).
22. A short CBS documentary on the exvangelical movement is available at https://

www.cbs.com/shows/cbs-news-specials/video/jBSOpwEP1_gFcxYqGIU_0PjxUqETIpGN/deconstructing-my-religion/; Blake Chastain podcast, https://exvangelicalpodcast.com/; Becca Andrews, "As a Teen, Emily Joy Was Abused by a Church Youth Leader; Now She's Leading a Movement to Change Evangelical America," *Mother Jones*, May 25, 2018, https://www.motherjones.com/crime-justice/2018/05/evangelical-church-metoo-movement-abuse/; Emily Joy blog, http://emilyjoypoetry.com/churchtoo; Bradley Onishi, "The Rise of #Exvangelical," Religion and Politics, April 9, 2019, https://religionandpolitics.org/2019/04/09/the-rise-of-exvangelical/, and "The 'Exvangelical' Movement Will Continue to Grow," Religion News Service, December 20, 2018, https://religionnews.com/2018/12/20/bradley-onishi-the-exvangelical-movement-will-continue-to-grow/; Chrissy Stroop website, https://cstroop.com/about/.

Chapter 1: Evangelicalism

1. For my earlier attempts to grapple with evangelicalism: David P. Gushee, *The Future of Faith in American Politics: The Public Witness of the Evangelical Center* (Waco, TX: Baylor University Press, 2008), 16–21; Gushee, ed., *A New Evangelical Manifesto: A Kingdom Vision for the Common Good* (St. Louis: Chalice Press, 2012), ix–xiii; Gushee and Isaac B. Sharp, eds., *Evangelical Ethics: A Reader* (Louisville, KY: Westminster John Knox Press, 2015), xv–xix; Gushee, *Still Christian: Following Jesus Out of American Evangelicalism* (Louisville, KY: Westminster John Knox Press, 2017), 52–55.
2. Intersubjectivity means a shared agreement between people on a given set of meanings or definition of a situation.
3. Alister McGrath, *Evangelicalism and the Future of Christianity* (Downers Grove, IL: InterVarsity Press, 1995), 19–23. McGrath spots uses beginning in the late fifteenth century, and traces its use in German, French, and English languages. An interesting recent study of the uses of the word is offered by Linford D. Fisher, "Evangelicals and Unevangelicals: The Contested History of a Word," in *Evangelicals: Who They Have Been, Are Now, and Could Be*, ed. Mark A. Noll, David W. Bebbington, and George M. Marsden (Grand Rapids: Wm. B. Eerdmans Publishing Co., 2019), chap. 7. Fisher discerns three main historical stages in the use of the word: (1) evangelical as anti-Catholic, (2) evangelical as true, primitive, or active faith, and (3) evangelical as the name for the reformist fundamentalist movement to be discussed in this section.
4. Mark A. Noll, "What Is 'Evangelical'?" in *The Oxford Handbook of Evangelical Theology*, ed. Gerald R. McDermott (New York: Oxford University Press, 2010), 19–34; Heinrich de Wall, "Evangelical," in *Religion Past and Present: Encyclopedia of Theology and Religion*, ed. Hans Dieter Betz et al. (Brill, 2011), accessed September 8, 2019, http://dx.doi.org/10.1163/1877-5888_rpp_SIM_04792; Lukas Vischer, "Evangelical," in *Encyclopedia of Christianity Online*, ed. Erwin Fahlbusch et al. (Brill, 2011), accessed September 8, 2019, http://dx.doi.org/10.1163/2211-2685_eco_E561.
5. D. G. Hart, in *Deconstructing Evangelicalism* (Grand Rapids: Baker Academic, 2004), says, "This book is about the way neo-evangelicals built the evangelical edifice and how academics have maintained the façade of the building commonly known as conservative Protestantism. . . . The first part of the book examines the scholarly construction of evangelicalism during the last twenty-five years, with chapters on religious history, social scientific studies of religion, and students of public opinion" (28–29). Chapter 1, "Religious History Born Again," 35–61, traces the way in which historians did this. Chapter 2,

"Evangelicalism and the Revival of Social Science," 63–84, traces the way in which sociologists like James Davison Hunter did this. Chapter 3, "Measuring Evangelicalism One Question at a Time," 85–106, traces the way in which pollsters did this.

On the pivotal role of pollsters, see also Robert Wuthnow, *Inventing American Religion: Polls, Surveys, and the Tenuous Quest for a Nation's Faith* (New York: Oxford University Press, 2015), 95–128.

6. Scottish historian David W. Bebbington argues:

Evangelical religion is a popular Protestant movement that has existed in Britain since the 1730s. It is not to be equated with any single Christian denomination, for it influenced the existing churches during the eighteenth century and generated many more in subsequent years. It has found expression in a variety of institutional forms, a wine that has been poured into many bottles. Historians regularly apply the term "evangelical" to the churches arising from the Reformation in the sixteenth and seventeenth centuries. The usage of the period justifies them. . . . Although "evangelical," with a lower-case initial, is occasionally used to mean "of the gospel," the term "Evangelical," with a capital letter, is applied to any aspect of the movement beginning in the 1730s. There was much continuity with earlier Protestant traditions, but . . . Evangelicalism was a new phenomenon of the eighteenth century. (*Evangelicalism in Modern Britain: A History from the 1730s to the 1980s* [London: Unwin Hyman, 1989], 1)

George M. Marsden writes:

"Evangelical" (from the Greek for "gospel") eventually became the common British and American name for the revival movements that swept back and forth across the English-speaking world and elsewhere during the eighteenth and nineteenth centuries. . . .

Being a style as well as a set of Protestant beliefs about the Bible and Christ's work, evangelicalism touched virtually all American denominations. These denominations, such as the Methodists, Baptists, Presbyterians, Congregationalists, Disciples of Christ, and others, had much to do with shaping American culture in the nineteenth century. . . .

Especially in its nineteenth-century heyday, then, evangelicalism was a very broad coalition, made up of many sub-groups. Though from differing denominations, these people were united with each other, and with persons from other nations in their zeal to win the world for Christ. (*Understanding Fundamentalism and Evangelicalism* [Grand Rapids: Wm. B. Eerdmans Publishing Co., 1991], 2–3)

Later in the book, Marsden suggests that "certainly one of the most remarkable developments in American religion since 1930 has been the reemergence of evangelicalism as a force in religious life" (63).

Mark A. Noll writes:

The specific sense of the term *evangelical* as used in this book . . . comes not out of continental Europe but from eighteenth-century Britain. It is a usage designating a set of convictions, practice, habits and oppositions that resemble what Europeans describe as "pietism." . . . The Continental pietist movements played a significant role in the beginning of evangelical movements in Britain, and the main themes of pietism anticipated the main themes of evangelicalism.

During the middle third of the eighteenth century, a similar series of interconnected renewal movements arose in England, Wales, Scotland, Ireland, and Britain's North American colonies. . . .

Two complementary perspectives are useful for defining the evangelical history that began with these revivals. On the one hand, evangelicalism was constituted by the individuals, associations, books, practices, perceptions and networks of influence shared by the promoters of the eighteenth-century revivals and their descendants. . . . Regarded from this angle, a history of evangelicalism is an effort to trace out an ever-expanding, ever-diversifying family tree with roots in the eighteenth-century revivals.

Yet evangelicalism was always also constituted by the convictions that emerged in those revivals and that drove its adherents in their lives as Christians. In this sense, evangelicalism designates a consistent pattern of convictions and attitudes that have been maintained over the centuries since the 1730s. (*The Rise of Evangelicalism: The Age of Edwards, Whitefield and the Wesleys* [Downers Grove, IL: IVP Academic, 2003], 17–19)

7. Gary Dorrien, *The Remaking of Evangelical Theology* (Louisville, KY: Westminster John Knox Press, 1998), 4. This book remains an extremely valuable theological assessment of evangelicalism from someone who does not identity as an evangelical.
8. The same people called themselves, or were called, variously, in stages, "fundamentalist," "neo-fundamentalist," "neo-evangelical," and then finally "evangelical," the term that stuck. That linguistic development is fascinating.
9. The National Council of Churches, "Member Communions," accessed September 7, 2019, http://nationalcouncilofchurches.us/member-communions/.
10. A study by the Pew Research Center in 2014 found that "14.7% of U.S. adults are affiliated with the mainline Protestant tradition—a sharp decline from 18.1% in 2007 . . . Despite overall U.S. population growth between 2007 and 2014, the total number of mainline Protestant adults has decreased by roughly 5 million during that time (from about 41 million in 2007 to 36 million in 2014)." Michael Lipka, "Mainline Protestants Make Up Shrinking Number of U.S. Adults," Pew Research Center, May 18, 2015, https://www.pewresearch.org/fact-tank/2015/05/18/mainline-protestants-make-up-shrinking-number-of-u-s-adults/.

From Public Religion Research Institute: "White mainline Protestants also experienced significant losses . . . dropping from 18% in 2006 to 13% in 2016." Robert P. Jones and Daniel Cox, "America's Changing Religious Identity: Findings from the 2016 American Values Atlas," PRRI, 2017, https://www.prri.org/wp-content/uploads/2017/09/PRRI-Religion-Report.pdf, 20.

Elsewhere, based in part on the General Social Survey, Robert P. Jones takes the data back to 1988, noting that mainline Protestants dropped "from 24 percent of the population in 1988 to 14 percent in 2012, at which time their numbers stabilized." Jones, "The Eclipse of White Christian America," *Atlantic*, July 12, 2016, https://www.theatlantic.com/politics/archive/2016/07/the-eclipse-of-white-christian-america/490724/.

Robert Wuthnow and John H. Evans put the membership of the six largest mainline denominations—the United Methodist Church, Evangelical Lutheran Church in America, Presbyterian Church (U.S.A.), Episcopal Church, American Baptists, and United Church of Christ—at 22 million in 2002, noting that the "members of these denominations make up the vast majority of American mainline Protestants." Introduction to *The Quiet Hand of God: Faith-Based Activism and the Public Role of Mainline Protestantism*, ed. Robert Wuthnow and John H. Evans (Berkeley: University of California Press,

2002), 4. Based on the "inclusive membership" of these six denominations, they count 21,295,819 mainline Protestants in 1947 and 21,737,146 in 1998. Their percentage of the total population obviously declined over time.

11. Kevin Kruse, *One Nation Under God: How Corporate America Invented Christian America* (New York: Basic Books, 2016); Lydia Bean, *The Politics of Evangelical Identity: Local Churches and Partisan Divides in the United States and Canada* (Princeton, NJ: Princeton University Press, 2016); Alison Greene, *No Depression in Heaven: The Great Depression, the New Deal, and the Transformation of Religion in the Delta* (Oxford: Oxford University Press, 2015).

    In his classic work *Righteous Empire* (New York: Dial Press, 1970), 177–87, Martin Marty suggests that the origin of the fundamentalist-modernist controversy was the emergence of a "two-party" split in late-nineteenth-century Protestantism that he calls "private" and "public" Christianities. The private party was focused on personal conversion and soul-saving. The public party was about addressing social problems using all relevant modern means. The private party evolved into fundamentalism, the public party into mainline Protestantism. The orientation of the underlying theologies tended to Pauline/atonement or Jesus/kingdom of God. This split has never really ended. The evangelicals hoped to resolve it but failed.

12. Dispensational premillennialists read the Bible and history to teach that God relates to the world through a series of seven distinct ages, or dispensations. We live in the penultimate of these ages, the church age. The last stage involves a seven-year tribulation, the return of Christ, and his establishment of a thousand-year kingdom ruled from Jerusalem. This movement is pessimistic, deterministic, ahistorical or mytho-historical, conspiratorial, and apocalyptic. This novel and, in my view, disastrous theology became an enormously important part of fundamentalism and later evangelicalism, with effects to this day.

    Inerrancy essentially means that the Bible is completely without error in any of its content. See chap. 2 for extended discussion.

13. A classic earlier study is George M. Marsden, *Fundamentalism and American Culture: The Shaping of Twentieth-Century Evangelicalism* (New York: Oxford University Press, 1980). See, more recently, Timothy E. W. Gloege, *Guaranteed Pure: The Moody Bible Institute, Business, and the Making of Modern Evangelicalism* (Chapel Hill: University of North Carolina Press, 2015).
14. Joel A. Carpenter, *Revive Us Again: The Reawakening of American Fundamentalism* (New York: Oxford University Press, 1997), chaps. 1–7.
15. George M. Marsden, *Reforming Fundamentalism: Fuller Seminary and the New Evangelicalism* (Grand Rapids: Wm. B. Eerdmans Publishing Co., 1987).
16. Marsden, 10.
17. Jon R. Stone, *On the Boundaries of American Evangelicalism: The Postwar Evangelical Coalition* (New York: St. Martin's Press, 1997), 20.
18. Donald W. Dayton, *Discovering an Evangelical Heritage* (New York: Harper & Row, 1976), 128–29, 133–34.
19. Robert Jewett, *Mission and Menace* (Minneapolis: Fortress Press, 2008), 259.
20. Hart, *Deconstructing Evangelicalism*, 24.
21. Carpenter, *Revive Us Again*, 155.
22. Formed in 1942, the National Association of Evangelicals (NAE) currently claims that it represents "more than 45,000 local churches from 40 different denominations and serves a constituency of millions," https://www.nae

.net/about-nae/, accessed November 2, 2019. For an early court history of the NAE, see James DeForest Murch, *Cooperation without Compromise: A History of the National Association of Evangelicals* (Grand Rapids: Wm. B. Eerdmans Publishing Co., 1956).

Envisioned by Billy Graham as an alternative to the more liberal *Christian Century*, *Christianity Today* was founded in 1956 under the editorship of Carl F. H. Henry. See "Our History," https://www.christianitytoday.org/who-we-are/our-history/, accessed November 2, 2019. For further discussion of the background and founding of *Christianity Today*, see Marsden, *Reforming Fundamentalism*, 157–71.

Founded in 1947 by the immensely popular radio evangelist Charles Fuller—with the help of a founding faculty that represented a veritable who's who of midcentury evangelicalism—Fuller Theological Seminary became widely regarded as twentieth-century evangelicalism's flagship nondenominational seminary. With more than 3,500 students, Fuller currently claims to be "the largest multidenominational seminary in the world," in "Our History," https://www.fuller.edu/our-history/, accessed November 2, 2019. For more on the history of Fuller Seminary and its role as the bellwether of neo-evangelicalism, see Marsden, *Reforming Fundamentalism*.

Currently representing more than 180 institutions around the world, the Council for Christian Colleges and Universities (CCCU) was founded in 1976 as "a broad association of Christian colleges that would support promotion and leadership activities for member schools and provide a unifying voice for Christian higher education in the public square," https://www.cccu.org/about/, accessed November 2, 2019.

By Francis A. Schaeffer: *Death in the City* (Chicago: InterVarsity Press, 1969); *He Is There and He Is Not Silent* (Wheaton, IL: Tyndale House Publishers, 1972); *How Should We Then Live?* (Westchester, IL: Crossway Books, 1976); Schaeffer and C. Everett Koop, *Whatever Happened to the Human Race?* (Old Tappan, NJ: F. H. Revell Co., 1979).

By Carl F. H. Henry: *The Uneasy Conscience of Modern Fundamentalism* (Grand Rapids: Wm. B. Eerdmans Publishing Co., 1947); *Remaking the Modern Mind* (Grand Rapids: Wm. B. Eerdmans Publishing Co., 1948); *Frontiers in Modern Theology* (Chicago: Moody Press, 1964); *Evangelicals in Search of Identity* (Waco, TX: Word Books, 1976).

Attempts at a consensus evangelical theology: J. I. Packer and Thomas C. Oden, *One Faith: The Evangelical Consensus* (Downers Grove, IL: InterVarsity Press, 2004); Kenneth S. Kantzer and Carl F. H. Henry, eds., *Evangelical Affirmations* (Grand Rapids: Zondervan, 1990).

23. The idea of evangelicalism as a culture of consumption is central to the project of Calvin College history professor Kristin Kobes Du Mez; see "There Are No Real Evangelicals; Only Imagined Ones," Religion News Service, February 6, 2019, https://religionnews.com/2019/02/06/there-are-no-real-evangelicals-only-imagined-ones/.
24. Christian Smith, *American Evangelicalism: Embattled and Thriving* (Chicago: University of Chicago Press, 1998), 14–15 (italics in the original).
25. Dayton, *Discovering an Evangelical Heritage*, 134–35.
26. Dayton, 128–34.
27. Donald W. Dayton and Robert K. Johnston, eds., *The Variety of American Evangelicalism* (Downers Grove, IL: InterVarsity Press, 1991), 251. See also

Dayton, "Holiness Churches: A Significant Ethical Tradition," *Christian Century* 92, no. 7 (February 26, 1975): 197–201; Dayton, "Whither Evangelicalism?," in *Sanctification and Liberation: Liberation Theologies in Light of the Wesleyan Tradition*, ed. Theodore Runyon (Nashville: Abingdon Press, 1981), 142–63; Dayton, "An Autobiographical Response," in *From the Margins: A Celebration of the Theological Work of Donald W. Dayton*, ed. Christian T. Collins Winn (Eugene, OR: Pickwick Publications, 2007), 383–426; Dayton and Douglas M. Strong, *Rediscovering an Evangelical Heritage*, 2nd ed. (Grand Rapids: Baker Academic, 2014).

28. Hart, *Deconstructing Evangelicalism*, 32, 10.
29. Bebbington, *Evangelicalism in Modern Britain*, 2–17; Marsden, *Understanding Fundamentalism and Evangelicalism*, 4–5; Timothy P. Weber, "Premillenialism and the Branches of Evangelicalism," in *Variety of American Evangelicalism*, 5–21.
30. Todd M. Brennaman, *Homespun Gospel* (New York: Oxford, 2014), examines the sentimental version of evangelical Christianity in the work of Max Lucado, Joel Osteen, and Rick Warren. His groundbreaking study reminds us that what passes for evangelical Christianity now varies dramatically, and that the doctrinaire neo-fundamentalism of Carl Henry and the like has little to do with the sentimental aesthetic offered in much populist evangelical Christianity.
31. Molly Worthen, *Apostles of Reason: The Crisis of Authority in American Evangelicalism* (New York: Oxford University Press, 2014).
32. A thorough recent treatment of the politics of white evangelicalism is found in Frances Fitzgerald, *The Evangelicals: The Struggle to Shape America* (New York: Simon & Schuster, 2017). Fitzgerald, a nonevangelical and a journalist, perhaps succumbs to reducing evangelicalism to its politics. But evangelicalism has earned that misreading to a very large extent.
33. Dayton describes it poignantly from his perspective as an evangelical student in the 1960s in *Discovering an Evangelical Heritage*, 1–6. He also illustrates the political conservativism of Charles Hodge and the Old School Presbyterians, forerunners of the new evangelicals of the 1940s, and thus of modern American evangelicalism (128–35).
34. Justin Randall Phillips, "Lord, When Did We See You? The Ethical Vision of White, Progressive Baptists in the South during the Civil Rights Movement" (PhD diss., Fuller Theological Seminary, 2013).
35. Daniel Burke, "Franklin Graham Wants the Nation to Pray for Trump on Sunday; but Other Christians Call It Propaganda," CNN, May 31, 2019, https://www.cnn.com/2019/05/30/us/franklin-graham-trump-day-of-prayer/index.html; Eliza Griswold, "Franklin Graham's Uneasy Alliance with Donald Trump," *New Yorker*, September 11, 2018, https://www.newyorker.com/news/dispatch/franklin-grahams-uneasy-alliance-with-donald-trump; Maggie Haberman, "Donald Trump Receives Backing from Jerry Falwell Jr.," *New York Times*, January 26, 2016, https://www.nytimes.com/politics/first-draft/2016/01/26/donald-trump-receives-backing-from-jerry-falwell-jr/; Joe Heim, "Jerry Falwell Jr. Can't Imagine Trump 'Doing Anything That's Not Good for the Country': The University President on Why Support from Evangelical Leaders for Trump Is Unbreakable," *Washington Post*, December 21, 2018, https://www.washingtonpost.com/lifestyle/magazine/jerry-falwell-jr-cant-imagine-trump-doing-anything-thats-not-good-for-the-country/2018/12/21/6affc4c4-f19e-11e8-80d0-f7e1948d55f4_story.

36. Two recent books sympathetic to evangelicalism have focused considerable attention on this problem. See Thomas S. Kidd, *Who Is an Evangelical? The History of a Movement in Crisis* (New Haven, CT: Yale University Press, 2019), as well as Noll, Bebbington, and Marsden, *Evangelicals*, chaps. 12–16.
37. Isaac B. Sharp, "The *Other* Evangelicals: The Marginalization of Liberal-Modernist, Barthian, Black, Feminist, Progressive, Arminian-Wesleyan-Pietist, and Gay Evangelicals and the Shaping of 20th Century U.S. American Evangelicalism" (PhD diss., Union Theological Seminary, 2019).
38. Sharp, 57.
39. David Hempton, *Evangelical Disenchantment: Nine Portraits of Faith and Doubt* (New Haven, CT: Yale University Press, 2008). Hempton's study assumes an evangelical tradition that goes back centuries. But it is striking that he traces evangelicalism's beginnings only to the eighteenth-century Anglo-American revivals (4).
40. Dorrien, *Remaking of Evangelical Theology*, 9.
41. Ibn 'Arabi, "Poem from the Diwān Written upon the Death of One of His Daughters," trans. Ralph Austin, Muhyiddin Ibn 'Arabi Society, http://www.ibnarabisociety.org/articles/poemsfromdiwan.html.
42. Jacob Alan Cook, "Evangelicals and Identity Politics: Reconsidering the World-Viewing Impulse" (PhD diss., Fuller Theological Seminary, 2018). This is another brilliant dissertation by one of my students, forthcoming from Fortress Press.
43. Sharp, "The *Other* Evangelicals," 60.

Chapter 2: Scripture

1. Peter Enns, *The Bible Tells Me So* (New York: HarperOne, 2014), and *How the Bible Actually Works* (New York: HarperOne, 2019); Christian Smith, *The Bible Made Impossible* (Grand Rapids: Brazos, 2011); Brian D. McLaren, *A New Kind of Christianity: Ten Questions That Are Transforming the Faith* (New York: HarperOne, 2010); Rob Bell, *What Is the Bible?* (New York: HarperOne, 2017); Emily Swan and Ken Wilson, *Solus Jesus: A Theology of Resistance* (Canton, MI: Read the Spirit Books, 2018), chaps. 1–3; Rachel Held Evans, *Inspired* (Nashville: Thomas Nelson, 2018).
2. Smith, *Bible Made Impossible*, viii. "Perspicuity" means clarity, plainness, intelligibility. For more detail, see Smith, 3–16.
3. For the text of the famous Chicago Statement on Biblical Inerrancy (1978), go to https://www.moodybible.org/beliefs/the-chicago-statement-on-biblical-inerrancy/.

   For a helpful introductory discussion of various theories of biblical inspiration, including uses of the terms "inerrancy" and "infallibility," see Don Thorsen and Keith H. Reeves, *What Christians Believe about the Bible: A Concise Guide for Students* (Grand Rapids: Baker Academic, 2012).
4. As noted in Isaac B. Sharp's discussion of Karl Barth's theology in "The *Other* Evangelicals: The Marginalization of Liberal-Modernist, Barthian, Black, Feminist, Progressive, Arminian-Wesleyan-Pietist, and Gay Evangelicals and the Shaping of 20th Century U.S. American Evangelicalism" (PhD diss., Union Theological Seminary, 2019).
5. For a fair and careful overview from an evangelical perspective, see Thorsen and Reeves, *What Christians Believe*, chap. 7.
6. C. S. Lewis, *Reflections on the Psalms* (London: Geoffrey Bles, 1958), 111–12.

7. Enns, *Bible Tells Me So*, 63: "The Bible looks the way it does because 'God lets his children tell the story,' so to speak."
8. Bell, *What is the Bible?*, 19.
9. Enns, *Bible Tells Me So*, 4.
10. Conservative evangelical David Dockery, in *Biblical Interpretation Then and Now: Contemporary Hermeneutics in the Light of the Early Church* (Grand Rapids: Baker Books, 1992), finds that early church figures agreed on the divine inspiration of Scripture, with a minority of voices also emphasizing the human role in biblical composition. No concept of inerrancy is mentioned in the book.
11. "The concept of biblical inerrancy first appeared among Protestant writers in the *late 17th century* to combat Roman Catholic appeals to tradition and the authority of the church. Spokesmen for the Protestant Reformation stressed both the self-sufficiency of the Scripture in interpreting itself and the essential accuracy of its text." Gardiner H. Shattuck Jr., "Inerrancy," in *Encyclopedia of American Religious History*, ed. Edward L. Queen, Stephen R. Prothero II, and Gardiner H. Shattuck Jr., 4th ed. (New York: Facts On File, 2018; italics added).
12. "The first of these conservative voices was Swiss Free Church professor Louis Gaussen (1790–1863), who *in 1840 published a defense of traditional biblical authority*: *Theopneustia: The Plenary Inspiration of the Holy Scriptures*. The book found an appreciative readership, especially at Princeton Theological Seminary, where it inspired several landmark books. In the 1880s, Princetonians A. A. Hodge (1823–86) and Benjamin B. Warfield (1851–1921) published *Inspiration*, which was followed in 1888 by Baptist Basil Manly Jr.'s volume *The Bible Doctrine of Inspiration* (1888)." J. Gordon Melton, "Inerrancy," in *Encyclopedia of Protestantism*, Encyclopedia of World Religions, 2nd ed. (New York: Facts On File, 2016; italics added).
13. D. G. Hart reviews thoroughly the historical debate about inerrancy in *Deconstructing Evangelicalism* (Grand Rapids: Baker Academic, 2004), 131–51.
14. Jaroslav Pelikan, *Whose Bible Is It? A History of the Scriptures through the Ages* (New York: Viking, 2005), chap. 1, provides a very helpful extended discussion of the oral roots and character of biblical texts.
15. Thorsen and Reeves, *What Christians Believe*, 132–34.
16. The book of Proverbs routinely says that the good are rewarded and the wicked punished in this life. God has established a moral structure that works itself out in human lives and history in this way. The book of Job centers on the great suffering of an innocent man. His friends respond with theological interpretations of Job's suffering that track with what we find in Proverbs. Job (the character and the book) rejects these interpretations. Indeed, the whole book seems to be a challenge to the theology expressed in a work like Proverbs. See chap. 4 for more.
17. Smith, *Bible Made Impossible*, viii.
18. John Goldingay, *Models for Scripture* (Grand Rapids: Wm. B. Eerdmans Publishing Co., 1994), 278.
19. Evans, *Inspired*, xiii.
20. McLaren, *New Kind of Christianity*, 78–86; Enns, *Bible Tells Me So*, 46; Bell, *What Is the Bible?*, 21.
21. Smith, *Bible Made Impossible*, chaps. 1–2.
22. Dale B. Martin, *Biblical Truths: The Meaning of Scripture in the Twenty-First Century* (New Haven, CT: Yale University Press, 2017), 95.

23. There is a nice discussion on "Scottish commonsense realism" as background to evangelical biblicism in Smith, *Bible Made Impossible*, 55–60. The assumption that any reader can easily discern God's truth by reading the common or plain sense of Scripture was based on ideas current during a particularly optimistic moment in philosophy, ideas that made their way into the work of the Old School Princeton Seminary fundamentalists Hodge and Warfield and did not fit with their otherwise pessimistic Calvinism.
24. Mark A. Noll, *The Civil War as a Theological Crisis* (Chapel Hill: University of North Carolina Press, 2006), 31–50.
25. Swan and Wilson, *Solus Jesus*, chap. 2. This is a common observation offered in pretty much every account of Christian theology written by those who have been harmed by powerful people's interpretation of the Bible: liberationist, feminist, womanist, LGBTQ, etc. See chap. 9.
26. A major theme in R. W. L. Moberly, *The Bible in a Disenchanted Age: The Enduring Possibility of Christian Faith* (Grand Rapids: Baker Academic, 2018).
27. The Septuagint, completed in the third century BCE, is the earliest extant Greek translation of the Hebrew Bible. The translation of the Hebrew Bible into Greek reflected the power of Greek culture at that period. The existence of the Septuagint is hugely important for the development of Christianity; for one thing, it is quoted more often than the Hebrew Bible in the New Testament; which was, of course, also written in Greek.
28. Peter Enns argues: "For Christians, the gospel has always been the lens through which Israel's stories are read—which means, for Christians, Jesus, not the Bible, has the final word." *Bible Tells Me So*, 65.
29. "The Bible is indeed a collection of writings much like others from the ancient world. . . . Arguments made for Christian faith nowadays cannot rest merely on the intellectual or cultural plausibility of the Bible. . . . They must rest instead on the living witness of the Church." Michael C. Legaspi, "The Church's Book," *First Things*, December 2018, 51.
30. Robert Jenson, *Canon and Creed* (Louisville, KY: Westminster John Knox Press, 2010), 55.
31. Marc Zvi Brettler, "My Bible," in *The Bible and the Believer: How to Read the Bible Critically and Religiously*, by Marc Zvi Brettler, Peter Enns, and Daniel J. Harrington, SJ (New York: Oxford University Press, 2012), 56.
32. In academic conferences, the difficulty as to what to call the text appears to be insuperable. Tanakh and Old Testament are terms used by Jews and Christians, respectively, about the same text (more or less), but one that has very different theological meanings in the two faith traditions. Hebrew Bible seems the most appropriate generic term, but when we are talking about Christians and our Bible, that is also not quite right. Oh well.
33. "Diaspora" is the technical term used to describe the dispersion of Jewish people all over the ancient Near East, the Mediterranean basin, and beyond, beginning with the forced Babylonian exile after 587 BCE. As language development goes, the term is sometimes also used to describe the mass dispersion of other populations, even today.
34. Pelikan, *Whose Bible Is It?*, 5.
35. "Second only to the Hebrew Bible (Tanakh), the Talmud (Hebrew for "study" or "learning") is the most important sacred text in traditional Judaism. It is a vast, multivolume compilation of legal, ethical, and allegorical discussions and debates conducted by the ancient rabbis over a period of several hundred

years. As such, it is a historical record of the founding generations of rabbinic Judaism . . . and the basic source of Jewish law as still observed by Orthodox Jews." Sara E. Karesh and Mitchell M. Hurvitz, "Talmud," in *Encyclopedia of Judaism*, Encyclopedia of World Religions, 2nd ed. (New York: Facts On File, 2016; published in digital format only, no page numbers available).

36. Paul Mendes-Flohr, *Martin Buber: A Life of Faith and Dissent* (New Haven, CT: Yale University Press, 2019), 158.
37. Quoted in Ariel Burger, *Witness: Lessons from Elie Wiesel's Classroom* (Boston: Houghton Mifflin Harcourt, 2018), 96–97.
38. Published in 1992, the Revised Common Lectionary is used by many of the liturgically inclined Protestant churches. It is an updated version of the Common Lectionary, published in 1982 by the Consultation on Common Texts, which was based on the Roman Catholic Church's Lectionary for Mass (1969). The Consultation on Common Texts, formed in the mid-1960s, includes representatives of the Roman Catholic Church and many Protestant denominations of North America. Consultation on Common Texts, *The Revised Common Lectionary* (Nashville: Abingdon Press, 1992); "Lectionary," in *The Concise Oxford Dictionary of the Christian Church*, ed. E. A. Livingstone (New York: Oxford University Press, 2013), 330.
39. Felix Just, SJ, PhD, "Lectionary Statistics," http://catholic-resources.org/Lectionary/Statistics.htm, as referenced in Charles Grondin, "Percentage of the Bible in the Lectionary," Catholic Answers, https://www.catholic.com/qa/percentage-of-the-bible-in-the-lectionary.

Chapter 3: Resources

1. Dale C. Martin, *Biblical Truths: The Meaning of Scripture in the Twenty-First Century* (New Haven, CT: Yale University Press, 2017), 56.
2. McClendon uses these phrases to describe a radical baptist way of reading Scripture, and he sees this move, when grounded in the faith community, as a positive thing. "The baptist vision is the way the Bible is read by those who (1) accept the plain sense of Scripture as its dominant sense and recognize their continuity with the story it tells, and who (2) acknowledge that finding the point of that story leads them to its application, and who also (3) see past and present and future linked by a 'this is that' and 'then is now' vision, a trope of mystical identity binding the story now to the story then, and the story then and now to God's future yet to come." James William McClendon Jr., *Systematic Theology*, vol. 2, *Doctrine* (Nashville: Abingdon Press, 1994), 45. I use the phrases negatively here for reasons I am outlining.
3. The *Didache*, which means "Teaching," is a crisp, brief statement of Christian moral teaching, worship regulations, and church order. The ethics section is sublime, in my view. This text is dated by most scholars to the late first century CE, which probably would make it an even earlier text than 2 Peter.
4. Martin, *Biblical Truths*, 56.
5. D. H. Williams, *Evangelicals and Tradition: The Formative Influence of the Early Church* (Grand Rapids: Baker Academic, 2005), 10. This book is part of an Evangelical Ressourcement series, entirely focused on a return to the ancient sources.
6. Robert E. Webber, *Ancient-Future Faith: Rethinking Evangelicalism for a Postmodern World* (Grand Rapids: Baker Books, 1999).
7. Thomas C. Oden, *Requiem: A Lament in Three Movements* (Nashville: Abingdon

Press, 1995); Oden, *The Rebirth of Orthodoxy: Signs of New Life in Christianity* (New York: HarperCollins, 2003); Oden, ed., Ancient Christian Commentary on Scripture series (Downers Grove, IL: InterVarsity Press, 1998–2010).

8. David P. Gushee, *Changing Our Mind: A Call from America's Leading Evangelical Ethics Scholar for Full Acceptance of LGBTQ Christians in the Church* (Canton, MI: Read the Spirit Books, 2014).
9. David P. Gushee, "Christian Ethics: Retrospect and Prospect," *Journal of the Society of Christian Ethics* 38, no. 2 (2018): 3–20.
10. My formative exposure to this horrible strand of ancient Christian tradition was Rosemary Radford Ruether, *Faith and Fratricide: The Theological Roots of Anti-Semitism* (New York: Seabury Press, 1974). By now the sources on this issue are abundant.
11. Jonathan Haidt, *The Righteous Mind: Why Good People Are Divided by Politics and Religion* (New York: Pantheon Books, 2012).
12. See *Catechism of the Catholic Church*, 2nd ed. (Rome: Libreria Editrice Vaticana, 1997), 1.3.36–38.
13. This theme is developed at length in David P. Gushee and Glen H. Stassen, *Kingdom Ethics: Following Jesus in Contemporary Context* (Grand Rapids: Wm. B. Eerdmans Publishing Co., 2016), chap. 9.
14. An excellent defense of taking seriously the role of human experience in discernment is offered in Emily Swan and Ken Wilson, *Solus Jesus: A Theology of Resistance* (Canton, MI: Read the Spirit Books, 2018), chap. 4.
15. For a great discussion, see Malcolm Gladwell, *Blink: The Power of Thinking without Thinking* (New York: Little, Brown, 2005).
16. Swan and Wilson, *Solus Jesus*, chap. 5, offers helpful methodological discussion about the role of the Spirit. Their rich work is post-evangelical but not post-Pentecostal.
17. Martin Buber, *I and Thou*, trans. Ronald Gregor Smith (Edinburgh: T. & T. Clark, 1937).
18. Albert C. Outler, *Theology in the Wesleyan Spirit* (Nashville: Tidings, 1975); Outler, *The Wesleyan Theological Heritage: Essays of Albert C. Outler*, ed. Thomas C. Oden and Leicester R. Longden (Grand Rapids: Zondervan, 1991); Outler, *Evangelism and Theology in the Wesleyan Spirit* (Nashville: Discipleship Resources, 1996).
19. Mark A. Noll, *The Scandal of the Evangelical Mind* (Grand Rapids: Wm. B. Eerdmans Publishing Co., 1994), 3.
20. David S. Dockery and David P. Gushee, eds., *The Future of Christian Higher Education* (Nashville: Broadman & Holman Publishers, 1999); Roger A. Ward and Gushee, eds., *The Scholarly Vocation and the Baptist Academy: Essays on the Future of Baptist Higher Education* (Macon, GA: Mercer University Press, 2008).
21. Harold Heie, *A Future for American Evangelicalism* (Eugene, OR: Wipf & Stock, 2015), esp. chap. 8. Heie served at evangelical schools, teaching at The King's College and Gordon College, and serving as vice president for academic affairs at Northwestern College in Iowa and Messiah College.
22. I refer especially to the infamous case of Larycia Hawkins at Wheaton College. See Ruth Graham, "The Professor Wore a Hijab in Solidarity—Then Lost Her Job," *New York Times*, October 13, 2016, https://www.nytimes.com/2016/10/16/magazine/the-professor-wore-a-hijab-in-solidarity-then-lost-her-job.html. Also, David P. Gushee, "Wheaton College, Doc Hawk, and

a Whole Heap of Trouble," Religion News Service, January 7, 2016, https://religionnews.com/2016/01/07/wheaton-hawkins-evangelicals-politics/; Gushee, "Why This Resolution of Hawkins Case Is Bad News for American Evangelicalism," Religion News Service, February 10, 2016, https://religionnews.com/2016/02/10/larycia-hawkins-wheaton-dreyfus-affair-evangelicalism/; Emily McFarlan Miller, "Whither Wheaton? An Evangelical College Ponders Its Future," Religion News Service, February 12, 2016, https://religionnews.com/2016/02/12/whither-wheaton-evangelical-college-ponders-future/.

I experienced considerable pressure at a conservative Christian university when I challenged US-sponsored torture after 9/11 and when I worked on climate change. I had not known these were points of evangelical doctrine.

23. Heie, *Future for American Evangelicalism*, 133. Heie is working from a typology of Christian higher education institutions that deploys the term "orthodox" to describe the kinds of schools dominant in officially Christian higher education. Such schools tend to have doctrinal statements and require all faculty to sign and adhere to them. His conclusion, after an entire career in such schools, is that they are too constrained in their quest for truth and too susceptible to constituency pressures.
24. Daniel Silliman, "Doubt Your Faith at an Evangelical College? That's Part of the Process," *Christianity Today*, August 30, 2019, https://www.christianitytoday.com/news/2019/august/evangelical-students-faith-crisis-christian-higher-ed-cccu.html.
25. Silliman, "Doubt Your Faith?" For the two-article series detailing her findings, see Jennifer L. Carter, "The Patterns of Religious Struggle among Undergraduates Attending Evangelical Institutions," *Christian Higher Education* 18, no. 3 (2019): 154–76; and "The Predictors of Religious Struggle among Undergraduates Attending Evangelical Institutions," *Christian Higher Education* 18, no. 4 (2019): 236–59.
26. Arthur Holmes, *All Truth Is God's Truth* (Grand Rapids: Wm. B. Eerdmans Publishing Co., 1977).
27. See David Kinnaman and Aly Hawkins, *You Lost Me: Why Young Christians Are Leaving Church . . . and Rethinking Faith* (Grand Rapids: Baker Books, 2011), chap. 7. Mark Noll pulled no punches in his critique of evangelicalism and science; see his *Scandal of the Evangelical Mind*, chap. 7.
28. There is a massive literature about the history of the relationship between faith and modern science. One of my favorites is James A. Connor, *Kepler's Witch* (New York: HarperCollins, 2004). See also Ian G. Barbour, *Religion and Science: Historical and Contemporary Issues* (San Francisco: HarperSanFrancisco, 1997); Barbour, *Religion in an Age of Science: The Gifford Lectures, 1989–1991* (San Francisco: Harper & Row, 1990); Barbour, *When Science Meets Religion* (San Francisco: HarperSanFrancisco, 2000); John Hedley Brooke, *Science and Religion: Some Historical Perspectives* (Cambridge: Cambridge University Press, 2014); Gary B. Ferngren, ed., *The History of Science and Religion in the Western Tradition: An Encyclopedia* (New York: Garland, 2000).
29. A fair-minded review is offered by Katharine K. Wilkinson, *Between God and Green: How Evangelicals Are Cultivating a Middle Ground on Climate Change* (Oxford: Oxford University Press, 2012).
30. These were the claims we were already making in 2006 with our evangelical declaration on climate change, of which I was the principal drafter. See "Christians

and Climate: An Evangelical Call to Action," http://www.christiansandclimate.org/.

31. David Wallace-Wells, *The Uninhabitable Earth: Life after Warming* (New York: Tim Duggan, 2019); Roy Scranton, *We're Doomed: Now What?* (New York: Soho Press, 2018).
32. Charles Pasternak, *Quest: The Essence of Humanity* (Chichester, UK: Wiley, 2003).
33. Here I am also thinking about Dietrich Bonhoeffer's famous claim: "The church is church only when it is there for others . . . not dominating but helping and serving. It must tell people in every calling what a life for Christ is, what it means 'to be there for others.'" *Letters and Papers from Prison*, Dietrich Bonhoeffer Works 8 (Minneapolis: Fortress Press, 2010), 503.
34. Not an expert on Erasmus, but hoping one day to become one, I cite Stefan Zweig, *Erasmus of Rotterdam* (New York: Viking Press, 1934), and Desiderius Erasmus, *In Praise of Folly* (1511; Princeton, NJ: Princeton University Press, 1941).
35. Zweig, *Erasmus of Rotterdam*, 149.

Chapter 4: God

1. David P. Gushee and Glen H. Stassen, *Kingdom Ethics: Following Jesus in Contemporary Context*, 2nd ed. (Grand Rapids: Wm. B. Eerdmans Publishing Co., 2016), chap. 1.
2. Walter Rauschenbusch, *Christianity and the Social Crisis* (1907; repr., Louisville, KY: Westminster/John Knox Press, 1991).
3. David P. Gushee, "An Introduction to the Ethics of Walter Rauschenbusch," in *Walter Rauschenbusch: Published Works and Selected Writings*, ed. William H. Brackney, vol. 2 (Macon, GA: Mercer University Press, 2018), vii–lxxviii; Brackney and Gushee, eds., *In the Shadow of a Prophet: The Legacy of Walter Rauschenbusch* (Macon, GA: Mercer University Press, 2020).
4. A good overview of Holocaust theology, with relevant citations, can be found in Richard L. Rubenstein and John K. Roth, *Approaches to Auschwitz*, 2nd ed. (Louisville, KY: Westminster John Knox Press, 2003), chap. 12.
5. My treatment of Littell is found in David P. Gushee, "Anti-Semitism, Christianity, and the Holocaust: An Essay in Honor of Franklin H. Littell," in *Legacy of an Impassioned Plea: Franklin H. Littell's* The Crucifixion of the Jews, ed. David Patterson (St. Paul: Paragon House, 2018), 141–56.
6. Bonhoeffer's last works, *Ethics*, Dietrich Bonhoeffer Works 5 (Minneapolis: Fortress Press, 2005), and *Letters and Papers from Prison*, Dietrich Bonhoeffer Works 8 (Minneapolis: Fortress Press, 2010), best reflect how Nazi atrocities were affecting his theology.
7. *Shoah* is a word in biblical Hebrew that means calamity. It has become widely used, especially among Jews, to name the Nazi genocide against the Jewish people.
8. One example of my participation is David P. Gushee, "Dialogue in Action," in *Jewish Christian Dialogue: Drawing Honey from the Rock*, ed. Alan L. Berger and David Patterson (St. Paul: Paragon House, 2008).
9. The most influential works for me: Martin Luther King Jr., *Strength to Love* (1963; repr., Minneapolis: Fortress Press, 2010); James H. Cone, *A Black Theology of Liberation* (Maryknoll, NY: Orbis Books, 1970); Howard Thurman, *Jesus and the Disinherited* (1949; repr., Boston: Beacon Press, 1996).
10. Katie G. Cannon, *Black Womanist Ethics* (Atlanta: Scholars Press, 1988); Emilie

Townes, *In A Blaze of Glory: Womanist Spirituality as Social Witness* (Nashville: Abingdon Press, 1995); Stacey Floyd-Thomas, *Mining the Motherlode: Methods in Womanist Ethics* (Cleveland: Pilgrim Press, 2006).

11. David J. O'Brien and Thomas A. Shannon, eds., *Catholic Social Thought: The Documentary Heritage* (Maryknoll, NY: Orbis Books, 1992).
12. Joseph Cardinal Bernardin, *Consistent Ethic of Life* (Kansas City: Sheed & Ward, 1988); John Paul II, *Evangelium Vitae: The Gospel of Life* (Washington, DC: US Catholic Conference, 2005).
13. Ronald J. Sider, *Rich Christians in an Age of Hunger* (Downers Grove, IL: Intervarsity Press, 1977); Tony Campolo, *Speaking My Mind* (Nashville: W Publishing Group, 2004); Jim Wallis, *The Call to Conversion* (San Francisco: Harper & Row, 1981).
14. Hal Lindsey, *The Late Great Planet Earth* (Grand Rapids: Zondervan, 1970).
15. Isaac B. Sharp, "The *Other* Evangelicals: The Marginalization of Liberal-Modernist, Barthian, Black, Feminist, Progressive, Arminian-Wesleyan-Pietist, and Gay Evangelicals and the Shaping of 20th Century U.S. American Evangelicalism" (PhD diss., Union Theological Seminary, 2019).
16. Gary Dorrien, *The Remaking of Evangelical Theology* (Louisville, KY: Westminster John Knox Press, 1998), chaps. 4–5.
17. The primary sources are many, but all these figures are discussed in Dorrien, *Remaking of Evangelical Theology*, or Sharp, "The *Other* Evangelicals."
18. *Night and Fog* (*Nuit et brouillard*), dir. Alain Resnais (Janus Films, 1955).
19. David P. Gushee, *The Righteous Gentiles of the Holocaust: A Christian Interpretation* (Minneapolis: Fortress Press, 1994).
20. Especially influential for me was Greenberg's "The Third Great Cycle of Jewish History" (New York: CLAL–The National Jewish Center for Learning and Leadership, 1987), available at https://rabbiirvinggreenberg.com/wp-content/uploads/2013/02/1Perspectives-3rd-Great-Cycle-1987-CLAL-1-of-3.pdf.
21. Prisoner testimony trans. Irving Greenberg, in Greenberg, *For the Sake of Heaven and Earth: The New Encounter between Judaism and Christianity* (Philadelphia: Jewish Publication Society, 2004), 21.
22. Elie Wiesel, *Night*, in *The Night Trilogy* (New York: Hill & Wang, 2008), 50.
23. Irving Greenberg, "Cloud of Smoke, Pillar of Fire: Judaism, Christianity, and Modernity after the Holocaust" (New York: Jewish Life Network, n.d.), https://rabbiirvinggreenberg.com/wp-content/uploads/2013/02/Cloud-of-Smoke-red.pdf, 23.
24. Baptist theologian Franklin Littell always used this language of "baptized Christians" to force his fellow Christians not to forget who did the killing. Littell, *The Crucifixion of the Jews* (New York: Harper & Row, 1975).
25. Perhaps best (or worst) symbolized today by the books and public statements of theologian John Piper; see http://www.desiringgod.org.
26. Clark Pinnock, *Most Moved Mover: A Theology of God's Openness* (Grand Rapids: Baker Academic, 2001), 1–2, 117–18, 131–34.
27. Hans Frei, *The Eclipse of Biblical Narrative: A Study in Eighteenth and Nineteenth Century Hermeneutics* (New Haven, CT: Yale University Press, 1974); George Lindbeck, *The Nature of Doctrine: Religion and Theology in a Postliberal Age*, 25th anniv. ed. (Louisville, KY: Westminster John Knox Press, 2009). See also Timothy R. Phillips and Dennis L. Okholm, eds., *The Nature of Confession: Evangelicals and Postliberals in Conversation* (Downers Grove, IL: IVP Academic, 1996). More recently on the evangelical side, see the highly sophisticated proposal by Kevin J. Vanhoozer, *The Drama of Doctrine: A Canonical-Linguistic*

Approach to Christian Theology (Louisville, KY: Westminster John Knox Press, 2005). For an overview of modern theology, see Kelly M. Kapic and Bruce L. McCormack, eds., *Mapping Modern Theology: A Thematic and Historical Introduction* (Grand Rapids: Baker Academic, 2012).

28. Peter Ochs, *Another Reformation: Postliberal Christianity and the Jews* (Grand Rapids: Baker Academic, 2011); Ochs, ed., *The Return to Scripture in Judaism and Christianity: Essays in Postliberal Scriptural Interpretation* (Eugene, OR: Wipf & Stock, 1993).
29. Elie Wiesel, quoted in Ariel Burger, *Witness: Lessons from Elie Wiesel's Classroom* (Boston: Houghton Mifflin Harcourt, 2018), 87.
30. Quoted in Paul Mendes-Flohr, *Martin Buber: A Life of Faith and Dissent* (New Haven, CT: Yale University Press, 2019), 294.
31. Greenberg, "On the Road to a New Encounter," in *For the Sake of Heaven and Earth*, 27.
32. Greenberg, 28.
33. Mendes-Flohr, *Martin Buber*, 294.
34. Sometimes he called it "Hebrew humanism." See Mendes-Flohr, *Martin Buber*, 171, 189, 190, 209, 212–13, 239. Buber was a Jewish refugee from Nazism who moved to Israel and spent the rest of his life there. He was grateful that the new State of Israel was born and concerned that its life and culture should be governed by "biblical humanism."
35. Bonhoeffer, *Letters and Papers from Prison*, 365–67, 473–82.
36. Greenberg, "Road to a New Encounter," 10. Christian historical theologian Jaroslav Pelikan makes the same suggestion in *Whose Bible Is It? A History of the Scriptures through the Ages* (New York: Viking, 2005), 250.
37. Greenberg, "Road to a New Encounter," 30.
38. This touches on the theological arguments made by the open and relational theism strand of evangelical theologian Thomas J. Oord. Making such arguments cost him his job at an evangelical school. See Oord, *God Can't: How to Believe in God and Love after Tragedy, Abuse, and Other Evils* (Grasmere, ID: SacraSage Press, 2019).
39. Greenberg, "Road to a New Encounter," 25. See also Terence E. Fretheim, *The Suffering of God: An Old Testament Perspective* (Philadelphia: Fortress Press, 1984).
40. Two favorite books on this theme are E. Frank Tupper, *A Scandalous Providence: The Jesus Story of the Compassion of God* (Macon, GA: Mercer University Press, 1995); and John Sanders, *The God Who Risks: A Theology of Providence* (Downers Grove, IL: InterVarsity Press, 1998). The suffering-God theme will be discussed in the next chapter.
41. Bonhoeffer, *Letters and Papers from Prison*, 479.

Chapter 5: Jesus

1. James D. G. Dunn, *Jesus according to the New Testament* (Grand Rapids: Wm. B. Eerdmans Publishing Co., 2019). All comments about Dunn are drawn from this book.
2. The Gospel of John is a wondrous text, much beloved by many Christians, deeply influential in the church's mystical and devotional traditions. John's Jesus has points of connection with the Jesus of the Synoptics, but the story reads very differently. He doesn't speak in parables. He clearly has a self-understanding as Son of God, speaks in "I am" sayings, and regularly focuses on his intimate and special relationship with God his Father. He almost never

mentions the kingdom of God but instead speaks in the language of being born again. He offers long discourses on the Holy Spirit, the command to love (one another, not everyone), the unity of the believing community, and his coming death (and resurrection) to which he submits his will readily. Fatefully, the adversaries in John are mainly called "the Jews," and the polemical relationship between Jesus and "the Jews" reaches a very high pitch, most notably in chap. 8, where Jesus describes the lying, murderous devil as their father (8:44). Despite scholarly efforts to reinterpret or soften the polemical language attributed to Jesus in John, this is the Gospel most easily read as theologically anti-Jewish. One reason I can't affirm an inerrant Bible is because I believe a number of New Testament texts, mainly but not exclusively in John, errantly set the church on a course of demonizing the Jewish people.

3. David P. Gushee and Glen H. Stassen, *Kingdom Ethics: Following Jesus in Contemporary Context*, 2nd ed. (Grand Rapids: Wm. B. Eerdmans Publishing Co., 2016), 86–93. After the first edition was published (2003), Glen used the language of "thin Jesus" and "thicker Jesus" to get at the same point; cf. Stassen, *A Thicker Jesus: Incarnational Discipleship for a Secular Age* (Louisville, KY: Westminster John Knox Press, 2013).
4. Dunn, *Jesus according to the New Testament*, chap. 1.
5. Dunn, 171.
6. Whether or not "virgin" is a mistranslation is a complicated question in biblical studies—not to mention in theological debate. It is a possible translation. Matthew and Luke appear to be the only biblical sources making the claim of the virgin birth, but both affirm the virgin birth as a matter of theological significance. Matthew and Luke are not using the same source material when they make their claims, which some suggest means they are arriving at the conclusion independently. By the second century the virgin birth of Jesus was apparently in circulation as a major theological belief. "Apart from some Jewish-Christian groups (e.g., the Ebionites; Jewish Christians) in the early period, no one raised serious doubts about the virginal conception prior to the rise of critical scholarship." Rowan D. Williams, "Virgin Birth," in *Encyclopedia of Christianity Online*, ed. Erwin Fahlbusch et al. (Brill, 2011), http://dx.doi.org/10.1163/2211-2685_eco_V.11.
7. On the apocalypticism of John and Jesus, see John Dominic Crossan, *The Historical Jesus: The Life of a Mediterranean Jewish Peasant* (New York: HarperCollins, 1992), chap. 11.
8. Whether "son" here means something like "my child" or points to Jesus' often-used term "Son of Man," or "a son of God," or "the Son of God," as Christians use the term, is much debated. See Marcus Borg, *Jesus: A New Vision* (New York: Harper & Row, 1987), 40–42.
9. An important theme in Bruce Chilton, *Rabbi Jesus: An Intimate Biography* (New York: Doubleday, 2000), 5–18.
10. Gushee and Stassen, *Kingdom Ethics*, chap. 1, "Jesus Began to Proclaim: The Reign of God," 3–20.
11. Gushee and Stassen, 6–7, 131, 135.
12. Gushee and Stassen, 3–20.
13. Albert Schweitzer, *The Quest of the Historical Jesus: A Critical Study of Its Progress from Reimarus to Wrede*, trans. W. Montgomery (1906; repr., New York: Macmillan, 1968). New Testament scholar Bart D. Ehrman also takes this approach in *Jesus: Apocalyptic Prophet of the New Millennium* (Oxford: Oxford University Press, 1999).

14. Gushee and Stassen, *Kingdom Ethics*, chap. 5 and throughout.
15. Paul J. Achtemeier, *Jesus and the Miracle Tradition* (Eugene, OR: Cascade Books, 2008); Rudolf Bultmann, *The New Testament and Mythology and Other Basic Writing*, ed. and trans. Schubert M. Ogden (Philadelphia: Fortress Press, 1984); Wendy J. Cotter, *The Christ of the Miracle Stories: Portrait through Encounter* (Grand Rapids: Baker Academic, 2010); Craig S. Keener, *Miracles: The Credibility of the New Testament Accounts* (Grand Rapids: Baker Academic, 2011); Léopold Sabourin, *The Divine Miracles Discussed and Defended* (Rome: Catholic Book Agency, 1977); Gerd Theissen, *The Miracle Stories of the Early Christian Tradition*, trans. Francis McDonagh, ed. John Riches (Edinburgh: T. & T. Clark, 1983); Graham H. Twelftree, ed., *The Nature Miracles of Jesus: Problems, Perspectives, and Prospects* (Eugene, OR: Cascade Books, 2017).
16. On Jesus' healing ministry and its theological and ethical significance, Gushee and Stassen, *Kingdom Ethics*, chap. 21.
17. James H. Cone, *The Cross and the Lynching Tree* (Maryknoll, NY: Orbis Books, 2013).
18. See Gary Dorrien, *Breaking White Supremacy: Martin Luther King Jr. and the Black Social Gospel* (New Haven, CT: Yale University Press, 2018), 18–19, 263–68, 312–14.
19. Howard Thurman, *Jesus and the Disinherited* (1949; repr., Boston: Beacon Press, 1976). See esp. chap. 5.
20. Miguel A. De La Torre, *Embracing Hopelessness* (Minneapolis: Fortress Press, 2017). See also Orlando O. Espín, *Idol and Grace: On Traditioning and Subversive Hope* (Maryknoll, NY: Orbis Books, 2014).
21. *Letters and Papers from Prison*, Dietrich Bonhoeffer Works 8 (Minneapolis: Fortress Press, 2010), 479.
22. "Finale" from *Godspell*, lyric and music by Stephen Schwartz. Lyrics available at https://genius.com/Stephen-schwartz-finale-godspell-lyrics.
23. Dunn, *Jesus according to the New Testament*, 88.

Chapter 6: Church

1. "Rates of religious attendance are declining. Over the last decade, the share of Americans who say they attend religious services at least once or twice a month dropped by 7 percentage points, while the share who say they attend religious services less often (if at all) has risen by the same degree." Pew Research Center, "In U.S., Decline of Christianity Continues at Rapid Pace," October 17, 2019, https://www.pewforum.org/wp-content/uploads/sites/7/2019/10/Trends-in-Religious-Identity-and-Attendance-FOR-WEB-1.pdf, 6.

   "Gallup finds the percentage of Americans who report belonging to a church, synagogue or mosque at an all-time low, averaging 50% in 2018. U.S. church membership was 70% or higher from 1937 through 1976, falling modestly to an average of 68% in the 1970s through the 1990s. The past 20 years have seen an acceleration in the drop-off, with a 20-percentage-point decline since 1999 and more than half of that change occurring since the start of the current decade." Jeffrey M. Jones, "U.S. Church Membership Down Sharply in Past Two Decades," Gallup, April 18, 2019, https://news.gallup.com/poll/248837/church-membership-down-sharply-past-two-decades.aspx.

   "An estimated 30,000 congregations shut their doors in the United States from 2006 to 2012." Rebecca Randall, "How Many Churches Does America Have? More Than Expected," *Christianity Today*, September 14, 2017, https://

www.christianitytoday.com/news/2017/september/how-many-churches-in-america-us-nones-nondenominational.html.

2. Joe E. Trull and James E. Carter, *Ministerial Ethics: Moral Formation for Church Leaders* (Grand Rapids: Baker Academic, 2004).
3. "Today, 17% of Americans say they never attend religious services, up from 11% a decade ago. Similarly, the decline in regular churchgoing is attributable mainly to the shrinking share of Americans who say they attend religious services at least once a week, which was 37% in 2009 and now stands at 31%." Pew Research Center, "Decline of Christianity," 12.
4. Nina Burleigh, "Trump and White Evangelicals: Support for President Grows, but Millennials Leave Movement," *Newsweek*, April 17, 2018, https://www.newsweek.com/trump-evangelicals-support-millennials-888267.
5. Dani Fankhauser, "11 Former Evangelicals Talk about What They Left Behind," Medium, July 22, 2019, https://medium.com/the-salve/11–former-evangelicals-talk-about-what-they-left-behind-479a614d57cb; Josiah Hesse, "'Exvangelicals': Why More Religious People Are Rejecting the Evangelical Label," *Guardian*, November 3, 2017, https://www.theguardian.com/world/2017/nov/03/evangelical-christians-religion-politics-trump; Bradley Onishi, "The Rise of #Exvangelical," Religion and Politics, April 9, 2019, https://religionandpolitics.org/2019/04/09/the-rise-of-exvangelical/.
6. I am not arguing here for an unbroken lineal descent from the apostles to this day, as this has been sundered by the churches' divisions. I am arguing that all churches need to retain meaningful contact with the taproot of the Christian Tradition, as discussed in chap. 3.
7. Dietrich Bonhoeffer, *Sanctorum Communio*, ed. Clifford J. Green, trans. Reinhard Krauss and Nancy Lukens (Minneapolis: Fortress Press, 1998); Bonhoeffer, *Life Together* and *Prayerbook of the Bible*, ed. Geffrey B. Kelly, trans. Daniel W. Bloesch and James H. Burtness, Dietrich Bonhoeffer Works 5 (Minneapolis: Fortress Press, 1996); Jennifer M. McBride, *The Church for the World: A Theology of Public Witness* (New York: Oxford University Press, 2011).
8. D. G. Hart, *Deconstructing Evangelicalism* (Grand Rapids: Baker Academic, 2004), 109–29.
9. Kristin Kobes Du Mez, *Jesus and John Wayne: How White Evangelicals Corrupted a Faith and Fractured a Nation* (New York: Liveright Publishing, 2020).
10. "Even as their numbers decline, American Christians—like the U.S. population as a whole—are becoming more racially and ethnically diverse. Non-Hispanic whites now account for smaller shares of evangelical Protestants, mainline Protestants and Catholics than they did seven years earlier, while Hispanics have grown as a share of all three religious groups. Racial and ethnic minorities now make up 41% of Catholics (up from 35% in 2007), 24% of evangelical Protestants (up from 19%) and 14% of mainline Protestants (up from 9%)." Pew Research Center, "America's Changing Religious Landscape," May 12, 2015, https://www.pewforum.org/2015/05/12/americas-changing-religious-landscape/.

    "Catholics in the U.S. are racially and ethnically diverse. Roughly six-in-ten Catholic adults are white, one-third are Latino, and smaller shares identify as black, Asian American, or with other racial and ethnic groups. The data also show that the share of U.S. Catholics who are Latino has been growing, and suggest that this share is likely to continue to grow. Indeed, among Catholic Millennials, there are about as many Hispanics as whites."

David Masci and Gregory A. Smith, "7 Facts about American Catholics," Pew Research Center, October 10, 2018, https://www.pewresearch.org/fact-tank/2018/10/10/7-facts-about-american-catholics/.

11. *The Catechism of the Catholic Church* (Vatican City: Libreria Editrice Vaticana, 2000); David J. O'Brien and Thomas A. Shannon, eds., *Catholic Social Thought: Encyclicals and Documents from Pope Leo III to Pope Francis* (Maryknoll, NY: Orbis Books, 2016).
12. Catholic Charities USA, https://www.catholiccharitiesusa.org/; Society of St. Vincent de Paul, https://www.svdpusa.org/.
13. Jacob Lupfer, "Catholic-Heavy Supreme Court Moves Right as the Church Moves Left," Religion News Service, July 11, 2018, https://religionnews.com/2018/07/11/catholic-heavy-supreme-court-moves-right-as-the-church-moves-left/; Jan-Werner Müller, "The Two Catholicisms: The Church between Tradition and Modernity," *Nation*, October 8, 2019, https://www.thenation.com/article/catholic-church-pope-francis-ross-douthat-james-chappel/; Michael J. O'Loughlin, "Catholic Leaders Confront Polarization but Skirt Polarizing Issues at Georgetown Forum," *America*, June 8, 2018, https://www.americamagazine.org/faith/2018/06/08/catholic-leaders-confront-polarization-skirt-polarizing-issues-georgetown-forum; Tom Roberts, "The Rise of the Catholic Right," *Sojourners*, March 2019, https://sojo.net/magazine/march-2019/rise-catholic-right.
14. Williamsburg Baptist Church, https://www.williamsburgbaptist.com/.
15. St. Luke's Episcopal Church, https://www.stlukesatlanta.org/; Christ Church Cathedral, https://cincinnaticathedral.com/.
16. Emily Swan and Ken Wilson, *Solus Jesus: A Theology of Resistance* (Canton, MI: Read the Spirit Books, 2018); Blue Ocean Faith, https://www.a2blue.org/.
17. Urban Village Church, http://www.urbanvillagechurch.org/.

Chapter 7: Sex

1. Justin Lee, *Torn: Rescuing the Gospel from the Gays-vs.-Christians Debate* (New York: Jericho Books, 2012); Amber Cantorna, *Refocusing My Family: Coming Out, Being Cast Out, and Discovering the True Love of God* (Minneapolis: Fortress Press, 2017); Jeff Chu, *Does Jesus Really Love Me? A Gay Christian's Pilgrimage in Search of God in America* (New York: Harper, 2013); Jennifer Knapp, *Facing the Music: My Story* (New York: Howard Books, 2014). See also Susan Cottrell, *"Mom, I'm Gay": Loving Your LGBTQ Child and Strengthening Your Faith* (Louisville, KY: Westminster John Knox Press, 2016); Brandan Robertson, *The Gospel of Inclusion: A Christian Case for LGBT+ Inclusion in the Church* (Eugene, OR: Cascade Books, 2019); Matthew Vines, *God and the Gay Christian: The Biblical Case in Support of Same-Sex Relationships* (Colorado Springs, CO: Convergent Books, 2014); and David P. Gushee, *Changing Our Mind: A Call from America's Leading Evangelical Ethics Scholar for Full Acceptance of LGBTQ Christians in the Church* (Canton, MI: Read the Spirit Books, 2014).
2. Linda Kay Klein, *Pure: Inside the Evangelical Movement That Shamed a Generation of Young Women and How I Broke Free* (New York: Touchstone, 2018).
3. William Loader, *The New Testament on Sexuality* (Grand Rapids: Wm. B. Eerdmans Publishing Co., 2012); Loader, *Making Sense of Sex: Attitudes towards Sexuality in Early Jewish and Christian Literature* (Grand Rapids: Wm. B. Eerdmans Publishing Co., 2013). This, by the way, is very important context for understanding Paul's condemnation of same-sex activity in that passage.

4. Robert Scheer, "The Playboy Interview with Jimmy Carter," *Playboy*, November 1, 1976.
5. David P. Gushee and Glen H. Stassen, *Kingdom Ethics: Following Jesus in Contemporary Context*, 2nd ed. (Grand Rapids: Wm. B. Eerdmans Publishing Co., 2016), chap. 13.
6. Nadia Bolz-Weber, *Shameless: A Sexual Reformation* (New York: Convergent Books, 2019), 171–74.
7. Gershon Winkler, *Sacred Secrets: The Sanctity of Sex in Jewish Law and Lore* (Northvale, NJ: Jason Aronson, 1998), 7.
8. Klein, *Pure*, 28.
9. Klein, 25, 27.
10. Robert Downen, Lise Olsen, and John Tedesco, "Abuse of Faith: 20 Years, 700 Victims: Southern Baptist Sexual Abuse Spreads as Leaders Resist Reforms," *Houston Chronicle*, February 10, 2019, https://www.houstonchronicle.com/news/investigations/article/Southern-Baptist-sexual-abuse-spreads-as-leaders-13588038.php; Daniel Avery, "Youth Minister at Anti-Gay Church in Illinois Charged with Sexually Exploiting Teen Boy," *Newsweek*, August 18, 2019, https://www.newsweek.com/pastor-gay-paxton-singer-harvest-bible-chapel-1454872; Bob Smietana, "James MacDonald Fired as Harvest Bible Chapel Pastor," Religion News Service, February 13, 2019, https://religionnews.com/2019/02/13/james-macdonald-fired-as-pastor-harvest-bible-chapel-by-church-elders/; Jeff Coen, "Claims against Willow Creek's Bill Hybels of 'Sexually Inappropriate' Conduct Are Credible, New Report Says," *Chicago Tribune*, February 28, 2019, https://www.chicagotribune.com/news/breaking/ct-met-willow-creek-church-bill-hybels-report-20190228-story.html.
11. Klein, *Pure*, chap. 4.
12. I am thinking of Søren Kierkegaard's famous line: "Purity of heart is to will one thing."
13. Klein, *Pure*, 9.
14. Klein, 140–41.
15. Joshua Harris, *I Kissed Dating Goodbye* (Colorado Springs, CO: Multnomah, 2003). The apology came in an Instagram post at https://www.instagram.com/p/B0ZBrNLH2sl/. Rob Picheta, "Joshua Harris, a Former Pastor Who Wrote Relationship Book, Says His Marriage Is Over and He Is No Longer Christian," CNN, July 29, 2019, https://www.cnn.com/2019/07/29/us/joshua-harris-divorce-apology-scli-intl/index.html.
16. In 1984 the estimated median age at first marriage was 25.4 for men and 23.0 for women. US Census Bureau, "Table MS-2. Estimated Median Age at First Marriage, by Sex: 1890 to the Present," last revised November 14, 2018, https://www.census.gov/data/tables/time-series/demo/families/marital.html.
17. In 2018 the estimated median age at first marriage was 29.8 for men and 27.8 for women. US Census Bureau, "Age at First Marriage."
18. In 1978, 59 percent of 18- to 34-year-olds were married. In 2018, 29 percent of 18- to 34-year-olds were married. US Census Bureau, "1978 and 2018 Current Population Survey, Annual Social and Economic Supplements," last revised November 14, 2018, https://www.census.gov/library/visualizations/2018/comm/percent-married.html.
19. Andrew J. Waskey, "Christian Reconstructionism," in *Culture Wars in America: An Encyclopedia of Issues, Viewpoints, and Voices*, ed. Roger Chapman and James Ciment, 2nd ed. (New York: Routledge, 2015), 115.

20. Sandra E. Garcia, "Tennessee Pastor Who Is Also a Detective Calls for L.G.B.T. People to Be Executed," *New York Times*, June 15, 2019, https://www.nytimes.com/2019/06/15/us/knoxville-pastor-grayson-fritts.html.
21. Antony Loewenstein, "US Evangelicals in Africa Put Faith into Action but Some Accused of Intolerance," *Guardian*, March 18, 2015, https://www.theguardian.com/world/2015/mar/18/us-evangelicals-africa-charity-missionaries-homosexuality; Nathalie Baptiste and Foreign Policy In Focus, "It's Not Just Uganda: Behind the Christian Right's Onslaught in Africa," *Nation*, April 4, 2014, https://www.thenation.com/article/its-not-just-uganda-behind-christian-rights-onslaught-africa/; Sheri Linden, "Review: 'God Loves Uganda' Looks at Missionaries, Anti-gay Bill," *Los Angeles Times*, October 17, 2013, https://www.latimes.com/entertainment/movies/la-xpm-2013-oct-17-la-et-mn-god-loves-uganda-review-20131018-story.html; Jeffrey Gettleman, "Americans' Role Seen in Uganda Anti-Gay Push," *New York Times*, January 3, 2010, https://www.nytimes.com/2010/01/04/world/africa/04uganda.html.
22. Emily Suzanne Johnson, *This Is Our Message: Women's Leadership in the New Christian Right* (New York: Oxford University Press, 2019).
23. Anthony Michael Petro, *After the Wrath of God: AIDS, Sexuality, and American Religion* (New York: Oxford University Press, 2015).
24. Bill Chappell, "Supreme Court Declares Same-Sex Marriage Legal in All 50 States," NPR, June 26, 2015, https://www.npr.org/sections/thetwo-way/2015/06/26/417717613/supreme-court-rules-all-states-must-allow-same-sex-marriages.
25. Mitchell Gold, ed., *Crisis: 40 Stories Revealing the Personal, Social, and Religious Pain and Trauma of Growing Up Gay in America* (Austin, TX: Greenleaf Book Group Press, 2008); Vicky Beeching, *Undivided: Coming Out, Becoming Whole, and Living Free from Shame* (New York: HarperOne, 2018); Cantorna, *Refocusing My Family*.
26. David P. Gushee, "Ending the Teaching of Contempt against the Church's Sexual Minorities," The Reformation Project Conference, Washington, DC, November 8, 2014, https://www.youtube.com/watch?v=G2o3ZGwzZvk; Gushee, "You're Hurting Me with Your Bible," Faith in America Community Dialogue, Jacksonville, FL, October 9, 2014, https://www.youtube.com/watch?v=6Mz5JbkFlok; Gushee, *Changing Our Mind*.
27. Tom Waidzunas, *The Straight Line: How the Fringe Science of Ex-Gay Therapy Reoriented Sexuality* (Minneapolis: University of Minnesota Press, 2015); Tanya Erzen, *Straight to Jesus: Sexual and Christian Conversions in the Ex-Gay Movement* (Berkeley: University of California Press, 2006); Michelle Wolkomir, *"Be Not Deceived": The Sacred and Sexual Struggles of Gay and Ex-Gay Christian Men* (New Brunswick, NJ: Rutgers University Press, 2006); Wayne R. Besen, *Anything but Straight: Unmasking the Scandals and Lies behind the Ex-Gay Myth* (New York: Harrington Park Press, 2003).
28. American Psychological Association, "Answers to Your Questions: For a Better Understanding of Sexual Orientation and Homosexuality" (Washington, DC: APA, 2008), www.apa.org/topics/sorientation.pdf; American Psychological Association, "APA Policy Statements on Lesbian, Gay, Bisexual, and Transgender Concerns" (Washington, DC: APA, 2011), https://www.apa.org/about/policy/booklet.pdf.
29. For a helpful discussion of the problems resulting from stigmatizing LGBT persons, see David G. Myers and C. Nathan DeWall, *Psychology*, 12th ed. (New York: Worth Publishers, 2018), 409–15.

30. Gushee and Stassen, *Kingdom Ethics*, 252–69; Gushee, *Changing Our Mind*, 99–105.
31. I offer an extensive treatment of this and other aspects of marriage in my widely ignored book, *Getting Marriage Right: Realistic Counsel for Saving and Strengthening Marriage* (Grand Rapids: Baker Books, 2003). Check it out; you might like it.
32. Klein, *Pure*, chap. 4.
33. Kate Julian, "Why Are Young People Having So Little Sex?" *Atlantic*, December 2018, https://www.theatlantic.com/magazine/archive/2018/12/the-sex-recession/573949/; Nicole Brodeur, "How Hookup Culture Makes College Students Afraid to Feel," *Seattle Times*, January 27, 2017, https://www.seattletimes.com/life/lifestyle/how-hookup-culture-makes-college-students-afraid-to-feel/; Leah Fessler, "A Lot of Women Don't Enjoy Hookup Culture—So Why Do We Force Ourselves to Participate?" *Quartz*, May 17, 2016, https://qz.com/685852/hookup-culture/; Ian Kerner, "Young Adults and a Hookup Culture," CNN, May 16, 2013, https://www.cnn.com/2013/05/16/health/kerner-hookup-culture/index.html.
34. "The share of U.S. adults reporting no sex in the past year reached an all-time high in 2018 . . . among the 23 percent of adults—or nearly 1 in 4—who spent the year in a celibate state, a much larger than expected number of them were 20-something men." Christopher Ingraham, "The Share of Americans Not Having Sex Has Reached a Record High," *Washington Post*, March 29, 2019, https://www.washingtonpost.com/business/2019/03/29/share-americans-not-having-sex-has-reached-record-high/.
35. I discuss the impact of divorce on children, based on research, in *Getting Marriage Right*, chap. 3.
36. Bolz-Weber, *Shameless*, 60.
37. Bolz-Weber, 139.
38. Brandan Robertson, *Gospel of Inclusion*.
39. Robertson, 95.
40. Robertson, 95–96.

Chapter 8: Politics

1. John A. Coleman, ed., *Christian Political Ethics* (Princeton, NJ: Princeton University Press, 2008); David P. Gushee, ed., *Christians and Politics beyond the Culture Wars: An Agenda for Engagement* (Grand Rapids: Baker Books, 2000); Oliver O'Donovan and Joan Lockwood O'Donovan, *Bonds of Imperfection: Christian Politics, Past and Present* (Grand Rapids: Wm. B. Eerdmans Publishing Co., 2004); O'Donovan and O'Donovan, eds., *From Irenaeus to Grotius: A Sourcebook in Christian Political Thought, 100–1625* (Grand Rapids: Wm. B. Eerdmans Publishing Co., 1999); C. C. Pecknold, *Christianity and Politics: A Brief Guide to the History* (Eugene, OR: Cascade, 2010).
2. Conservative evangelicals often draw their models of rule from biblical figures such as kings and emperors. They frequently speak as if it is inappropriate to criticize "God's anointed ruler." They regularly express support for predemocratic modes of civil government like Puritanism. Many evangelical churches are led by pastors who have few checks on their power, who teach that men should lead their families constrained only by (their understanding of) God's will. And so on. Christian ethicist Luke Bretherton is wise in making his priority the renewal of Christian commitment to democracy and democratic participation. See his *Christ and the Common Life: Political*

Theology and the Case for Democracy (Grand Rapids: Wm. B. Eerdmans Publishing Co., 2019).

3. Mark A. Chancey, Eric M. Meyers, and Carol L. Meyers, eds., *The Bible in the Public Square: Its Enduring Influence in American Life* (Atlanta: SBL Press, 2014); Frances Flannery and Rodney A. Werline, *The Bible in Political Debate: What Does It Really Say?* (New York: Bloomsbury T&T Clark, 2016); Jione Havea, ed., *Scripture and Resistance* (Lanham, MD: Lexington Books/Fortress Academic, 2019); Cynthia Briggs Kittredge, Ellen Bradshaw Aitken, and Jonathan A. Draper, eds., *The Bible in the Public Square: Reading the Signs of the Times* (Minneapolis: Fortress Press, 2008); Gregory W. Lee and George Kalantzis, eds., *Christian Political Witness* (Downers Grove, IL: IVP Academic, 2014).
4. Kimberly Winston, "'Christian America' Dwindling, Including White Evangelicals, Study Shows," Religion News Service, September 6, 2017, https://religionnews.com/2017/09/06/embargoed-christian-america-dwindling-including-white-evangelicals-study-shows/; Jacob Lupfer, "Evangelical Christians Need an Exit Ramp from Trumpism," Religion News Service, January 28, 2019, https://religionnews.com/2019/01/28/evangelical-christians-need-an-exit-ramp-from-trumpism/; Ryan Burge, "Why Politics May Kill White Churches," Religion News Service, May 29, 2019, https://religionnews.com/2019/05/29/why-politics-may-kill-white-churches/; Peter Wehner, "The Deepening Crisis in Evangelical Christianity," *Atlantic*, July 5, 2019, https://www.theatlantic.com/ideas/archive/2019/07/evangelical-christians-face-deepening-crisis/593353/; Scott Slayton, "New Study Shows Growing Political Differences between Older and Younger Evangelicals," Christian Headlines, September 3, 2019, https://www.christianheadlines.com/contributors/scott-slayton/new-study-shows-growing-political-differences-between-older-and-younger-evangelicals.html.
5. Donald W. Dayton, *Discovering an Evangelical Heritage* (New York: Harper & Row, 1976).
6. Dayton, 1–6.
7. Jim Wallis, *The Call to Conversion* (San Francisco: Harper & Row, 1981), xvii–xix.
8. Isaac B. Sharp, "The *Other* Evangelicals: The Marginalization of Liberal-Modernist, Barthian, Black, Feminist, Progressive, Arminian-Wesleyan-Pietist, and Gay Evangelicals and the Shaping of 20th Century U.S. American Evangelicalism" (PhD diss., Union Theological Seminary, 2019), chap. 4.
9. Justin Randall Phillips, "Lord, When Did We See You? The Ethical Vision of White, Progressive Baptists in the South during the Civil Rights Movement" (PhD diss., Fuller Theological Seminary, 2013); Jacob Alan Cook, "Evangelicals and Identity Politics: Reconsidering the World-Viewing Impulse" (PhD diss., Fuller Theological Seminary, 2018).
10. Cook, "Evangelicals and Identity Politics," chap. 3.
11. Sharp, "The *Other* Evangelicals," chap. 3.
12. Sharp, chap. 3.
13. Grant Wacker, *One Soul at a Time: The Story of Billy Graham* (Grand Rapids: Wm. B. Eerdmans Publishing Co., 2019), part 3.
14. Matthew Avery Sutton, *American Apocalypse: A History of Modern Evangelicalism* (Cambridge, MA / London: Belknap Press, 2014).
15. Paul McGlasson, *Choose You This Day: The Gospel of Jesus Christ and the Politics of Trumpism* (Eugene, OR: Wipf & Stock, 2019), chap. 3.

16. McGlasson, 68.
17. Hal Lindsey, *The Late Great Planet Earth* (Grand Rapids: Zondervan, 1970); Tim LaHaye and Jerry B. Jenkins, *The Left Behind Series Complete Set* (Carol Stream, IL: Tyndale House, 2008).
18. Joel Edward Goza, *America's Unholy Ghosts: The Racist Roots of Our Faith and Politics* (Eugene, OR: Wipf & Stock, 2018). The next four paragraphs are from my review of Goza's book, "How Did American Racism Get to This Point?," *Christian Century*, December 26, 2019, https://www.christiancentury.org/review/books/how-did-american-racism-get-point. Page numbers from Goza are cited in the text.
19. David R. Swartz, *Moral Minority: The Evangelical Left in an Age of Conservatism* (Philadelphia: University of Pennsylvania Press, 2012); Brantley W. Gasaway, *Progressive Evangelicals and the Pursuit of Social Justice* (Chapel Hill: University of North Carolina Press, 2014); Mark A. Lempke, *My Brother's Keeper: George McGovern and Progressive Christianity* (Amherst: University of Massachusetts Press, 2017).
20. Randall Herbert Balmer, *Thy Kingdom Come: How the Religious Right Distorts the Faith and Threatens America* (New York: Basic Books, 2006); John Clifford Green, Mark J. Rozell, and Clyde Wilcox, eds., *The Christian Right in American Politics: Marching to the Millennium* (Washington, DC: Georgetown University Press, 2003): Matthew Avery Sutton, *Jerry Falwell and the Rise of the Religious Right: A Brief History with Documents* (Boston: Bedford/St. Martin's, 2013); Clyde Wilcox, *Onward Christian Soldiers? The Religious Right in American Politics* (Boulder, CO: Westview, 1996).
21. Balmer, *Thy Kingdom Come*, 13–17.
22. David P. Gushee, *The Future of Faith in American Politics: The Public Witness of the Evangelical Center* (Waco, TX: Baylor University Press, 2008), 47–55.
23. From a typical Falwell speech:

    "I believe that Americans want to see this country come back to basics, back to values, back to biblical morality, back to sensibility, and back to patriotism. Americans are looking for leadership and guidance. It is fair to ask the question, 'If 84 per cent of the American people still believe in morality, why is America having such internal problems?' We must look for the answer to the highest places in every level of government . . .

    It is now time to take a stand on certain moral issues, and we can only stand if we have leaders. We must stand against the Equal Rights Amendment, the feminist revolution, and the homosexual revolution. We must have a revival in this country." (Falwell, *Listen, America!* [New York: Bantam Books, 1982], 17)
24. Ron Sider, "LGBT Rights, Religious Freedom, and the Democrats," *Ron Sider Blog*, November 6, 2019, https://ronsiderblog.substack.com/p/lgbt-rights-religious-freedom-and.
25. Lupfer, "Evangelical Christians Need Exit Ramp"; Christina Zhao, "Nearly Three-Quarters of White Evangelicals Approve of Donald Trump," *Newsweek*, July 22, 2019, https://www.newsweek.com/nearly-three-quarters-white-evangelicals-approve-donald-trump-1450610; Philip Schwadel and Gregory A. Smith, "Evangelical Approval of Trump Remains High, but Other Religious Groups Are Less Supportive," Pew Research Center, March 18, 2019, https://pewrsr.ch/2HsERvG; Frank Newport, "Highly Religious, White Protestants Firm in Support for Trump," Gallup, April 9, 2019, https://news.gallup.com/opinion/polling-matters/248384/highly-religious-white-protestants-firm-support-trump.aspx; Robert P. Jones, "White Evangelical Support for

Donald Trump at All-Time High," Public Religion Research Institute, April 18, 2018, https://www.prri.org/spotlight/white-evangelical-support-for-donald-trump-at-all-time-high/. The books about the evangelical embrace are beginning to flow; two important ones are Paul A. Djupe and Ryan L. Classen, eds., *The Evangelical Crackup? The Future of the Evangelical-Republican Coalition* (Philadelphia: Temple University Press, 2018); and John Fea, *Believe Me: The Evangelical Road to Donald Trump* (Grand Rapids: Wm. B. Eerdmans Publishing Co., 2018). For broader perspective, Robert P. Jones, *The End of White Christian America* (New York: Simon & Schuster, 2016).

26. McGlasson, *Choose You This Day*, 72–75.
27. Ta-Nehisi Coates, "The First White President," *Atlantic*, October 2017, https://www.theatlantic.com/magazine/archive/2017/10/the-first-white-president-ta-nehisi-coates/537909/.
28. Jacob Cook, "Toward an Incarnational Theology of Identity," in David P. Gushee and Reggie L. Williams, eds., *Justice and the Way of Jesus: Christian Ethics and the Incarnational Discipleship of Glen Stassen* (Maryknoll, NY: Orbis Books, 2020), chap. 2.
29. David P. Gushee and Glen H. Stassen, *Kingdom Ethics: Following Jesus in Contemporary Context*, 2nd ed. (Grand Rapids: Wm. B. Eerdmans Publishing Co., 2016), 3–20.
30. O'Donovan and O'Donovan, *Bonds of Imperfection*; O'Donovan and O'Donovan, *From Irenaeus to Grotius*; J. Philip Wogaman, *Christian Ethics: A Historical Introduction* (Louisville, KY: Westminster/John Knox Press, 1993); Pontifical Council for Justice and Peace, *Compendium of the Social Doctrine of the Church* (New York: Burns & Oates, 2005).
31. Richard A. Spinello, *The Encyclicals of John Paul II: An Introduction and Commentary* (Lanham, MD: Rowman & Littlefield, 2012); Pope Francis, *Lumen Fidei* (San Francisco: Ignatius Press, 2013); Pope Francis, *Laudato si'* (San Francisco: Ignatius Press, 2015); *Vatican Council II: The Conciliar and Postconciliar Documents*, trans. Austin Flannery (Collegeville, MN: Liturgical Press, 2014); *Catechism of the Catholic Church* (London: Bloomsbury Continuum, 2019).
32. Gen. 1; John 3:16; Rom. 5:18–19; 1 Cor. 15:20–22; 2 Cor. 5:16–21; Phil. 2:5–11; Col. 1:19–20.
33. Jennifer M. McBride, *The Church for the World: A Theology of Public Witness* (New York: Oxford University Press, 2011).
34. *Catechism of the Catholic Church*; David P. Gushee, ed., *A New Evangelical Manifesto: A Kingdom Vision for the Common Good* (St. Louis: Chalice Press, 2012).
35. Gushee and Stassen, "Salt, Light, Deeds: The Church's Public Witness in an Unbelieving World," chap. 10 in *Kingdom Ethics*, 195–214.
36. Emily McFarlan Miller, "China Tariffs Could Lead to a 'Bible Tax' in the US, Say Christian Publishers," Religion News Service, June 21, 2019, https://religionnews.com/2019/06/21/china-tariffs-could-lead-to-a-bible-tax-in-the-us-say-christian-publishers/; Robert Barnes, "Supreme Court Declines Case of Photographer Who Denied Service to Gay Couple," *Washington Post*, April 7, 2014, https://www.washingtonpost.com/politics/supreme-court-wont-review-new-mexico-gay-commitment-ceremony-photo-case/2014/04/07/f9246cb2-bc3a-11e3-9a05-c739f29ccb08_story.html; David G. Savage, "Supreme Court Revisits Wedding Cakes and Same-Sex Marriages," *Los Angeles Times*, April 11, 2019, https://www.latimes.com/politics/la-na-pol-supreme-court-wedding-cake-religion-gay-rights-20190411-story.html;

Jessica Glenza, "How the Religious Right Gained Unprecedented Access to Trump," *Guardian*, January 31, 2019, https://www.theguardian.com/us-news/2019/jan/30/donald-trump-administration-religious-right-access.

37. Micah Schwartzman, Chad Flanders, and Zoë Robinson, eds., *The Rise of Corporate Religious Liberty* (New York: Oxford University Press, 2016); Geoffrey R. Stone and Lee C. Bollinger, eds., *The Free Speech Century* (New York: Oxford University Press, 2019).
38. Lew Daly, *God's Economy: Faith-Based Initiatives and the Caring State* (Chicago: University of Chicago Press, 2009); Rebecca Sager, *Faith, Politics, and Power: The Politics of Faith-Based Initiatives* (New York: Oxford University Press, 2010).

Chapter 9: Race

1. I heard this comment at the symposium on James Cone, the founder of modern black liberation theology, and immediately recorded it.
2. Willie James Jennings, *The Christian Imagination: Theology and the Origins of Racism* (New Haven, CT: Yale University Press, 2011), 6.
3. J. Kameron Carter, *Race: A Theological Account* (Oxford: Oxford University Press, 2008), 4.
4. Reggie L. Williams, *Bonhoeffer's Black Jesus: Harlem Renaissance Theology and an Ethic of Resistance* (Waco, TX: Baylor University Press, 2014), 40.
5. Black bodies as suspect, criminal, dangerous, polluting, exotic, alluring, repelling, *other*; the white gaze and how we "see" black skin, black bodies, black people, or fail to see them—this has become a major theme in black theology and ethics, for very practical reasons. How people, such as police officers, *see* black bodies is clearly a matter of life and death. See Kelly Brown Douglas, *Stand Your Ground: Black Bodies and the Justice of God* (Maryknoll, NY: Orbis Books, 2015); M. Shawn Copeland, *Enfleshing Freedom: Body, Race, and Being* (Minneapolis: Fortress Press, 2010); Eboni Marshall Turman, *Toward a Womanist Ethic of Incarnation: Black Bodies, the Black Church, and the Council of Chalcedon* (New York: Palgrave Macmillan, 2013); Rima Vesely-Flad, *Racial Purity and Dangerous Bodies: Moral Pollution, Black Lives, and the Struggle for Justice* (Minneapolis: Fortress Press, 2017); Brian Bantum, *Redeeming Mulatto: A Theology of Race and Christian Hybridity* (Waco, TX: Baylor University Press, 2010); *The Death of Race: Building a New Christianity in a Racial World* (Minneapolis: Fortress Press, 2016).
6. See Vincent Lloyd and Andrew Prevot, *Anti-Blackness and Christian Ethics* (Maryknoll, NY: Orbis Books, 2017).
7. Noted in David P. Gushee, *The Sacredness of Human Life: Why an Ancient Biblical Vision Is Key to the World's Future* (Grand Rapids: Wm. B. Eerdmans Publishing Co., 2013), 178–96.
8. Note that this interpretation of Rom. 1:18–32 implicitly (and now explicitly) rejects Paul's association of same-sex sexual activity with this spiral of moral degradation. In *Changing Our Mind* (Canton, MI: Read the Spirit Books, 2014), I discuss how the debauched and sexually predatory practices of slaveholders and the Roman elite may account for the inclusion of same-sex activity in this passage.
9. The complete text of the address and all sources: David P. Gushee, "2018 AAR Presidential Address: In the Ruins of White Evangelicalism; Interpreting a Compromised Christian Tradition through the Witness of African-American Literature," *Journal of the American Academy of Religion* 87, no. 1 (March 2019): 1–17.

10. *Narrative of the Life of Frederick Douglass* (1845; repr., New York: Dover Publications, 1995), 71.
11. *Crusade for Justice: The Autobiography of Ida B. Wells* (Chicago: University of Chicago Press, 1991), 154–55.
12. James H. Cone, *The Cross and the Lynching Tree* (Maryknoll, NY: Orbis Books, 2011), 102.
13. Cone, 132.
14. *The Autobiography of Malcolm X as Told to Alex Haley* (1964; repr., New York: Ballantine Books, 2015), 376.
15. James Baldwin, *The Price of the Ticket* (New York: St. Martin's, 1985), xix–xx.
16. Albert J. Raboteau, *American Prophets: Seven Religious Radicals and Their Struggle for Social and Political Justice* (Princeton, NJ: Princeton University Press, 2016), 96–97.
17. Christine Leigh Heyrman, *Southern Cross: The Beginnings of the Bible Belt* (New York: Alfred A. Knopf, 1997); Paul Harvey, *Christianity and Race in the American South* (Chicago: University of Chicago Press, 2016); see also James L. Gorman, Jeff W. Childers, and Mark W. Hamilton, eds., *Slavery's Long Shadow: Race and Reconciliation in American Christianity* (Grand Rapids: Wm. B. Eerdmans Publishing Co., 2019).
18. "Report on Slavery and Racism in the History of Southern Baptist Theological Seminary," Southern Baptist Theological Seminary, 2018, https://sbts-wordpress-uploads.s3.amazonaws.com/sbts/uploads/2018/12/Racism-and-the-Legacy-of-Slavery-Report-v3.pdf.
19. Allen Guelzo, *Abraham Lincoln: Redeemer President* (Grand Rapids: Wm. B. Eerdmans Publishing Co., 1999).
20. Most recently, Henry Louis Gates Jr., *Stony the Road: Reconstruction, White Supremacy, and the Rise of Jim Crow* (New York: Penguin Press, 2019).
21. For a very important recent treatment, see Donald G. Mathews, *At the Altar of Lynching: Burning Sam Hose in the American South* (Cambridge: Cambridge University Press, 2018).
22. A new volume reflects the current state of the conversation: William H. Brackney and David P. Gushee, eds., *In the Shadow of a Prophet: The Legacy of Walter Rauschenbusch* (Macon, GA: Mercer University Press, 2020).
23. Paula J. Giddings, *Ida: A Sword among Lions* (New York: HarperCollins, 2008); Ida B. Wells, *The Light of Truth: Writings of an Anti-Lynching Crusader* (New York: Penguin Books, 2014); cf. Angela D. Sims, *Lynched: The Power of Memory in a Culture of Terror* (Waco, TX: Baylor University Press, 2016). The powerful continuing salience and terror associated with lynching for many African Americans must be clearly understood. It appears in many novels and in black theology and ethics. For a very early treatment in womanism, see Emilie M. Townes, *In a Blaze of Glory: Womanist Spirituality as Social Witness* (Nashville: Abingdon Press, 1995).
24. Ralph E. Luker, *The Social Gospel in Black and White: American Racial Reform, 1885–1912* (Chapel Hill: University of North Carolina Press, 1991); Gary Dorrien, *The New Abolition: W. E. B. Du Bois and the Black Social Gospel* (New Haven, CT: Yale University Press, 2015); Ronald C. White Jr., *Liberty and Justice for All: Racial Reform and the Social Gospel* (New York: Harper & Row, 1990); Dorrien, *Breaking White Supremacy: Martin Luther King Jr. and the Black Social Gospel* (New Haven, CT: Yale University Press, 2018).
25. Raboteau, *American Prophets*, 97.

26. National Black Evangelical Association, founded in 1963, http://www.the-nbea.org/; National Hispanic Christian Leadership Conference, founded in 2001, https://nhclc.org/. Compare the National Latino Evangelical Coalition, a more politically progressive group, http://www.nalec.org/. For a time I served on the NALEC advisory board.
27. See William E. Pannell's bracing 1970 essay, "The Evangelical Christian and Black History," chap. 3, and John Perkins's 1982 essay, "Love Is Stronger Than Hate," chap. 7, in *Evangelical Ethics: A Reader*, ed. David P. Gushee and Isaac B. Sharp (Louisville, KY: Westminster John Knox Press, 2015).
28. Edward Gilbreath, *Reconciliation Blues: A Black Evangelical's Inside View of White Christianity* (Downers Grove, IL: Intervarsity Press, 2006).
29. NAACP, https://www.naacp.org/; Southern Christian Leadership Conference, https://nationalsclc.org/; Family Research Council, https://www.frc.org/; American Family Association, https://www.afa.net/.
30. Randall Kennedy, *The Persistence of the Color Line: Racial Politics and the Obama Presidency* (New York: Pantheon Books, 2011).
31. Ta-Nehisi Coates, *We Were Eight Years in Power: An American Tragedy* (New York: One World Publishing, 2017).
32. Stacey Floyd-Thomas, "My Jesus is P-H-A-T: A Womanist Response to Glen Stassen's Invitation to Incarnational Discipleship in the Name of a Thicker Jesus," in David P. Gushee and Reggie L. Williams, eds., *Justice and the Way of Jesus: Christian Ethics and the Incarnational Discipleship of Glen Stassen* (Maryknoll, NY: Orbis Books, 2020), chap. 4.
33. David Emmanuel Goatley, *Were You There? Godforsakenness in Slave Religion* (Maryknoll, NY: Orbis Books, 1996).
34. Kelly Brown Douglas, *Sexuality and the Black Church: A Womanist Perspective* (Maryknoll, NY: Orbis Books, 1999), 93; Renita Weems, "Reading Her Way through the Struggle: African American Women and the Bible," in *Stony the Road We Trod: African American Biblical Interpretation*, ed. Cain Hope Felder (Minneapolis: Fortress Press, 1991), 60–61. One of my favorite examples of this kind of creative reinterpretation is found in Delores S. Williams's treatment of the Hagar story. See her *Sisters in the Wilderness: The Challenge of Womanist God-Talk* (Maryknoll, NY: Orbis Books, 1993). Similar themes surface in Native American and Latino/a theologies and biblical studies. Conquest and colonization in the name of Scripture tends to cause that. See Loida I. Martell-Otero, Zaida Maldonado-Perez, and Elizabeth Conde-Frazier, eds., *Latina Evangelicas: A Theological Survey from the Margins* (Eugene, OR: Cascade Books, 2013).
35. See Brian J. Blount, *Then the Whisper Put on Flesh: New Testament Ethics in an African American Context* (Nashville: Abingdon Press, 2001).
36. See David L. Chappell, *A Stone of Hope: Prophetic Religion and the Death of Jim Crow* (Chapel Hill: University of North Carolina Press, 2004).
37. Raphael G. Warnock, *The Divided Mind of the Black Church: Theology, Piety, and Public Witness* (New York: New York University Press, 2014).
38. The entirety of Baldwin's semiautobiographical debut novel, *Go Tell It on the Mountain* (New York: Dell, 1952), can be considered such a critique, but it is elsewhere in his work as well.
39. Katie G. Cannon, *Black Womanist Ethics* (Atlanta: Scholars Press, 1988), introduction.
40. Stacey Floyd-Thomas, *Mining the Motherlode: Methods in Womanist Ethics* (Cleveland: Pilgrim Press, 2006).

41. Anthony B. Pinn, ed., *By These Hands: A Documentary History of African American Humanism* (New York: New York University Press, 2001), 319–26; see also Melanie L. Harris, "Womanist Humanism: A New Hermeneutic," in *Deeper Shades of Purple: Womanism in Religion and Society*, ed. Stacey M. Floyd-Thomas (New York: New York University Press, 2006), 211–25.
42. Among many other sources, see Marcia Y. Riggs, *Plenty Good Room: Women Versus Male Power in the Black Church* (Eugene, OR: Wipf & Stock, 2003); Kelly Brown Douglas, *Black Bodies and the Black Church* (New York: Palgrave Macmillan, 2012).
43. Douglas, *Sexuality and the Black Church*; Traci C. West, *Disruptive Christian Ethics: When Racism and Women's Lives Matter* (Louisville, KY: Westminster John Knox Press, 2006); Pamela R. Lightsey, *Our Lives Matter: A Womanist Queer Theology* (Eugene, OR: Pickwick, 2015); Horace L. Griffin, *Their Own Receive Them Not: African American Lesbians and Gays in Black Churches* (Eugene, OR: Wipf & Stock, 2006); Thelathia Nikki Young, *Black Queer Ethics, Family, and Philosophical Imagination* (New York: Palgrave Macmillan, 2016).
44. Douglas, *Sexuality and the Black Church*, 11–12.
45. Douglas, 12, 73. The theme is throughout womanist literature. See Katie Geneva Cannon, Emilie M. Townes, and Angela D. Sims, eds., *Womanist Theological Ethics: A Reader* (Louisville, KY: Westminster John Knox Press, 2011), chaps. 6–8, essays by Cheryl Townsend Gilkes, M. Shawn Copeland, and Douglas.
46. My most-read black authors focusing on politics include, in historical order, W. E. B. DuBois, James Baldwin, Martin Luther King Jr., Malcolm X, Cornel West, Michael Eric Dyson, and Eddie Glaude.
47. Richard Hughes, *Myths America Lives By: White Supremacy and the Stories That Give Us Meaning* (Urbana: University of Illinois, 2018).
48. Chanequa Walker-Barnes, *I Bring the Voices of My People: A Womanist Vision for Racial Reconciliation* (Grand Rapids: Wm. B. Eerdmans Publishing Co., 2019).
49. Ibram X. Kendi, *How to Be an Antiracist* (New York: One World, 2019).

Index of Bible References

Index of Names and Subjects